# SIMON

# SIMON

*ROSEMARY SUTCLIFF*

*Illustrated by*
RICHARD KENNEDY

OXFORD UNIVERSITY PRESS
*Oxford New York Toronto Melbourne*

*Oxford University Press, Walton Street, Oxford* OX2 6DP

OXFORD LONDON GLASGOW
NEW YORK TORONTO MELBOURNE WELLINGTON
KUALA LUMPUR SINGAPORE JAKARTA HONG KONG TOKYO
DELHI BOMBAY CALCUTTA MADRAS KARACHI
NAIROBI DAR ES SALAAM CAPE TOWN

*First published 1953*
*Third edition 1979*

ISBN 0 19 271442-2

*Printed in Great Britain by Richard Clay (The Chaucer Press) Ltd.,*
*Bungay, Suffolk*

FOR MY MOTHER
*with love*

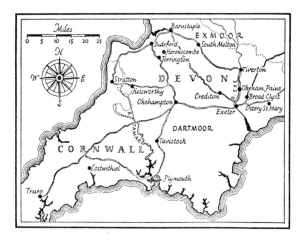

## Author's Note

Most history books deal with the final campaign of
the Civil War in a single paragraph, and the Battle of
Torrington they seldom mention at all. In this story
I have tried to show what that final campaign in the
west was like, and to re-fight the battles fought over
my own countryside. Most of the people I've written
about really lived ; Torrington Church really did
blow up, with two hundred Royalist prisoners and
their Parliamentary guard inside, and no one has ever
known how it happened, though Chaplain Joshua
Sprigg left it on record that the deed was done by
' one Watts, a desperate villain '.

I should like to thank the people—especially Miss
Margaret Bourdillon and Colonel Crookenden, CBE,
DSO—who helped me to find out the many things I
needed to know for the making of this book.

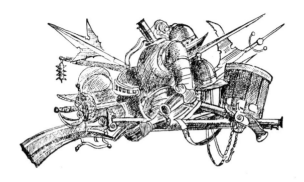

# Contents

# The Golden City of Manoa

IN the deep sunshiny window recess of Dr Odysseus Hannaford's study, two boys sprawled side by side. One, the slighter
and taller of the two, wore doublet and breeches of holly-leaf
green that made the tawny hair rising in a defiant crest from his
forehead seem red as flame by contrast; tawny eyes, a disdainful
beak of a nose, a wide laughing mouth—this was Amias Hannaford, the doctor's son. The other, clad in puritan's grey, was
his friend Simon Carey, a square dependable-looking boy with a
shock of barley-pale hair, bleached silver at the ends by the sun
of the past summer, which had burned his skin to berry brown.

There was a bowl of apples on the polished sill between them,
and they were both in a state of joyful thanksgiving. It was not

that they actually wanted Mr Braund, their harassed school-master, to have one of his bilious turns—they rather liked him, as a matter of fact, and certainly wished him no ill; but if he had to have one, then they were glad and grateful that he should have it on such a day as this. For ever since dawn the wind had been rising, and now it was blowing half a gale from the south-west. The long grass in the doctor's garden lay over in silvery swathes before the gusts, and the tangle of lilac and guelder-rose at the garden end was a swaying lashing turmoil from which the brown and coral leaves came whirling down. It was a day of shining blue and russet, dancing to the wild music of the gale; a day to make the heart leap after adventure; and the two in the Doctor's window gave thanks loudly for Mr Braund's bilious spell that had set them free as the wild sou'wester for all that afternoon.

Simon was almost as much at home as Amias in the deep window recess, for the village of Heronscombe, from which he rode in every morning on the odd-job pony, was too far off for him to go home again at noon; so he always had his dinner at the Doctor's house, and in winter, when the lanes were turned to quagmires, he often slept there too, sometimes for several nights together. It was he who had removed the apples from the side chest, to stay the pangs of hunger while they waited for dinner.

They took great care to eat fair, each taking an apple at the same moment, and every time they finished an apple, they un-picked what was left of the core and tried which of them could spit the pips farthest.

'I can spit farther than you can,' said Amias, with conscious superiority.

'Well, you've got that hole where your front tooth came out,' Simon pointed out reasonably. 'That makes a difference, you know.' He took careful aim at a large cobble in the path. 'Got it! How about *that*?'

'Wind behind it,' said Amias, and reached for another apple.

Simon let it pass. He never argued with Amias; and besides, he felt too contented to argue with anyone, sprawling there in the windy sunshine, with the whole afternoon an unexpected gift before him. So he took another apple—a golden apple, flecked with coral and crimson, and fragrant as a flower—and bit a large piece out of it, squinting happily at the juicy white hollow with tooth-marks round its edge.

'I say! *That* was a good one.' An exultant shout from Amias made him look up. 'Right into the middle of that clump of marigolds! I'll wager Sir Walter Raleigh couldn't have spat farther than that!'

Simon measured the distance with his eyes. 'It's a long way,' he agreed. 'But I expect Sir Walter could spit mighty far!'

Sir Walter Raleigh was their most particular hero. Simon had learned to read from his 'Discovery of Guiana', in the great calf-bound copy of Hakluyt's *Voyages* at home; and during the past summer holidays, when Amias was spending harvest-time with him, they had pored in the evenings over Sir Walter's accounts of great rivers and wide plains, of golden cities which he had never quite found, and birds of white and crimson and carnation, that fluttered through the steaming forests.

'Of course, Sir Walter mightn't have got a front tooth out,' Amias ruminated.

The door behind them opened as Tomasine Blackmore came in to set the table, and instantly the October gale swooped in through the window with a shout. Golden leaves whirled in after it and all the room was in a hurly-burly. The cloth on the side chest took wings, upsetting a box of red-pepper lozenges and a pot full of earth in which Amias, who was of an inventive turn of mind, had lately planted an apple-core with a cherry stone embedded in the middle of it, hoping to grow a tree that would bear cherries as big as apples. A pile of the Doctor's papers scattered to the four corners of the room, and the heavy curtains billowed out, flapping like the sails of a ship when she comes about. Then the door slammed shut with a crash that brought a shower of plaster down from the low raftered ceiling. Almost before they knew what had happened, the boys felt a hand twisted in the neck-band of each, and they were jerked backward into the room and set on their feet with a tooth-shaking thump.

'I say—why——' began Amias.

'We're sorry; we didn't think it would do that,' Simon said, looking up rather anxiously into Tomasine's wrathful face as she slammed the window shut.

'I dare say,' said Tomasine, much put out. 'Opening the window with the wind in this direction! Will 'ee look at thicky mess? Now 'ee can clear 'un up while I sets the table, or there'll be no dinner for either of 'ee.'

It was a threat which Tomasine was quite capable of carrying out, and they set to work in a great hurry, Amias gathering up the broken pot and sweeping the scattered earth into a pile, while Simon, still holding the remains of his apple in one hand, collected the red-pepper lozenges, blew the earth off them, and put them back in their box. While lying on his stomach under the drug-chest, groping for the last one, he found something. 'I say, Amias,' he called, his voice slightly muffled by the cobwebs. 'There's some more of your cherry-apple earth here, and a sort of *thing* with it that we must have dug up at the same time.'

'What kind of thing?' demanded Amias, who had just found the cherry-apple core under the table.

But at that moment Dr Hannaford appeared in the doorway, stripping off his heavy riding-gloves as he came, and Simon pushed the Thing down the front of his doublet, and wriggled out backwards from under the chest in a hurry. Dr Hannaford stood with his legs planted well apart, and surveyed them out of very blue eyes under bushy badger-grey brows. 'Ah!' said Dr Hannaford in an amused rumble that seemed to come from the middle of his deep chest. 'A little gardening, I presume, Amias? And Simon trying his hand at dispensing lozenges? I always thought that it was Amias who planned to be a doctor, while Simon grew things. Strange how easily one can be mistaken.'

Both at once, they began to explain; but Dr Hannaford was peering at the box of lozenges in Simon's hand. 'I am sure that Grannie Halfyard will find the apple-juice a great improvement,' he said, 'but the cobweb is a mistake. Cobwebs for an open wound, not for a sore throat, no.'

Simon hastily removed the cobweb; and a few moments later, Tomasine having brought in the broiled mutton and prunes and departed again, slamming the door, they gathered round the

4

leather-topped table. The two boys stood behind their stools with bowed heads and folded hands while the Doctor said Grace, adding, as he had done ever since the troubles started, a plea that God might bless His most Gracious Majesty King Charles, and confound his enemies in Parliament. Simon always found that part of Grace rather confusing, because when his own father mentioned the King in family prayers each evening, it was to pray that he might be brought to his senses before he ruined England. So he was glad when Grace was over, and he could forget about it until next time.

Simon liked having dinner with Dr Hannaford. He liked the low-ceiled room, which, although it was called the study, and served as living-parlour, was almost as full of pestles and mortars, instrument cases and pill-boards and pitch-pots as the surgery next door. The walls were lined with shelves in which books on herbs and surgery and astronomy rubbed shoulders with drug-jars of thick green glass or grey lambeth pottery, each with its name on it in gold: mercury and camomile, camphor and opium, making a kind of shadowy tapestry with stray sparks of light and colour in it, that Simon found oddly fascinating. The smell of the study was fascinating too: a mixture of drugs and herbs, the leather bindings of old books, a faint suggestion of mice, and the warm sweetness of apples; and Simon sniffed contentedly as he ate his dinner and listened to the Doctor reading extracts from the book which was open on the table beside him.

It was Dr Hannaford's custom to read at meals, for the simple reason that he had no leisure to read at any other time; and generally he read extracts aloud to the two boys. Today it was a new book, *The Circulation of the Blood*, by a Dr William Harvey of St Bartholomew's Hospital, and Simon did not find it very interesting; but Amias, who was passionately interested in how things worked, found it enthralling.

It was not until dinner was nearly over that Simon remembered the Thing he had found under the chest. He took it out of his doublet and looked at it in the palm of his hand. It was a chrysalis of some sort, brown and shiny, and very large, with a queer little tail turned up over its back like the handle of a jug. Simon had never seen one quite like it before. He held it out to

5

the Doctor, while Amias sprawled across the table for a closer
view. 'It was in the earth in the pot that got broken,' he said.
'What is it, do you think, sir?'

'It's a kind of grub thing,' said Amias, and poked it. 'With
a hard skin,' he added.

Dr Hannaford brought out his square horn-rimmed spectacles.
He had eyes like a hawk, but he had worn glasses in his youth to
make him look learned, and they had become a habit. Balancing
them on the end of his nose, he peered through them at the brown
thing in Simon's hand. Then he shook his head. 'Save that
it is some sort of chrysalis, I greatly fear that I cannot satisfy your
thirst for knowledge. Had it been a morbid humour, now, or
a spasmodic contraction of the thorax, I could have told you all
about it; even a conjunction of Saturn with Mercury: but a
chrysalis—no, my education has been neglected.'

'You don't know at *all* what sort?' Simon was surprised and
disappointed, because usually the Doctor knew the answer to any
question you might ask him.

'I have not the slightest idea,' said Dr Hannaford, returning his
spectacles to his pocket. 'You had best ask Pentecost Fiddler,
the next time you meet him. There are very few living creatures
he does not know, at least to bow to, I should imagine.'

Across the table the eyes of the two boys met, bright with
sudden excitement. Here was the perfect adventure for this
golden afternoon. They did not speak, for they seldom needed
to put their plans into words, each to the other. but from that
moment the whole thing was settled. Pentecost Fiddler was
something of a legend in those parts; he came and went as fitfully
as an April wind, he and the battered fiddle that had given him
his name; and wherever he appeared, at wake or wedding or
country fair, he was welcomed for his playing, that could set the
feet of an old man dancing and draw the heart out of a maid.
From Hartland to South Molton, every man, woman and child
was his friend when they chanced to meet him. But nobody
ever went near him when he was at home; nobody ever went
up the wooded valley below his cottage without crossing their
fingers or turning their coats inside out. For Pentecost lived
alone in a clearing of the woods beyond the Torridge, in a place

where it was not good for a mortal man to live. Once, the cottage had been lived in by ordinary folk, but that was long ago. The fairy flowers grew in what had once been the garden—white foxgloves and vervain and elder—and everyone knew what that meant. From time out of mind the place had been called Solitude, and a place does not get such an odd, uncanny name for nothing; and since no man could live comfortably on Fairy Ground unless he was on very intimate terms with the rightful owners, it stood to reason that Pentecost was kin to Good Folk.

Therefore, to visit Pentecost in his own fastness and ask him what sort of moth the brown chrysalis belonged to would be an adventure worthy of this heaven-sent half-holiday. They made no mention of their plans to anybody, because an adventure should never be made public beforehand. When dinner was over and the Doctor had gone back to his doctoring, they simply got a box to put the chrysalis in, lest it should find the inside of Simon's doublet uncomfortably warm, and set out.

They went down through the garden and out on to Castle Hill, Amias leading and Simon at his heels. Amias always led in all their doings, partly because he was eleven and Simon was only ten and three-quarters, partly because he was the kind who leads and has brilliant ideas, whereas Simon was the kind who follows loyally, and does his best to save the brilliant ideas from ending in disaster. The wind was roaring up from the south-west, churning the bracken into a wild golden sea, and lashing through the waist-high furze with a shrilling like the outgoing tide on a pebbly beach; and the boys flung themselves into it, running and shouting for the joy of the autumn gale. They charged over the edge of the hill, down the ridged sheep-tracks that zigzagged through the furze, travelling at breakneck speed, for long practice had made them sure-footed as mountain sheep; and arrived at last, breathless and laughing, on the river-bank just above Taddi-port.

Taddiport was a disreputable clump of cottages, and the Manor mill huddled under the sheer bluff of Castle Hill. It was joined to the town of Torrington high above by the steep straggle of Mill Street, which hung down so like a disgraceful tail that one almost expected it to wag when the town was pleased. More often than

7

not when going that way the boys crossed Mill Street and continued down-stream, to ford the river by one of the many stickles; but today, for no particular reason, they elected to cross like Christians by the hump-backed bridge where the seeding willow-herb grew between the arches.

On the farther bank they stopped to pass the time of day with a friend, a lean and lounging man with one watery blue eye, and a ferret in his pocket.

'Mitching from school, my dears?' inquired the one-eyed man, with sympathy.

'No. Schoolmaster has the stomach ache, and we have a holiday,' Amias told him; and they went on, past the chapel of the old leper hospice, and into the woods beyond, where the wind through the trees roared like a high sea and one had to shout to make oneself heard above it; and all the woods were full of flying sunshine and the shrivelled leaves whirling down the gale.

'This is the Orenoque!' Amias shouted presently, when, having worked their way down-river almost as far as Rotherne bridge, they reached the tiny half-choked stream that came down the valley of Solitude. 'And if we follow it, it will bring us to the Golden City of Manoa that the Spaniards called Eldorado.'

So the woods became the great and rich country of Guiana, and the muddy trickle running down to join the Torridge was a great silver river, winding through forests of huge trees among whose branches fluttered Sir Walter Raleigh's birds of white and crimson and carnation. The two explorers pushed on in huge excitement, until they found themselves far up the winding valley; here they halted and looked at each other, suddenly a little scared.

'Perhaps he's not at home,' said Simon, and then felt ashamed, because his voice sounded hopeful.

'Of course we could turn our doublets inside out,' suggested Amias. 'We should be quite safe then. But perhaps he wouldn't like it.'

Simon shook his head. 'It would be sort of *untrusting* to call on him like that,' he agreed.

So they went on with their doublets still right side out, which

8

took quite a lot of courage. They had left the stream now, and were pushing up the wooded hillside, guided by nothing but the smell of adventure in their eager noses.

A few steps more, and quite suddenly the woods fell back, and they were on the edge of the clearing they had come to look for. Solitude lay aside from the main valley, in a little hollow of the hills, sheltered from the wind which surged through the tree-tops all around; and the quietness of it, under the roof of roaring wind, gave the place an odd feeling of sanctuary. Elder trees ringed it round, dripping with dark berries beloved of thrush and blackbird; crab trees drooped branches of little russet apples almost to the long grass where the coral leaves of the bird-cherry lay thick. Seeding periwinkle and wild geranium told where once a tended flower-patch had been. The tangle was so thick that it was a few moments before the two boys, halting on the wood-shore and looking about them, could pick out the tumbledown cottage on the far side. Then they both saw it at the same instant.

'There 'tis!' exclaimed Amias, pointing.

'I say, what a queer place,' said Simon, with bated breath.

'I wonder if Pentecost *is* there.'

'Umm. So do I.'

For a moment, neither of them moved, then Amias squared his shoulders and strode forward. 'Come on, let's go and see.'

Simon marched after him, clutching the box in which was the brown chrysalis. They made their way through the tangle to the open doorway of the cottage, and halted again. The cottage was so low that the roof came down almost to their eye-level: once it had been thatched, but now the rotten reeds were covered over with moss like emerald velvet; the open door looked as though it had not been shut for years; the threshold was choked with nettles, and there was no sign of anybody inside.

'Let's knock,' said Amias, and rapped gently at the open door.

They listened, but nothing happened; then they scuffled their feet and called politely, 'Pentecost, are you at home?'

Still nothing happened.

'He's out,' said Amias, between exasperation and relief. He gazed thoughtfully at the door for a few moments, and then made

9

up his mind. 'Well, I don't see why we should come all this way for nothing. I'm going to take a look inside.'

'I don't think we ought to,' said Simon flatly.

But Amias sniffed at him—he had a peculiarly insulting sniff—and advanced right into the doorway. Simon followed as in duty bound, and they stood together peering into the gloom, their hearts thumping uncomfortably. Neither of them knew what they had expected to see, but what they did see in the farthest and darkest corner was a dim white shape that suddenly spread its arms and swept forward right into their faces, with a piercing mournful cry that made their blood jump. They sprang back, and for an instant, as they turned to run, they caught sight of a strange oval face with huge eyes, then the thing was planing away on ghost-white silent wings.

'It was only a white owl,' shouted Amias. 'Only a silly old white owl!' And he laughed, and shouted it to the trees. 'A white owl—a white owl!' But he did not stop running until he reached the edge of the clearing, and neither did Simon.

In the shelter of the woodshore, they halted and faced each other.

'A white owl; that was all it was,' said Amias.

'Silly, to be scared off by a white owl,' said Simon slowly. 'I'm going back.'

'Come on,' commanded Amias; and back they went.

They had just reached the doorway again, when they heard a new sound, so like the shriller overtones of the gale that at first they were not sure they had heard it at all; then, as they stared into each other's startled faces, rising shrill and sweet and clear above the turmoil, the sound of a fiddle playing, not a tune, but simply an accompaniment to the wind in the trees.

They spun round, and there, leaning against the trunk of a bird-cherry, with his fiddle tucked beneath his chin, stood Pentecost Fiddler. He was watching them under the brim of his slouch hat, and the moment they looked round he stopped playing and came forward, a mocking smile curving his long lips.

'So you thought you'd have a good look at the warlock's lair, while the warlock was out, did ye, my fine young gentlemen?' said Pentecost, looking down at them.

'We didn't!' said Amias indignantly. 'We came to see you. We didn't know you were out.'

'And then the white owl flew out of your house, and—we ran away; and so of course we had to come back again,' added Simon, who was painfully truthful.

'Ah, yes, poor Bess. Her would be more startled than you were.'

'Is she yours?' asked Amias.

'No more than I be hers. Her shares the shelter of my roof now and again, that is all.' He drew his bow slowly across the strings, making for a few moments a kind of soft regretful music that had no tune in it, and looking thoughtfully at the two boys the while. Then he broke off, and demanded mockingly, 'Weren't you afeared to come here-along? Haven't you heard that Pentecost Fiddler be kin to the Fairy Kind? Bain't you afeared that I shall witch you into white mice? Abracadabra, hellebore and toadflax. Grrr!'

The boys stood their ground, though with quaking stomachs, and gazed back at him. For a wonder, it was Simon who answered first, grinning with sudden friendliness up into the fiddler's strange dark face.

'No,' said Simon.

'Good,' nodded the fiddler. 'And now, do 'ee tell me why you did come.'

Simon had forgotten about the chrysalis; it had never been much more than an excuse for the adventure. But now he remembered it, and held out the box. 'We found this in some earth that we dug up,' he said breathlessly. 'At least, we put the earth in a pot to grow something special in, and then we broke the pot, and that was how we found it; and we don't know what it is, and we thought maybe you could tell us.'

Pentecost tucked his fiddle and bow under one arm and, opening the box, took out the chrysalis. For a little while he was silent, turning it over and over in his thin brown hands. Then he asked, 'Was there any bindweed close by where you dug 'un up?'

'Oh yes; it grows all over the bank that we got the earth from,' Amias put in.

11

' Aye, I thought as much. 'Tis a chrysalis of one o' the hawk moths. I've only seen but one like it before, and I can't tell 'ee its name because it bain't got one, so far as I know. The caterpillar has a li'l crimson horn in the middle of its head, like as it might be a li'l unicorn. You could call it a Unicorn Moth; that 'ud be as good a name for it as any.'

' What shall we feed it on? ' asked Simon.

' You won't need to feed 'un at all. Put it in a dark place, and maybe 'twill turn into a moth, come the spring. If the moth was to lay eggs, and the eggs was to hatch into caterpillars, then you'd need to feed them on the leaves of the bindweed.'

' I see. We'll not forget. Thank you very much,' said Simon, as he took back the chrysalis in its box.

Amias, who had been standing first on one leg and then on the other, put in, ' I say, Pentecost, could we see inside your cottage? '

' 'Twould be a fine tale to tell, for sure, wouldn't it, young maister? That you set foot inside Pentecost Fiddler's door.' The man's voice had grown mocking again.

' We shouldn't tell anyone,' said Amias.

' We don't tell about things.' Simon backed him up.

Pentecost's mouth quirked at the corners. ' Come in, then,' he said, and led the way indoors.

It was very dark in the one-roomed hovel, for there was no window, only the open door behind them; and it smelled musty because of the rotten thatch. But there were fresh rushes piled against one wall for a bed, with an old horse-blanket to cover them, a clean pitcher in one corner, and a skillet and an iron spoon hanging beside the hearth; and most surprisingly and wonderfully, on the rough shelf above it, the model of a ship with all sails set. A lovely little ship, roughly, yet skilfully made, and so full of life that she seemed to hover on the edge of movement, as though next instant would bring her dipping forward out of the shadows like a gull in the hollow of a wave.

' Ah, I thought you'd like her,' said Pentecost, laying his fiddle on the bed-place as the boys made for the hearth and stood gazing up at the shelf on which she stood. He took her down, handling her deftly and gently, as he had handled the chrysalis, and carried her to the light.

'Did you sail in her?' asked Amias, while Simon touched the prow with one careful finger.

'Aye, I've been a ship's fiddler in my time,' said Pentecost. 'Sit on the capstan head, I would, playing me fiddle to keep the time, while the capstan hands 'ud go tramp-tramping round and round, and the anchor cable coming dripping in, and the lads aloft in the rigging, ready to break out the sails. I finished with the sea half-a-dozen year agone, but maybe I'll go back one day, me and the old fiddle.'

'What was her name?' asked Amias.

'The *Destiny*. Sir Walter Raleigh's *Destiny*. The first ship ever I served in, she were; and she were Sir Walter's last.'

'You mean you actually served under Sir Walter Raleigh?' shouted both boys at the same instant.

Pentecost took the model away from them and returned it to its shelf. 'Aye, on thicky last voyage.'

'I say, tell us about it,' Amias begged.

'Playing me fiddle in a waterside tavern, Deptford way, I was, when Sir Walter come in. He stands listening for a bit, and then he says: "How'd you like to make a fortune? How'd you like to plunge your hands in your very own gold, up to the elbows?" "I'd like that proper," I says, "but where be the gold?" And he sits down on a beer cask (he was a bit weak in the legs, after fifteen years caged in the Tower), and he says: "In El Dorado. All there waiting to be dug out of the dark earth; but I needs a capstan fiddle for my ship, afore us can get it." So I says, "I'm your man."'

'That was when King James let him out of the Tower to fetch him gold from the New World?' put in Simon.

They were sitting in a row on Pentecost's bed by that time, with Pentecost in the middle, his fiddle across his knees, and an eager listener on either side.

'Yiss, that was it. But it weren't only the gold he went for, 'twas for the adventure. One last adventure, look 'ee; and he knowed well enough it were his last. I heard him one night, talking to his son as went with him. "Walt," he says, "us'll show this new weak-kneed breed what Elizabeth's seamen were; us'll drub the Dons out of Guiana, if need be," he says. "And after that—maybe a longer and a swifter voyage than this; but there's good shipmates of mine awaiting at the landfall." And then he says something that sounds as if it comes out of a book, about the Islands beyond the Sunset, and the trees of golden apples as grows there.'

'The Hesperides!' Amias chimed in excitedly. 'Father's got that book.'

The fiddler nodded. 'Aye, that were the name he called 'em by . . . But there weren't no Isles of Golden Apples; weren't no gold at all; and the boy was killed before a Spanish fort; and Sir Walter Raleigh come home to face the music. Plenty of other countries he could have gone to; the French would have been glad enough to have him, and there's some would have cut and run for it; but he wouldn't strike his colours to do a thing like that, not my old Captain.'

'And so King James put him back in the Tower and cut his head off, to please the Dons,' said Amias fiercely, after a little silence. 'King Charles wouldn't ever have done a mean thing like that.'

'Tell some more about Sir Walter,' said Simon.

'Nay, my dears, that be enough for one day; and 'tis time you was on your way back to Torrington. Maybe another time I'll tell 'ee more,' said Pentecost, and drawing his long legs under him he got up.

The two boys scrambled to their feet, and stood gazing up at him. 'We can come again, then?' said Simon hopefully.

'Aye, come along when you like. But don't 'ee go upsetting Bess if her should be here and I should be from home.'

'We won't,' they promised. 'And thank you, Pentecost,' and Simon picked up the box with the chrysalis in it, which had all but escaped his mind again.

'Oh, we almost forgot,' said Amias, turning in the doorway, 'We know your name, but perhaps you don't know ours: I'm Amias Hannaford, and he's Simon Carey.'

''Tis a maister fine thing for a man to know the names of his guests,' said the Fiddler, and his eyes twinkled under his drooping hat-brim. 'Good day to 'ee, my dears.'

'Good day,' they said, and they went out.

14

Pentecost Fiddler did not come to the door to see them off, and when they halted on the woodshore and glanced back the cottage looked completely derelict once more.

'You wouldn't think anyone lived there at all,' said Simon.

'No,' Amias agreed thoughtfully. 'You know, if you were wanting somewhere to hide, Solitude would be an awfully good place. I'll wager if Sir Walter Raleigh had hidden here, King James would never have found him to cut his head off.'

'If you didn't know it was here, you'd never find it,' Simon said, and as they plunged away into the trees he added triumphantly, 'and if you *did* know it was here, you'd be scared of coming to look, because of the Good People—everybody except us, that is.'

It had been an adventure worthy of the wild golden afternoon, and the full splendour of it held them silent until they had almost got back to Taddiport. Then Simon dropped the chrysalis box, the lid fell off, and the chrysalis fell out, and they had to scramble after it among the bramble roots.

'Got it,' Simon said, and put it carefully back in the box. 'Funny, it being a sort of unicorn,' he said.

Amias peered at the chrysalis, his eyes brightening with an idea.

'We could say, "As sure as unicorns can fly," and "as sure as unicorns lay eggs," and everybody'd think we were quite mazed —and all the time it would be true.'

'Umm,' said Simon, and put the lid on again.

Neither of them mentioned the matter farther, but from that day forward 'As sure as unicorns' became a kind of private catch-phrase between the two of them.

## II

# *The Last Day's Freedom*

ON a still September afternoon Simon and Amias lay up in the high orchard behind Lovacott. It was their last day of freedom, for next morning they were riding for Tiverton, to become scholars at Blundell's School; and in the intervals of helping to get in the harvest, they had taken leave of all their old haunts: no mean task, for they knew and loved every inch of the country for miles around. They were just back now from a long day in the Taw valley; and only the day before they had been to say good-bye to Pentecost. In the year since that wild autumn afternoon when they had called on him with the unicorn chrysalis—which had most disappointingly failed to turn into a moth—Pentecost Fiddler had become a great friend; and Solitude, in the character of the Golden City of Manoa, had known them very often, though they had contrived to keep their visits secret from the rest of the world. Now it would know them no more until Christmas time. The last day was nearly over, and the next four years stretched ahead very drearily, lit by only the short holidays at Christmas and Harvest. The one consolation was that they would be in it together. Nothing was quite unbearable so long as they were in it together, not even school.

' Oh, I *wish* we were sixteen!' said Amias, plucking up a grass stem and biting it savagely.

' Four years,' groaned Simon. ' Oh well, they'll pass, I suppose; and then I shall come home and help Father farm Lovacott, and you'll be prenticed to *your* father. You'll make a mighty funny doctor.'

' I shall make a very good doctor,' said Amias, with conviction. He took the grass stem out of his mouth and squinted at the bitten end. ' Only I should like to have a few adventures first. Run away to sea or something. I'd have my long bright rapier, and go and fight people; Barbary Pirates, perhaps—or I might *be* a pirate.' He warmed to his theme, with a kindling eye. 'I'd do things like Sir Walter Raleigh did: go looking for gold in the New World, and sacking Spanish cities and things; a red beard I'd have, and I'd be the Terror of the Spanish Main! *Then* I'd come home and be apprenticed to Father. You could come too, and be my trusty Master Gunner.'

'Ye-es,' said Simon.

If Amias turned pirate, then Simon would certainly be his Master Gunner, because where Amias led, Simon followed, loyally digging him out of the trouble his brilliant ideas so often got him into. But all the same, he thought, it would be good, when one was through with the Spanish Main, to come home to Lovacott.

From where he lay, up here in the high orchard, he could look down through the dipping branches of the old cider trees and see Lovacott: the house and outbuildings, the home paddock and his mother's beloved garden close, like the heart of a flower of which the three petals were the three big demesne fields, Sanctuary and Salutation in the valley, and Twimmaways joining the orchard just behind him and sloping over the hill-top towards the village. His father had once tried to change the names of Sanctuary and Salutation into Easter and Wester Meadows, but tradition had been stronger than him, and the two fields remained Sanctuary and Salutation, as they had been when they were held from the shaven-headed monks of Fris'tock Priory. The Careys had held Lovacott and the village of Herons-combe, first from the monks and then in their own right, from the days of Agincourt, and the place was in their blood. Back in Elizabeth's reign, when so many of their kind had built themselves grand new houses and left the old one to become the farm, Simon's grandfather had refused to do any such thing, merely adding a kitchen door and more windows to the house-place, and building a range of farm buildings on the south side, so that the courtyard need no longer have the midden and the pigs in it. So the Careys had remained at Lovacott, fitting into it as perfectly as a nut fits its brown shell; and at the thought of tomorrow's leave-taking, a stab of homesickness shot through Simon. All the

17

same, if Amias wanted a Master Gunner, of course he had only to say the word.

'Lovacott would make a splendidly good fortress,' Amias said, after they had chewed grass in silence for a bit. 'I mean, the way it's built solid all round the courtyard, and with Diggory's gatehouse and all. Of course we'd have to stop up the kitchen door and all those outside windows, so that the enemy couldn't climb in through them.'

'Who'd be the enemy?' Simon asked.

Amias considered. 'Of course if this was up north, we could have the Scots, like last year when they came over the border and all down through Northumberland.' He sniffed. 'Them and their old Covenant!'

'Well, I think it would be very exciting to have a Covenant, and sign it in one's own blood, and meet out on the Moors with a Bible in one hand and a sword in the other,' argued Simon.

Amias thought so too, but as the Covenanters were against the King, and Amias was a passionate Royalist, he could not very well admit it. So he changed the subject. 'It would be just as good if Cornwall was a hostile country; then the Cornish might come reiving over the border, and we could have a siege. We'd leave loopholes in the windows, and fire through them—like this.' He demonstrated, squinting along the barrel of an imaginary matchlock. 'And your mother and the maids could load for us.'

'Mouse too,' put in Simon firmly. Mouse was his small sister, and he often found her rather a trial, but he was not going to have her left out of the fun, all the same.

'All right, Mouse too. And we could climb up on the gatehouse roof and pour boiling lead on their heads—ssswsh!—like that.'

'We could have all the things out of the armoury,' added Simon.

Like all farms and manor houses, Lovacott had to provide certain weapons and pieces of armour for the county Militia. In the small farms this might be only an ancient helmet—a morion— and perhaps a pike that first saw service in King Hal's army. But Lovacott, beside John Carey's own equipment as Lieutenant of the Torrington Company, provided three back-and-breasts and morions, and a motley collection of pikes and matchlocks; and they were stored in a small room between the house and the stables, which was called the armoury in consequence. Only a few days before, Simon had helped his father and Diggory to overhaul those ancient and fascinating weapons, just as most people, up and down the country, were overhauling their weapons that summer. For the old trouble that had been twenty years a-brewing between King and Parliament was all too surely coming to a head at last. Simon knew that, of course, and the grimness of his father's face as he tested the straps of a breast-plate had stuck in his mind, so that he remembered it again now, and the memory gave him a solemn feeling in the pit of his stomach.

'Of course, if they got up here into the high orchard, we'd have to make a sortie, and drive them out,' Amias was saying. 'Otherwise they might be able to shoot down into the court-yard.'

Simon did not answer. Between the branches of the apple trees the sky was turning clear and colourless as crystal. The shadows of the hawthorn wind-breaks had reached out, all across the fields, and the green of pasture and the gold of arrish were quenched with evening. Tomorrow, Diggory's son Tom would begin ploughing Sanctuary, ready for the autumn sowing; but Simon would not be there to see it. A heron came lapping lazily home against the quiet sky, following the pass through the hills between Taw and Torridge, which herons had followed since the world began, thereby giving Heronscombe its name. Simon watched it out of sight, the solemn feeling deepening in his stomach; and he didn't want to talk about fighting in the high orchard, or Lovacott being besieged, not any more.

So when Amias began to work out a brilliant plan for blowing up the enemy with their own gunpowder, he gave him a violent push and said, 'Yah! You've got gunpowder on the brain! What happened when you tried inventing that new kind, last year?'

Amias shoved back. ''Twas proper fine gunpowder! The best gunpowder ever was—as sure as unicorns!'

'Yiss! And it blew your eyebrows off and set fire to the study table, and I had to use all the stock-jar of dill-water to put it out—

Yow! Get off my innards!' for Amias had hurled himself upon him with a war-shout.

They tumbled over and over like puppies in mock fight, until there was no more breath left in them, and then rolled apart, laughing and gasping, and lay quiet. Simon had forgotten the solemn feeling in his stomach.

At that moment, round the corner of the farm buildings appeared the little bent figure of Diggory Honeychurch. Diggory lived in the gatehouse, with his pippin-round wife Phoebe, and was steward, horseman, and friend to the Careys. It was his proudest boast that so long as there had been a Carey at Lovacott, there had been a Honeychurch to serve him. And indeed, to look at him, one might have thought that it had been the same Honeychurch all that time, for he was as gnarled as any thorn root, and skin, hair and clothes alike were the colour of drought-parched earth. Chancing to look up into the orchard at that moment, he caught sight of the two boys and waved, shouting something.

Simon cupped his hands and shouted back, 'Can't hear!'

'Rizpah!' bellowed Diggory, also making a trumpet of his hands. 'Foal!'

'It's *come*?' yelled Simon.

'Yiss!'

Simon was afoot in an instant and racing down the hill. 'It's Rizpah's foal!' he shouted over his shoulder to Amias, who came hurtling after him. 'It's come, after all!' and he flung himself down through the russets and mazard cherry trees of the lower orchard, and through the wicket gate into the garden close.

Rizpah was his father's sorrel mare, and his father had promised him the expected foal to replace the odd-job pony for which he would soon be getting too big. It would be the first horse of his own that he had ever possessed; and he had hoped, and prayed and wished on the new moon that it might arrive before he had to go away to school. He had almost given up hope; and now Rizpah had done it for him, after all. With a triumphant shout he hurtled in at the open kitchen door, across the hall and out into the courtyard, with Amias racing at his winged heels; and the startled doves exploded upward in a flurry as he swerved stable-ward, skidding on the cobbles.

Diggory was there before them and holding the half-door shut, having scuttled back from the farmyard for the purpose. 'Softly now!' he scolded, as they came to a panting halt before him. 'Do 'ee want to startle the poor li'l toad from here to Kingdom Come?'

'Is it a filly or a colt?' demanded Simon, edging round him.

'Proper fine li'l colt. Yiss, 'ee can go in now—like Christians, mind!' and the old man let go of the half-door. The two boys went in like Christians. 'There!' said Diggory. 'You won't see a finer foal nor that in a month of Sundays! Will 'em, Rizpah, my maid?'

Rizpah stood where the last rays of the westering sun, slanting into her stall through the doorway, fell full on her satiny rust-red flank: not for nothing had she been named Rizpah, which means a hot coal. Her long neck was curved as she nuzzled at the new-born foal standing on tottering legs beside her, and her eyes were huge and soft.

''Oppin' about and suckin' already!' said Diggory, with a satisfied chuckle, as the foal butted against his mother, tail awag like a brown feather behind his narrow little rump.

'Rizpah,' said Simon, 'he's a beauty!'

The mare swung her gentle head towards him, nickering softly with pleasure as he drew his hand down her nose; then she turned her attention to her son once more.

Simon did the same, surveying the little creature with the warm pride of ownership. Only one thing disappointed him. 'I hoped he'd be really red, like Rizpah.'

Diggory snorted. 'Now did 'ee ever see a foal borned the colour 'twas going to be when 'twas growed?' He put his old gnarled hands on either side of the little thing as it drew back from its mother, and turned it into the light, while the two boys crowded closer and the mare looked on anxiously. 'Look at the red glint in his coat. He'm be so red as his dam in a few months —redder. He'm be so red as any fox that ever stole a goose, by the time he'm growed, sure 'nough. Look close—there where the light ketches 'un.'

Simon and Amias looked, and saw that sure enough there was a red glint in the soft apricot-buff of the foal's coat. His muzzle was like dark velvet, white-flecked just now with his mother's milk; his eyes were dark and scarey, and the long lashes that shadowed them were gold-tipped in the sunset light. He blinked, standing insecurely on wide-planted legs; and Simon's heart went out to him.

'I say, he *is* a beauty!' said Amias. 'What are you going to call him?'

'I don't know yet. What do you think?'

'If you gave him a very *red* sort of name——' began a small voice behind them, and looking round they saw Mouse hovering on the outskirts of the group.

Nobody had heard her come, but it was always like that with Mouse, hence her name, though she had been christened Marjory. It was infuriating, this silence of hers, and made it almost impossible to keep anything secret from her; but both boys were bound to admit that whatever she found out about them and their affairs she never told to anyone else.

'Hullo! Where did you spring from?' demanded Simon, rather ungraciously.

Mouse advanced into their midst, and stood looking at the foal. 'From the house,' she said. 'I heard you go through and I thought it must be Rizpah's baby, so I came to see. His tail's just like a feather.'

'What did you say about calling him a red sort of name?' demanded Amias, who hated people to wander from the point and leave their sentences unfinished.

'If you gave him a very red sort of name, perhaps it might help him to grow red. Simon was saying he *wanted* him to grow red.'

'That's a good idea,' nodded Simon. 'You've hit on a sensible notion for once, Mouse. Amias, what's the reddest name you can think of?'

'Scarlet,' said Amias promptly, while Mouse, pleased at the unwonted praise, smiled at both boys until a large dimple which she very seldom showed appeared in her left cheek.

'All right,' said Simon. 'We'll call him Scarlet. I say, Diggory, when can we begin breaking him?'

But it was another voice that answered, and turning quickly

they saw Mr Carey in the stable doorway, with a couple of field spaniels at his heels. 'Not until he's rising three years old,' said Simon's father. 'A horse broken younger than that is too often a horse spoiled.'

They faced him respectfully, hands behind their backs. 'He's simply splendid,' said Simon, 'and, Father, we're going to call him Scarlet.'

'That seems quite a reasonable name.' Simon's father studied the little group with cold light-grey eyes that always made Amias remember his latest evil-doings. 'Does it seem to you that Rizpah may be feeling a little crowded, with quite so many admirers in her stall? Suppose you three come outside. Oh, and, Marjory, your mother wants you in the still-room.'

They trooped after him; and Mouse scurried away to her mother, while old Diggory remained behind to make much of Rizpah, who was his darling.

Outside in the courtyard, Simon said in an eager rush, 'Thanks for giving him to me, Father. He's—he's *splendid*!'

'I am glad he comes up to your expectations. You realize you will have to help break him when he's old enough,' said Mr Carey, closing the half-door of the stable. 'Amias, your pony is ready for you, as you see, and it is time that you were on your way home. Your father will want to see a little of you, I imagine, on this last evening before you go to school.'

'Yes, sir, I'll go now,' said Amias, who was much more in awe of Simon's father than he was of his own; and crossed to where his fat pony stood with its bridle looped over the hitching-post. He mounted into the saddle and wheeled the fat little creature towards the gateway. 'Good night, sir. 'Night Simon. See you tomorrow.'

'Wait for me by the market,' Simon called.

Pony and rider disappeared under the arch of the gatehouse, and Simon heard the hoofbeats tittupping up the rutted wagon-way. The sky above the roofs of Lovacott was deepening to lavender, and the wings of the wheeling doves were no longer gilded, as they had been a while back, but grey. Soon the candles would be lit in the deep mullioned windows: and when they were lit tomorrow evening, Simon would not be there to see. Another

23

stab of homesickness pierced him through and through. ' Oh, I *wish* tomorrow would never come ! ' he burst out. ' If only you *knew*——'

John Carey's stern manner and cold grey eyes made people think him a hard man, and so he was, but he and Simon had always understood each other. ' Believe it or not, Simon, I do know,' he said. ' I remember quite distinctly wishing desperately that I might wake up with the smallpox, the last evening before I went away to school.' Then, as Simon looked up at him miserably, he added, ' It isn't really so unbearable, you know, once you get used to it.' He put a hand on the boy's shoulder, and they went indoors, followed by the spaniels Jillot and Ben.

III

# *A Toast to the King*

Aʟʟ through that winter and the spring that followed, the wildest rumours were rife in the West Country. The Irish Papists were coming to join their English fellows and the Protestants were to be massacred: another St Bartholomew's Eve. There was a plan to blow up London. There was a French fleet in the Channel, waiting the King's word to attack. Worst of all, in the eyes of Devon men, who had greater cause than the rest of England to remember the Inquisition, Charles was in league with Spain.

Simon and Amias contrived not to think about all this. They both knew in their heart of hearts that there was going to be civil war—one day. But it might not be yet awhile, and it did not bother them much, not while the summer lasted and there were so many other things to think about. Now and then Amias would speak of some new rumour, especially the one about blowing up London, for mines and explosives always interested him intensely;

25

but when that happened, Simon would say, ' Oh, don't let's talk about it,' and they would forget again.   It was better so.

They had forgotten more completely than usual, one afternoon, half-way through the summer holidays.   It was a burning blue-and-golden afternoon, after a week of storms, and they had been up-river all day simply messing around, watching for a certain otter of their acquaintance, bathing in the dark pool under the hanging oakwoods where the leeches fastened on to you no matter how careful you were, and had to be pulled off afterwards; and now they were going home for supper.

The furze was a blaze of gold, bean-scented in the August sunshine, as they climbed by their usual paths up Castle Hill, and the sheep lay in every patch of shade, too hot even to graze. Nothing stirred among the furze but a darting goldfinch or a linnet.   The boys were hot too; their shirts stuck to them, and their arms and legs were flecked with horsefly bites, which in some odd way seemed only to add to their contentment, their sense of a day well spent.   They were drenched with sunshine, half asleep as they walked.   They had seen the otter and there was nearly a fortnight of the holidays left.   Tomasine had promised damson tarts and gingerbread for supper, and afterwards, if no one was taken unexpectedly ill, Dr Hannaford, who was no mean swordsman of the old school and had given them lessons in the noble art of fence ever since they were big enough to hold a foil, had promised to show them a certain deadly thrust in tierce which he now considered them skilled enough to be trusted with.   Alto-gether, life seemed very good, and if they had been cats they would have purred.

The study, when they entered it by way of the window, seemed very dark after the golden dazzle of the world outside, where the peonies and late roses of the untidy garden burned like flowers of coloured flame; and it was a few seconds before they saw that Dr Hannaford was there already.   He was standing at the side chest, with his back to them, and he could only just have arrived, for he was emptying instruments from the deep pockets of his riding-coat.   Next instant he swung round on them, and even through the green-and-crimson cloud that the darkness after the sunshine had spread before his eyes, Simon knew that the Doctor was in a state of blazing excitement, and his own heart gave an odd lurch.

'Have you heard the news?' Dr Hannaford demanded.

'What news, Father?'

The doctor's bright blue eyes were shining like a boy's, and his big voice was bigger than usual. 'The King has raised his standard, two days ago, at Nottingham!'

There was a long silence, and then Amias let out a triumphant whoop. 'That'll finish Parliament's nonsense! I say, Father, it's simply splendid!'

'Splendid? Aye, it's that,' Dr Hannaford said, and suddenly his voice grated, 'but Devon will have no part in the splendour.'

'Why not? What d'you mean?'

'Parliament has levied an army of ten thousand men—that news came this morning also—and Sir Samuel Rolle is at this moment raising the Militia to join it. Didn't you hear the uproar in the town?'

'We came up over the Common. Father—it's not true, is it? It *couldn't* be!'

Dr Hannaford flung his gloves on the chest top as though he were flinging them in Sir Samuel's face. 'Ah, but it is,' he said bitterly. 'No matter, the King's Majesty will hold his own against such mealy-mouthed gentry, yes!' Then, with a sudden change of manner, he turned to the carved wall-press in which he kept his more precious drugs : litharge of gold and silver, ground sapphire, crystal and topaz, and the like; and unlocking it with a curiously fretted key, set the door wide. A pungent smell of the contents floated out, and reaching up to the top shelf while Amias watched him, he brought out a flask which he set on the table. A strangely shaped flask with a long slender neck and fat shoulders, which cast a wonderful quivering stain of greenish golden light on to the leather table-covering, where the sun shone through it. Returning to the press, Dr Hannaford brought out three glasses, tall and slender, of blown glass that was faintly golden, opening at the lip like the trumpet of some fragile flower. 'These originally came from Venice,' he said, handling the lovely frail things as Pentecost Fiddler handled the little *Destiny*, as he set them on the table. 'And this '—he picked up the flask and set to work

27

on the cork, talking the while, his big voice sunken to a reflective rumble—' is from Tuscany; the last of three that I brought home with me from my student days at Padua University. There's all the gold of a Tuscan summer in this flask, and something of my own youth too. One day, when you're old, you two, you'll understand that. I had meant to broach it on the day that Amias passed out of his apprenticeship; but we'll put it to a nobler use, a use worthy of it.' He poured the thin golden wine into his own glass, and a little into the other two; then straightened, holding his glass aloft so that the sunlight burned in it like some great jewel.

'We will drink to his most Gracious Majesty King Charles—to his success in arms, and the downfall of his enemies.'

Amias stepped forward eagerly to take up his glass, but Simon never moved. He had stood perfectly still, from the first, staring down at the table, his hands rigid at his side, and a feeling of cold emptiness growing inside him.

'Oh, wake up, Simon,' said Amias, standing with his own glass raised, his cheeks flushed and his tawny eyes blazing with eagerness.

Simon raised his head slowly, and looked at the Doctor. He said, 'I—I'm not going to drink success to the King.'

There was a long, leaden silence that seemed to drag on and on. He saw the unbelief turn to angry amazement in the faces of the other two, as they stared at him; and he stared back, his head up and his eyes steady. But the cold emptiness was deepening and deepening within him; and it seemed to him that the gold had fallen like shining dust from the August afternoon.

'Good grief! What wicked nonsense is this?' rumbled Dr Hannaford at last.

Simon said, 'My father says the King is ruining England with his Scottish quarrels and his foreign pacts, and his wars that he always loses because he puts his favourites in command whether they know anything about fighting or not.'

Dr Hannaford's bushy brows were twitched together, and he had begun drumming on the back of a chair with his fingers. 'If Parliament ties the King's hands at every turn, by refusing him the money he needs for his wars, how can he win them?' he demanded.

'My father says that stopping the money is the only thing Parliament can do to hold the Kingdom from ruin,' said Simon, ' *and* my father says that unless the King learns better—unless he's *taught* better—soon there'll be no more freedom in England, for he grows into more and more of a tyrant every year.'

'He is the King,' said Dr Hannaford. 'He has the Divine Right!'

'My father says there's no such thing. He says there's one law of right and wrong for everybody, and being the King makes no difference. And I think so too.'

Amias broke in, stammering with outraged astonishment. 'But Simon, you *can't* mean—Simon, don't you understand? *I'm* for the King!'

Simon turned his head as though his neck was stiff, and looked at him. Ever since they were three years old, and the Doctor had brought out his small son on his saddle-bow when he came to tend Diggory for the flux, it had been the two of them, Amias leading, Simon following. But now it was over; it could not be like that ever again. It was hard to break the habit of his whole remembered life, but it had to be done. 'You can be for whom you like,' he said. 'I am for Parliament, like my father,' and he watched the sudden hurt bewilderment in Amias's eyes harden into scorn. 'I'm going now,' he said. 'I've got to get home and tell my father, because he's in the Militia.'

'Simon'—Dr Hannaford was no longer angry, but only desperately worried and sorry—'I had no idea that it would be like this. I know of course that your father had these—these ideas, but I find it hard to believe that he would really come out into rebellion against his King. Are you sure beyond all doubt?'

'Yes—and if he wouldn't, I would.'

'Then there's no more that I can say. Good-bye, Simon.'

'Good-bye, sir.' Simon turned to Amias, and held out his hand, but the other boy set down his glass and whipped both hands behind him.

'I do not shake hands with the King's enemies,' he said, as coldly and grandly as any veteran of the King's wars.

Simon's own hand dropped to his side, and he grew very

white. 'Thank you for reminding me,' he said, every whit as cold as Amias. '*I* do not shake hands with people who——' He broke off, and turning on his heel stalked out of the room as proudly as if he had been going to instant execution.

Behind him, Dr Hannaford sighed and glanced at the back of his son, who had swung away and was staring, with hunched shoulders, out into the burning August evening.

Simon went round to the stables. Jem, the doctor's man, was out and he was glad of it, for he did not want to have to speak to anybody just then. He saddled and bridled the fat pony and, leading him out into the street, mounted and set out for home. Avoiding the Market Square, where he knew most of Torrington would be gathered (indeed he could hear the uproar as he wheeled the pony into an alleyway), he cut across into Calf Street, where the crowds were thinner. But even there the people thronged up and down, loud voiced and with faces eager or scared, solemn or reckless, as the case might be, reading the freshly posted notices announcing the call-up of the Militia. Edging the pony slowly through the crowds, he emerged at last near the tumble-down cottages of Goosey Green, where the road forked, one road following the moorland ridge to Barnstaple, the other passing close to Stevenstone, the great house of the district. Both roads led home, but usually Simon took the ridgeway, because he loved the high moors. He took it now, but without knowing that he did so, striking his heel into the pony's flank to urge it into a canter. He wanted to ride like the wind; he wanted the thunder of hooves in his ears and the wind of his going whistling by; speed and noise and shouting to outdistance and drown the misery within him; but the fat old pony declined to do more than a canter, and very soon dropped back into its usual trot, despite all that he could do to urge it on.

So Simon rode home, forgetting, for the first time in his life, to look for the distant view of Bideford Bay that opened to him just before the Chapel Path turned down to Heronscombe.

As he rounded the corner of Salutation, Scarlet, who was grazing there, tossed his head and came up at a gallop, whinneying. Scarlet was red as a fox now, full of joyous fire from his little yearling crest to the plumy sweep of his tail. But Simon rode on

unheeding, and Scarlet, who was used to being petted and talked to on every occasion, stuck an indignant head over the gate, and stared after him like a spoiled child that has been snubbed for no reason.

A few yards farther on, Simon met two local men coming down the wagon-way, each with a bundle of accoutrements. Evidently the news had arrived before him and already the Militiamen were collecting their equipment from the Lovacott armoury. They gave him Good evening, and he returned their greeting; but after he had gone by, the two turned and looked after him.

'Young Maister looks a bit whitish round the gills,' said one. 'Scared, maybe.'

But the other shook his head. 'Looked to me more like a was tizzy 'bout something. Thicky quiet chaps, they'm allus the most passionful when they'm roused.'

The dogs came yelping to give him their usual welcome as he turned in through the gatehouse, and as he dismounted Mouse came bolting out to meet him, her face white and scared. 'Father wants you in the parlour,' she said. 'Oh, *Simon*, Father's going away to fight the King this evening!'

'I know. Get Tom to rub Captain down, will you?' Simon dropped the pony's reins over the hitching-post and went in to answer his father's summons.

Mr Carey was standing before the empty hearth, and the two dogs ran to him, snuffing unhappily at his feet. He was fastening the strap of his lobster-tail helmet, and he swung round as the boy entered, and stood looking across the room to him. Simon was used to the sight of his father in buff and steel, ready for the monthly training-musters, but as he checked on the threshold, it seemed to him that he was looking at a stranger: for the face in the shadow of the helmet was grimmer than he had ever seen his father's face before.

'Well, Simon, I suppose you know that we are at war?'

Simon nodded. 'Yes, Father. It's all over Torrington that the King has set up his standard at Nottingham.'

'And the wind blew it down again, the same night,' added his father quickly. 'I am away to join my Company this evening.'

Simon came a step nearer, and begged with desperate eagerness. 'Take me with you, sir! I'm very strong, and I could easily pass for fifteen, I'm sure.'

His father shook his head. 'This isn't a business for schoolboys.'

'But I can shoot, and handle a horse better than many others who are older than I am,' protested Simon.

'I know you can; but I have not the remotest intention of taking you with me,' said John Carey. Then his face lost some of its grimness. 'Come here.'

Simon came, and his father put both hands on his shoulders and looked down at him.

'Listen, Simon—because I do not know when I may see you again, and so you must remember what I say now. I have given Diggory orders for carrying on the demesne, and your mother has the affairs of the Manor in charge; and I wish you to go back to Blundell's next term as usual, unless the war conditions should prevent you. Nobody knows what may happen. It is like setting light to stubble in a dry year: only the Lord of Hosts knows where the blaze will end. If the countryside becomes too unsettled, you may not be able to get through; but you are to go on with your schooling as long as you can. You understand?'

'Yes, Father.'

'If I should be killed, you will be master of Lovacott. Look after your mother and sister, and remember that you can't drive the likes of Diggory and Tom. Always be just in your dealings with them, and they will be just in their dealings with you; and never be too proud to take advice. Diggory knew how to farm this land before I was breeched.'

Again Simon nodded, but without a word.

'Never neglect family prayers, never be afraid to make a stand for what you believe to be right. And whatever you do, if you have occasion to buy a calf, remember that a good Red Devon should have his legs set well out at the corners! He'll grow to them; but a calf with its legs set near and close will be a mean small beast when 'tis grown.'

'I'll remember,' said Simon.

33

' Good.   That's all—except that if the war is not over by your sixteenth birthday——'

' Yes, sir? '   Simon interrupted.

' Take Scarlet and join the Parliamentary Army.'   Mr Carey dropped his hands from his son's shoulders, and took up the heavy cavalry sword that had been lying on the table.

' I hope the war isn't over by then,' Simon said fiercely.   ' Can I put on your sword for you? '   He took it from his father, and began to fasten the heavy buckles he had fastened so often before. His father's voice made him check and look up.

' Simon, have you and Amias come to the parting of the ways over this? '

Simon muttered something indistinctly.   His fingers were still on the buckles, but his eyes, bright with misery, were raised to the long silver-hilted rapier that hung by its warm crimson slings above the mantle.   Once, there had been a pair of them, for his grandfather had been a two-sword man, in the fashion of forty years before, and had carried his twin blades, Balin and Balan, in a double sheath.   But he had given Balin to Dr Hannaford when he went to Padua University and first had need of a sword; and since then Balan had hung solitary above the mantle.   Dr Hannaford had promised his blade to Amias when he was old enough to go armed; would *he* have to wait until he was sixteen, Simon wondered.   Balan belonged to Simon already; it had been his ever since his grandfather had left it to him; and ever since he could remember he had seen it hanging there, one of the familiar things of life; but now, quite suddenly, it seemed to him that the long blade in its double sheath looked very lonely.

' Son against father, brother against brother, friend against friend,' said John Carey, testing the buckles.   ' Civil war is a hideous thing.   Don't hope for it to last, Simon.'

They went out together, followed by the dogs, into the long hall, where the thick sunlight of the August evening slanted in through the windows and lay in golden puddles on the stone-flagged floor, and the remains of supper were still on the table.

Simon's mother, with the maids and Mouse at her heels, came in from the kitchen at the same moment, carrying the pack containing the ten days' ration of wheaten biscuit and strong yellow cheese which all ranks of the Militia must carry with them to a muster.

'Anne,' said Simon's father, 'have you done with that pack? It's time I was away.'

'Quite ready, John.' Simon's mother set it down on the chest beside the open house-place door, and turned to him as he came towards her down the hall. Mouse was crying in a subdued frightened way, and so were the two maids and old Phoebe Honeychurch; but Simon's mother smiled—at least her mouth smiled. 'You'll be in Torrington before it's really dark. I've put in three clean shirts; they will last you until we can make arrangements.' But when Simon's father put his arms round her to say good-bye, she clung to him desperately, with her cheek pressed against the blacked steel of his cuirass. 'Oh John, John, you will come home soon, won't you?'

'That is as God wills,' said John Carey. 'Keep a good heart, beloved.' He put her away from him, and slinging the pack over his shoulder went out to his horse, which Diggory was walking to and fro in the courtyard. He spoke to the old man, paused an instant to test the girths and make sure his long horse pistols were safe in their holsters, then swung into the saddle. The others crowded round him; Mouse was standing at his stirrup, her small tear-stained face raised to his; Simon was patting the chestnut's glossy neck.

'Good-bye, Marjory. Be a good maid while I am gone,' said Mr Carey. 'Good-bye, Simon. Stand back both of you—no, don't come out into the lane.' Over their heads he looked for an instant at Simon's mother; then he turned his horse toward the gatehouse, and clattered out of sight.

The little group in the house-place doorway stood listening to Hector's hoof-beats growing fainter and fainter down the wagon-way. Simon was feeling much older than he had done when he got up that morning. In the last few hours he had broken with Amias, and he was lonely, with a desolation of loneliness such as he had never known before. And now his father had ridden off to fight for the things he thought right, and the weight of responsibility for Lovacott and his womenfolk felt very heavy on his shoulders.

The sound of hoof-beats was quite gone now, and the startled doves were fluttering down into the courtyard again. One landed on little pink feet close beside the door-sill.

Simon's mother turned back into the house, looking very much as usual. 'Simon, have you had your supper?' she asked.

Simon shook his head. He had forgotten about supper.

'Oh, my dear, you must be so hungry—come and have it this moment. Mouse, sweeting, don't cry like that; it will only make you sick—it always does.' She turned on the scared maids with little shooing gestures. 'Run along, Meg; run along now, Polly. Have you no sewing nor spinning waiting to be done?'

War might come; the skies might fall; but Simon's mother would see to it that her husband had clean shirts, her family were fed, and her maids not idle.

# IV

# Horsemen from the West

SIMON leaned against the rough stone wall of the smithy, and gazed idly across the hummocky field-corner round which the lane curved like a horseshoe, to the church and straggling cottages of Little Torrington. He had ridden over to see Matthew Weeks about a litter of pigs, and had hoped to be home again by dusk; but only a mile on the homeward way Scarlet had cast a shoe, and he had had to turn back to have it seen to. It was a nuisance, but it couldn't be helped, so he waited patiently.

The village had a very peaceful look in the early autumn quiet of 1644, so that it was hard to believe that England had been at war within herself for more than two years. Edgehill and Newbury were battles of the past, as well as a score of lesser fights. Parliament had triumphed at Marston Moor two months ago, and the Earl of Essex, overrunning the south, had driven Sir Ralph Hopton, the Royalist General, back into Cornwall. Leaders were rising out of the chaos, their names becoming household words; Prince Rupert and his brother Maurice, Hopton and Astley, for the King; and for Parliament, Fairfax and Waller, and a certain East Anglian squire, Oliver Cromwell, who had ideas of his own about raising armies. The whole country was in a turmoil, and yet always, between the marching armies, the ordinary life of ordinary folk went on : wool was woven and tin mined, the harvest gathered in, and the fields ploughed for the autumn sowing, people married or died or were born, and Sunday dinners were cooked.

In Little Torrington, children were playing between the cottages, and there were Michaelmas daisies and a golden tide of Good-bye Summer in the little gardens. Two women stood in their doorways, discussing somebody's shameless behaviour, and

37

their voices came to Simon clearly across the field corner. A lean pig rooted contentedly among the yellow cabbage-leaves in a garbage pile, and on the brown hillside beyond the church a man was ploughing, with a wheeling crying cloud of gulls behind him.

Leaning there, with the quick ring of the smith's hammer in his ears, and his eyes on the distant plough team, Simon found himself thinking idly back over those two years. During the first few months, his father had been one of the Barnstaple Garrison, serving under Colonel Chudleigh, who had built the fort at Bideford—for North Devon too had had their leader at the outset; and James Chudleigh had led his men out to victory again and again, until his name began to have a ring to it that was almost magic. Simon had seen him once riding by, a young man laughing into the high March wind, and understood why his men followed him as a guiding flame. Then had come the day when the garrisons of the three towns had marched out to head off Hopton's advance from Launceston (for Cornwall had risen staunch for the King as Devon had done for Parliament). They had been defeated, and news of the disaster, filtering back into Devon, had brought with it the almost unbelievable tidings that James Chudleigh, taken captive by the King's men, had turned his coat for the sake of freedom and a Colonelcy in the Royalist Army ! The bright flame had been only a jack-o'-lantern, after all; and when it flickered out, some of the heart seemed to go from the men who had followed it. A few weeks later, after Bideford and Torrington had fallen, Barnstaple had yielded without a fight, leaving Plymouth to stand alone for Parliament in the West Country.

Prince Maurice had occupied Barnstaple, and the Militia and train-bands in the town had been disbanded. Simon's father had come home in a cold rage against Colonel James Chudleigh. There had been a wonderful pie of mazard cherries for supper, Simon remembered—his mother was famous for her mazard pies—and the door had opened and they had looked up, and there he was standing in the doorway. He had come in and taken his place at table, but he hadn't been able to eat the mazard pie. They hadn't dared speak to him about what had happened; they hadn't dared try to comfort him, and the next morning he had ridden off to join Essex's army in the Home Counties. They had not seen him since, though they had word from time to time. Barnstaple was back in Parliamentary hands this last month and more, but that was not likely to bring him home, for he was serving in the north, now, with Lord Leven's army, to which he had somehow become joined after Marston Moor.

And Simon himself? He had obeyed his father's order and continued his schooling as best he could. So had Amias. But they had not ridden the Tiverton road together, nor shared the same school bench, nor spoken when they passed. Then last April Prince Maurice had wanted men, all the men he could raise, for an attack on Lyme. The news had reached Tiverton on a market day; and Amias had gone to answer the call. He had not run away in the night, that was not Amias's way; he had simply walked out, during the midday break. He had turned in the gateway, his tawny eyes dancing, and waved to the crowded playground. 'I'm through with inky schoolboys! I'm off to join the Prince.' And he had disappeared into the market-day crowds before anyone realized what he was about. Save that he had sent to claim Balin from his father (Simon knew that from Tomasine, who was still his friend if they chanced to meet), he had not been heard of again.

Abruptly, Simon turned and went into the smithy, where the smith, with Scarlet's hoof between his leather-aproned knees, was putting the finishing touches to the new shoe. He glanced up as Simon entered, then returned to his task, while Scarlet slobbered at the back of his neck. 'There, me beauty,' he said, a few moments later, parting his knees so that the round hoof came down with a ringing crash on to the cobbles. " Proper fine horse, young maister. And ye'd never think a'was newly broken. Stands so still as a Christian, to be shod! That'll be sixpence, but if so be as you bain't got it on you, any time you're passing will do.'

' I've got it somewhere.' Simon felt inside the breast of his jerkin, while Scarlet advanced a hopeful nose, with soft lips nuzzling. ' No, you zany, it's not sugar.'

' Will Mr Carey be coming back, now Barnstaple be held for Parliament again?' asked the smith.

' I shouldn't think so. He seems to be with Lord Leven's troops for good and all.' Simon produced the sixpence, and paid it over into the grimy palm outheld to receive it.

' My niece be wed to a Barnstaple man serving under Colonel Lutterel as led the revolt and turned the Cavaliers out. Proper fine show 'twas, so they do tell me.'

' Proper!' agreed Simon.

' Don't seem like the war's going to be over yet awhile, for all that.'

' If 'tisn't over by the New Year, I'm off to join the Army,' Simon said, and turned to free Scarlet from the ring in the wall to which he had been secured. His hand was already on the headstall, when above the murmur of the forge fire there rose a distant uproar, a confused splurge of shouting and the drumming of horses' hooves, followed by a sharp crack like a breaking twig. Dropping his hand from the headstall, Simon strode back to the doorway. A soft scurry of rain blew in his face as he rounded the corner of the smithy wall, making him blink, and when his sight cleared, the first of a knot of horsemen had appeared over the hill-crest to his left, and were riding hell for leather towards the village, with the unmistakable look of men pursued. The peace of the scene was shattered as by a blow, children rushed squealing for their own doors, the rootling pig departed at a canter. Somewhere behind the riders sounded again that sharp crack like a breaking twig. Then the first wave of buff-and-steel-clad horsemen had pulled out of the lane and were heading for the church, fanning out over the hummocky grass so that the horses on the nearer flank swept by within a few yards of where Simon stood.

' My days! What be 'appening?' shouted the smith, appearing round the corner of the smithy to join him.

' Running fight, seemingly,' Simon shouted back. The horses swept on, wild-eyed, with labouring blood-streaked flanks, their riders crouching low and tense in their saddles, in a smother of flying mud and streaming manes and drumming hooves. ' Looks as if they're going to make a stand in the churchyard.'

Wave after wave of desperate horsemen were drumming up the lane and across the fields, and in the distance, topping the rise,

Simon could see the forefront of the pursuit. As the last knot of fleeing riders swept past the smithy, the report of a horse-pistol cracked through the tumult, and one of them jerked in his saddle, swayed, and crashed down on to the churned grass, while his horse plunged on riderless.

''Ware there! He'll be ridden down!' Simon sprang forward into the path of the following horsemen. An upreared head with wild eyes and rolling mane blotted out the sky, and the thunder of hooves stunned and deafened him as he dragged the fallen man clear; and next instant the first wave of the pursuit torrented past.

'Give me a hand,' he shouted to the smith, and between them they lifted the fugitive and carrying him inside, laid him down in a clear space beside the anvil. Scarlet was snorting and trembling, but Simon had no time to console him just then.

'Be 'un a Parlyment man?' demanded the smith, in a doubtful bellow, above the noise of the hunt as it thundered by to hurl itself against the desperate defenders of the churchyard.

Simon had dropped on one knee beside the man, and was unfastening the worn buff coat to expose the bullet-wound in the base of his neck. 'I don't know,' he said. 'I think so.' It had not occurred to him to wonder whether the man was friend or foe, he had simply seen that he was in danger of being ridden down, and acted accordingly. Certainly the hair which curled wildly back from his forehead was long, and the square linen collar turned down over his buff coat was edged with point lace, but Simon had seen hair as long and lace as fine on a Parliamentary officer before now. Moreover, he thought that in the fleeting glimpse he had caught of the pursuing Standard, he had recognized the arms of Sir Francis Storrington, a Royalist of Royalists.

It was a shallow wound, though bleeding freely, and the man, who to judge by the lump on his temple had been knocked out in his fall rather than by the bullet, was already beginning to stir. Simon dragged back the stained shirt and looked up at the smith. 'The ball's not still there, is it?'

The smith bent forward to look, then shook his head. ''Tis

41

no more'n a gash; best tie 'un up—if so be as you think 'un be a Parlyemnt man.'

The fugitive's eyes opened suddenly, with a dull bewilderment in them, and with a savage exclamation he tried to struggle up.

Simon pressed him back. 'Stay still, till I bind up your hurt; you're bleeding like a stuck pig.'

'What I asks is,' said the smith doggedly, 'be you a Parlyment man, or be you not?'

The wounded man squinted at him for a moment, then, as the question sank in, said faintly but with extreme clearness, 'You babbling splay-footed lunatic, of course I'm a Parliament man,' and shut his eyes again. But an instant later, as his head began to clear, he made another attempt to rise. 'What's happened? I must go after the rest—I——'

'You've been shot,' Simon told him, tearing his own rather grimy kerchief into strips. 'And you fell just outside here. You'll be all right when I've tied you up.'

The other gave a little groan of weary remembrance rather than pain, and rubbed the back of one hand across his forehead. Simon saw now that he was young, not more than two or three and twenty, with a round, freckled face and snub nose. 'For the Lord's sake be quick! What's happened to the rest of the Cavalry?'

'They are making a stand round the church, out yonder. If you don't stop squirming about, how *can* I tie up this gash?'

'Oh, perdition to that! What's happening out there?' The young man had strained up on to one elbow and was staring round at the doorway.

Simon glanced up at the smith, and jerked his head in the same direction. The smith ambled over to it, and disappeared, and a few moments later he was back, grinning. 'Fine old to-do,' he reported. 'They'm shooting from the church tower now. Looks like they'm holding their own, what's more.'

The young man relaxed at his words and lay down once more, and Simon was able to get on with his task. As he strained the first strip tight, his patient flinched sharply, and then apologized. 'Sorry. I'm about at the end of my tether. We all are. It's a long way from Lostwithiel.'

42

'Lostwithiel?'

'Oh, of course, you wouldn't know; but you will soon enough. We got drubbed at Lostwithiel.'

The smith bent forward to peer at him. 'What happened, then?' he demanded. 'Do 'ee tell us what happened, my dear soul.'

'Goring and Grenville made a sudden drive across our rear and—trapped us,' said the young man, muzzily. 'Essex got away—I believe he got away—but the Infantry couldn't, and poor old Daddy Skippon was left to hand over the whole lot.' He gave a dreary laugh. 'We only got out because My Lord Goring was drunk, so mazy drunk he couldn't stop us.'

Amid the tumult of battle outside, the sudden hush in the smithy was like a bubble of utter silence, broken only by Scarlet's scared fidgeting. 'Then—do you mean the war is over—we're beat?' Simon demanded.

'No! Not by a long shot! The Royalists are bound to give our Foot a pass—a safe conduct back to Plymouth or Portsmouth when they've disarmed them. They can't feed five thousand prisoners, and even that brute Grenville can't hang so many— there wouldn't be trees enough in Cornwall to go round. Daddy Skippon will bring his troops home somehow; and the whole of the Horse got away—leastwise, unless the rest have fared no better than we have. We ran into a blazing regiment of the King's men up on the moor 'bout six miles from here, and we were too done to beat them off . . . Go and see what's happening outside.'

Simon knotted off the makeshift bandage and, getting up, crossed to the doorway and made his way round to the corner of the smithy, from which he could get a clear view of the church. He had been longer than he knew, tending the hurt of the man behind him, and the running fight had become a grim and desperate struggle for the churchyard. The King's men seemed everywhere, pressing in from all sides against the churchyard wall, behind which the defenders, some afoot, some still on horseback, were battling stubbornly for the makeshift breastwork. Some of the horses had been tethered among the dark yew trees close in to the church, and stood quiet, too spent to resent the uproar all

43

around them. From the bell-slits in the tower an occasional crack and a puff of blue smoke, whipped away by the September wind, told where a marksman was at work; but on both sides the shooting was dying down, mainly, Simon guessed, from lack of powder and ball; and it seemed that the fight was going to be finished hand-to-hand with the sword.

All this he shouted back as well as he was able to the wounded man; and a short while later he caught his breath in a gasp of excitement, as, without any warning, the fight began to break up once more. He could not see what had happened, but suddenly the Royalists round the gate swayed back. They rallied, pressing fiercely in once more, and once more gave ground. A hoarse cheer went up from the churchyard, and the defenders hurled themselves against the weakened place in the attack. The grey light glinted on many leaping blades; and Simon found himself yelling, he didn't know what—and beside him, someone else was yelling too. He glanced round and saw the young officer clinging to the rough stone wall, and rocking on his feet. 'Done it! Done it, by the Lord Harry!'

In other places now, all round the churchyard, the Royalists were being forced back; and the men of Essex's Horse were swinging into the saddle once more. For a few wild minutes of charge and counter-charge, victory seemed to hang in the balance;

44

then another yell burst from Simon's companion. 'They're running! Praise be! They're finished!'

It was quite true. Hurled back by a grim, exultant wave from the churchyard, the King's troops were falling back upon each other, streaming away in confusion; and after them poured the men of Essex's army, cheering as they spurred their weary horses.

The time that followed seemed to Simon a wild dream of men and mud and horses, and a score of separate skirmishes wheeling and whirling through the village and across the fields; and a turmoil that grew fainter and fainter in the distance, until it was gone. He found that his companion was wringing him violently by the hand, and then sitting down suddenly on a convenient baulk of timber, and sliding quietly from it to the ground in a dead faint.

By the time Simon, with the smith's help, had contrived to bring him round again, the whole thing was over and the Parliamentary troops beginning to gather once more round the church. Like gnats in the first sunshine after a storm, the villagers were appearing from their cottages, and the young officer staggered to his feet and demanded his steel cap, which still lay where it had fallen, against the smithy wall. Simon brought it, and he clapped it on with a flourish, and set out to rejoin his comrades, without more ado. 'Though I do say I'm a bit weakly,' he said cheerfully, zigzagging like a snipe in the general direction of the church.

Simon grabbed him from the edge of a headlong fall, and put a steadying arm round him. 'Well, you've had a good crack on the head,' he said, 'and you'll get another if you go falling over your feet like that.' Together they crossed the open ground, where men and horses lay crumpled on the hummocky turf or among the Good-bye Summer in little ruined gardens.

'Up there, towards the door—that's Colonel Ireton,' directed the other, as they reached the church, and Simon obeyed.

There were a good many wounded already in the churchyard, and others being brought in by their comrades, and nobody took any particular notice of them as they made their way up the rough path. A knot of officers were standing in the west door of the church, talking earnestly together, and Simon's fugitive staggered clear of his arm and joined them. A ruddy hawk-nosed man

45

swung round to him, exclaiming, 'Colebourne! I imagined you were dead.'

'No, sir. Reporting back for duty,' grinned the other, doffing his steel cap in salute.

Colonel Ireton nodded, and turned away to give some order to a grizzled corporal, while the young officer sat down thankfully on a tombstone, and called to a passing trooper, 'Jenks, have you seen anything of my horse?'

'Tethered round the north side of the church, sir,' said Trooper Jenks; and then, his eye falling on Simon: 'Hi, you! Come and give a hand here.'

It was falling dusk by now, and with the food and clean rags which the Colonel had ordered to be brought from the cottages, some of the villagers were bringing up lanterns to light the tending of the wounded, who had mostly been gathered in the church. The lights came jiggiting up between the tombstones and the dark yew trees, turning the scarlet yew berries to strung jewels, making the soft rain shine as it fell, and filling the church, when they reached it, with a golden radiance that seemed more fitted to a festival than to the grim business in hand. Simon worked hard, that evening, among the wounded of both armies, while outside the church, and at the Sanctuary door and the windows, the troopers stood with drawn swords, in grim readiness for an attack. But no attack came. Evidently Sir Francis Storrington's men had had enough for one night. The food had been issued and eaten, and most of the wounds tended, and presently, as Simon knelt in the porch, steadying someone's forearm while somebody else got the bullet out, he realized that the hawk-nosed officer was standing by, in earnest talk with a younger man.

'If we can reach Barnstaple, we can get rations and fresh horses, or at least bait these, Richard.'

The other shrugged. 'And get away over Exmoor afterwards. Yes, but how in the Lord's name are we to get to Barnstaple?'

Colonel Ireton swung round to the knot of villagers who yet hung about the church door. 'Is there any man here able and willing to act as our guide to Barnstaple?'

There was no answer, and after a few moments he spoke again.

46

'It is needful that we should reach Barnstaple before dawn. Do any of you know the way, or know anyone who *does*?'

A long silence, and then someone suggested, helpfully, ''Twould be easy enough, maister, but the road goes through Torrington, and Torrington be in the Cavaliers' hands, do 'ee see?'

'I know that, you fool!' Colonel Ireton's voice was biting. 'It is precisely because Torrington is in enemy hands, that I need a guide for the cross-country journey.'

Another silence. The village people seldom travelled more than a few miles from their own homes; Torrington was their market town, and Barnstaple quite beyond their ken. Then Simon, having finished his task, rose slowly. He knew the Barnstaple road, since he had travelled it several times when his father was in the garrison, and when the direct road from Herons-combe was closed by spring floods; and with Amias in the old days he had explored every mile of the country round Torrington. He said, 'I'll take you. We can fetch a half-circle round Torring-ton, and join the ridge road farther on.'

Colonel Ireton looked him up and down in the lantern-light. 'You are sure of the way? We cannot afford to be led into a bog.'

'I know the way well, sir,' Simon said. He saw that the soldier was searching his face to make sure that he was trust-worthy, and he returned the look, levelly. 'I'll not lead you into a bog—or a trap.' By way of giving some proof of good faith, he added, 'My father served in the Barnstaple garrison until the capitulation. He's with Lord Leven and the Covenanters now.'

'All right,' said Colonel Ireton abruptly. 'We'll trust you.'

'I'll go and fetch my horse from the smithy, sir.'

The other gave his quick pecking nod, and turned to issue orders for the bestowing of such of the wounded as must be left behind, while Simon made his way back to the smithy. There was no sign of the smith, but Scarlet was still secured to the ring in the wall, and greeted him with a shrill whinny when he appeared in the doorway. The horse was still shivering and sweat-ing, his ears pricked and the whites of his eyes showing, and

Simon talked to him, drawing one hand again and again down his nose while with the other he freed the headstall.

A few minutes later he was back in the churchyard once more, leading Scarlet with him, and talking to him still, softly and encouragingly.

The troopers were already swinging into their saddles; the order to march was given, and before the dusk had quite yielded to the friendly darkness, Simon found himself riding beside Colonel Ireton, at their head, as they defiled out through the churchyard gate and down the village street, where faces dim-seen in the light of open doorways strained to watch them go by. There were close on six hundred men behind him, and it was his responsibility to get them safely to Barnstaple before dawn, and as he settled his feet in his stirrups and bent his head into the soft rain, he was filled with a queer quick excitement.

Presently the villagers of Langtree roused from their sleep to hear horses trotting through the dark. Later, a miller woke to hear the splashing of a multitude through the ford below his mill. He went to the window, but could see nothing for the darkness and the driving rain, and after he had heard the last horse away down the Weare Giffard road he went grumbling back to bed.

Simon had been worried about Weare Giffard, for the Hall was a Royalist stronghold, and a brush with the troops there might bring reinforcements from Torrington down upon them; but there was no possible way of avoiding the village. He had explained this to Colonel Ireton, who replied that since there was no help for it, the risk must be taken. But the deep mud muffled their hoofbeats, and riding on the verges of the lane, and the soft ground between the cottages and the river, they got through safely, and took to the steep coombs beyond.

In more than one lonely farm, strung in a wide curve about Torrington, people woke and listened anxiously before going to sleep again, and in the morning pointed out to each other the tracks and drove-roads churned to a quagmire by the passing of many horses.

It was a hard ride for men who were already exhausted, and many of them wounded besides; but in the first sodden cobweb light of dawn, Simon brought his scarecrow army over the brow

48

of the last hill and down towards the pale glint of the river and the thickly manned breastworks on Barnstaple Bridge.

'There's Barnstaple,' he said, in a kind of weary croak. 'I think I'd best be getting home now, sir,' for he had suddenly remembered that his mother might be worried about him.

'You've done a good night's work, lad,' Colonel Ireton said, and put his hand into the pocket under the skirt of his buff coat. Then he hesitated, looked at Simon in the growing light, and changing his mind, took it out empty. 'When next you write to your father in Lord Leven's army, tell him that you helped to save Essex's Bodyguard from being wiped out.'

They shook hands, and Simon, wheeling his horse clear of the column, sat to watch them go by, looming up in the grey light, mired leg-weary horses, and men blind with fatigue, who looked as if they kept in the saddle more by instinct than any power of their own. One or two of them turned their heads to glance at him in passing; the rest were too exhausted even for that.

If he had been a few months older, Simon thought, he might have been one of them.

Almost at the rear of the column, the young officer he had tended in the smithy looked round as he passed, and made him a wide cheerful gesture of farewell; but he was rocking in the saddle. Simon waved back. He sat watching until the town barriers had been dragged aside and the last rider had straggled through; then he turned Scarlet's weary head towards home.

A few days later Barnstaple was in Royalist hands again, after a five-day siege by Lord Goring. But long before that, Colonel Ireton and his tattered squadrons had got safely away over Exmoor, to rejoin the forces of Parliament.

## V

## *Fiery Tom*

TOWARDS evening of a day some months later, Simon came riding into the Royal town of Windsor, where the great New Model Army was being built. While the last stragglers from Lostwithiel were yet coming in, old Sir William Waller had warned the Committee of Both Kingdoms. ' Sirs, I tell you fairly that unless you form a properly unified army, you will not win this war,' and the Committee had at last, now that it was almost too late, taken his advice. The army that he had demanded was being formed, and Simon had come to join it. More than a week had passed since, having turned sixteen, he had said good-bye to his family and Lovacott and set out, but he had ridden Scarlet all the way, and that had meant a slower journey than if he had ridden post. However, here he was, with a pair of long horse-pistols in his holsters that had been a parting gift from his mother—flint-lock pistols, the very latest thing—and he and the new Model Army were beginning together. The thought made him sit very upright in his saddle and look about him with bright, eager eyes.

It was yet early in February, and the poplars and elms of the river-meadows were bare, while the flickering water of the Thames reflected back a thin sunshine that had no warmth in it; but already the crimson flush of the willows told of rising sap, and there was that faint quickening in the air which is the first sign of spring while it is still a long way off. And high above the bare trees and the steep russet roofs of the town rose the great round Keep of Windsor Castle, grey, and somehow triumphant as a fanfare of trumpets, looking as though it had not been built by hands, but had grown out of the very stuff of England.

Simon had been watching the Keep ever since it first came in sight, but as he turned into the narrow street, it was hidden from his sight by the crowding roofs and overhanging upper storeys of the houses. Not that he would have had leisure for looking at it now, anyway, when all his attention must be given to getting Scarlet safely through the crowds that thronged and jostled up and down the crooked ways. Country folk and towns-folk, rich merchants in well-cut doublets, and beggars showing their sores in the kennel, a street-corner preacher in black gown and Geneva bands, a vendor with caged linnets for sale, a group of laughing girls with market-baskets on their arms; and everywhere, soldiers and yet more soldiers. Simon looked at them all, but particularly at the soldiers, because soon he would be one of them.

They were a motley crew, some in rags, some in scarlet coats stiff with newness; some gaunt and toughened with long campaigning; many still ruddy from the plough or pale from the counting-house desk, for the new Model Army was as yet only an army in the making.

Stopping to ask his way from a small wizened man whose scarlet coat was faced with shrieking yellow, Simon rode on until the high curtain-wall and ancient towers of the Castle began to peer over the gables and down into the thronged streets, and he came to one of the gateways. There was no ditch on this side of the Castle, for it had long since been filled in, and crowding hovels grew right to the curtain-wall as toadstools crowd against a tree-trunk, and a lane simply turned between two houses and led straight in through Henry VIII's gate. Simon followed the lane, and reining up, appealed to the sentry on duty. ' I want to see the colonel.'

' Which colonel? ' demanded the sentry.

' Any colonel of Horse.'

' Sergeant! ' shouted the sentry.

The sergeant appeared from the guard-room, and looked at Simon hard.

' Cove here wants a colonel of Horse—any colonel of Horse,' said the sentry.

' What for, sir? ' demanded the sergeant, doubtfully.

' I want to join the Army,' said Simon.

A young officer in the usual scarlet coat, who chanced to be passing, swung round at the sound of his voice, and letting out a yelp of surprise, came striding to join the group. ' You! ' he cried. ' Well, of all the——'

Simon looked at him blankly for an instant, and then suddenly the gay freckled face under the jaunty feathered hat seemed to alter, and he remembered it as he had seen it last, grey and haggard and stained with blood. It was the man he had pulled from under the hooves of a Royalist horse at Little Torrington!

' You! ' echoed Simon, and bent down from the saddle to wring his hand. ' How's your neck? '

' Sound as a bell, and right as a blazing trivet! You're a good surgeon.' The young officer's eyes were dancing up at him, his huge mouth curling almost into his ears. ' You've come to join us? '

' Yes.' Simon nodded. ' Where and how do I find a colonel? '

' Oh, to hell with colonels! It's the General for you, my lad —and he's down here today too. Come along and we'll catch him before he starts back again. All right, sergeant, a friend of mine; I'll see to this.'

With a breathless sense of being caught up and hurried along by a wave against which it was useless to fight—not that he had the least desire to fight—Simon abandoned himself to whatever might happen next, and dismounting, obediently led Scarlet back into the main street.

52

'I say, this is luck! A timely meeting!' his companion was saying. 'My name's Barnaby Colebourne. What's yours?'

'Simon Carey,' said Simon, slightly dazed. '*Who* did you say we were going to see?'

'The Lord-General, Sir Thomas Fairfax. *You* know.'

Yes, but surely we don't need to bother *him*!' Simon protested, as they shouldered back into the shifting crowds of Thames Street.

Barnaby Colebourne explained rapidly and at the top of his voice, as he pushed forward across the street. 'We do if you're going to join my Regiment. Fairfax's Horse, we are, and so the General is our Colonel, if you see what I mean.'

Simon saw, rather hazily, and was just opening his mouth for another question, when they arrived before the courtyard arch of a great inn, over which hung a brilliantly coloured sign showing the blue-and-gold insignia of the Garter.

'Here we are,' said Barnaby Colebourne, and with Simon and Scarlet at his heels, turned in through the dark tunnel of the archway. They emerged in a cobbled courtyard where two horses were being walked up and down before the house door; and after handing Scarlet over to the care of an hostler, Simon followed his new friend into a shadowy hall where several soldiers were standing about, and up a broad flight of stairs, past the doleful-looking sentry on duty at its foot.

'Of course we could have gone to Major Disbrow,' said Barnaby casually. 'Most of the Colonel's duties fall on him really, but the Lord-General is more likely to listen to reason.'

There was another man on duty before a door at the end of the long upstairs gallery, and a young officer of the Staff, a Galloper, kicking his heels by the window. Barnaby spoke to him, and he disappeared into the next room, and after a few moments came back and left the door open for them.

They went in and the door shut behind them, and Simon found himself in a panelled room where a low fire was smoking badly on the hearth. A man writing at a table in the middle of the room glanced up for an instant at their entrance, and then went on writing; while another man in the dark clothes of a secretary sat by him, ready to take the finished paper.

After the noisy streets, it seemed very quiet here, with no sound save the faint, harsh scratching of the quill pen over the paper; and Simon had plenty of time to take stock of the writer, who he supposed must be General Sir Thomas Fairfax. The Commander-in-Chief was dark; that was the first thing one noticed about him: dark as a gipsy, and gaunt as a scarecrow under the gay scarlet of his uniform coat, with black unruly hair hanging about his cheeks and neck. With nothing of his down-bent face visible save the frowning black brows and great beaked nose, he had a most forbidding aspect; and seeing his gloves and riding-whip beside him on the table, and remembering the horses being walked up and down in the courtyard, Simon began, first to feel that they had not chosen a very good moment to bother him, and then to wish fervently that they had not come to bother him at all, but gone to Major Disbrow, whoever he might be, instead.

The great man finished his writing and laid down the pen, sanded the sheet and handed it to the man beside him, saying in a slow very pleasant voice, 'Three copies, John—no, four. Colonel Pride had better have one.' Then he turned his attention to the pair waiting before him. Now that he was looking up, his dark face no longer seemed forbidding, for the eyes did much to redeem its harshness. Also, Simon saw to his surprise that he was quite young—not more than two or three and thirty. The scar of an old wound showed livid on cheek and temple, and he put up one hand for an instant to cover it, as though he was still very conscious of the disfigurement; then let his hand fall back to the table.

'Yes, Colebourne? You wished to see me?'

Barnaby stepped forward, doffing his hat in salute. 'Yes, sir. This is Simon Carey, a friend of mine, and he wants to join the Regiment; so I brought him along to you, sir.'

The General turned his head in the quick alert way he had, and studied Simon in silence for a few moments. Then he nodded, as though satisfied with what he saw. 'How old are you?'

'Sixteen, sir.'

'You have seen no fighting before, I take it?'

'Only as an onlooker, sir,' said Simon.

Barnaby made a quick movement forward, and Fairfax turned to him. 'Yes, Colebourne?'

'He's the guide who got us safely through to Barnstaple, after Lostwithiel, sir.'

Fairfax studied Simon again. 'That was a good night's work,' he said slowly. (Indeed, all through the interview Simon found the slowness of the General's speech an odd contrast to the quickness of his looks and movements.)

'Thank you, sir.'

'I haven't got a cornet, yet, sir; beg pardon, sir,' said Barnaby, insinuatingly.

'What about Cornet Wainwright?'

'He——' Barnaby hesitated, and then plunged on. 'I know he thinks he has a right to the post, but seniority isn't everything, and—do you think he's quite the man for the job?'

'Don't you?'

'Frankly, no, sir.'

The General's left brow shot up, and he leaned forward, arms folded on the table. 'Tell me why,' he suggested.

'Well, sir, he's too touchy about his dignity, for one thing, and he's got a sarcastic way with him that doesn't go down well.'

'He has the makings of a good officer, none the less.'

'But not for the Second Troop, sir.' Barnaby was speaking quickly, and very much in earnest. 'My men are mostly old Ironsides, and a good many of them are Anabaptists and so on, too, and that doesn't make them any easier to handle. They're the salt of the earth, sir, but they're a pretty hard lot, and if Cornet Wainwright started his airs and graces on them, they'd—they'd be more inclined to spank him than salute him!'

The General's dark face kindled suddenly into a smile that made him seem for an instant like an eager boy; then it was gone, and only a trace of it lingered in his eyes. 'That sounds like indiscipline, Captain-Lieutenant Colebourne.'

'No, sir; human nature,' said Barnaby with a grin.

'And you think Carey, here, would have a better chance of success with these ravening wolves of yours?'

'Yes, sir—and Colonel Ireton would speak for him, I'm sure. So would Richard Cromwell.'

'You have met him only once before?' mused Fairfax. 'Ah well, the circumstances of the meeting being what they were, that might be enough. We won't trouble Colonel Ireton or Captain Cromwell.' Turning back to Simon, he began to question him closely: of course he could ride? Had he ever used pistols? . . . Simon's answers to these and sundry other questions evidently satisfied him, for finally he pushed back his chair and got up, saying, 'Very well, Colebourne. I bow to your judgement. John Rushworth, see to it. You have the details correctly?'

The grey-haired secretary glanced at a slip of paper on which he had been writing and read out, 'Simon Carey, to be commissioned as Cornet of the 2nd Troop, Fairfax's Horse.'

Fairfax nodded, then turned to Simon again. 'You will receive your Commission from the Committee of Both Kingdoms in the course of a day or two. In the meanwhile, get your equipment and report to Major Disbrow.'

Simon drew himself up even straighter than he had been standing before and said rather breathlessly, 'Thank you, sir! I—I'll do my level best to be worthy of it.'

'I know that.' Fairfax picked up his gloves and moved toward the fire. 'I wish you a good evening, Colebourne. Good evening, Carey.'

A few moments later they were outside the door again, and clattering downstairs.

'A friendly soul, the Lord-General,' said Barnaby with satisfaction, as they crossed the courtyard where the horses were still being walked up and down before the door. 'Never too busy to talk to small fry man-to-man and listen to what one has to say. Now for the Quartermaster; I'm off duty, so I'll come too. We'll leave your horse here and pick him up later on the way back to Quarters. Oh, but wait a moment——'

They had just emerged into the street, when he stopped in his tracks and turned to point upward. 'Look up there.'

Simon followed the line of his pointing finger, and saw a mass of drooping Colours that hung motionless in the quiet air, brilliantly, glowing blue and gold and white in the fading light of the February afternoon, from the open oriel window above him. 'Those are our Regimental Standards,' Barnaby was explaining. 'The big ones on the left are the Colours of Fairfax's Foot, and the smaller ones on lances are the Standards of Fairfax's Horse; one for each Company and Troop, you see. That's ours, second from the left, and the black leopard above is Sir Thomas's personal Standard. They are always housed where everyone can see them, partly to show where Regimental Headquarters is, and partly because—well, because they belong to each one of us, and so we all have the right to see them, not only in action and on parade, but all the time.'

Simon stood gazing up at the motionless Standards, especially at the second from the left, the Standard of his own Troop, which one day he would carry into action. His heart beat high with resolve to be worthy of his trust; visions of honour and chivalry and the Glory of Arms rose within him, and pride in the cause for which he would soon be fighting . . . Then he woke to the fact that Barnaby was shouting in his ear that he was blocking up the way; and suddenly he flushed crimson, and turned to follow his new friend up the street.

Several hours later, Simon was sitting up in his shirt in the pallet bed which had been made up for him on the floor of Lieutenant Colebourne's chamber. The White Hart was not a fine large inn such as the Garter next door, and with the sixteen officers of Fairfax's Horse quartered there, space was limited; and there was another pallet in the small room, as well as the narrow trucklebed on the edge of which Barnaby himself was seated, still half-clad, and tenderly polishing a pair of truly wonderful boots. They were of yellowish leather, very soft, and with turn-down tops so enormous that Simon wondered very much how it was possible to walk in them at all.

Simon was dog-tired, and the hours since his interview with Fairfax seemed like a crowded dream. In company with Barnaby Colebourne he had gone to report to Major Disbrow, a lean brown little fighting man with an eye of blue steel. The two senior troops or companies of each regiment had no captain, but were under the direct command of the colonel and major, and in them the work of the captains mostly fell to the lieutenants, who were superior beings to other lieutenants in consequence. This, being the 2nd, was Major Disbrow's Troop, and Barnaby was its Captain-Lieutenant. Those were two of the few positive facts that Simon had discovered that evening, and he clung to them as to a spar in a sea of chaos. Leaving Major Disbrow, they had repaired to the Quartermaster's Office farther up the town, and to various magazines and depots to draw his equipment and see about his uniform. The scarlet coat faced with blue which was the uniform of both Fairfax's Regiments had had to be altered slightly, and would not be ready until next day. But his sleeveless buff coat (second-hand and somewhat worn and weather-stained) and his heavy spurred boots and steel cap were now stacked with Barnaby's in the corner; and from the back of the one chair which the room possessed hung his new sword in its crimson slings. He had been half-minded, before he left home, to take Balan with him, as Amias had taken Balin; but he had realized that though it was a rapier of the old sort, with a cutting edge as well as a point for thrusting, it would not be a good weapon for fighting on horseback, and he would do better to wait until he reached Windsor. Now he had his heavy Cavalry blade, the real thing, and he sat and hugged his knees, feasting his eyes on it, while Barnaby polished and re-polished those preposterous boots.

They had collected Scarlet from the Garter stables and brought him here to the White Hart. Then there had been supper in a long room that seemed over-full of loud voices, long legs and tobacco smoke. He had a confused memory of a dark-eyed resentful looking youth a year or two older than himself, who he had gathered was Cornet Wainwright; and of a long ropey Yorkshireman with a merry eye, who Barnaby had whispered to him was Ralf Marjory, one of Cromwell's old Ironside captains. All the rest had been just faces, grim or merry, ruddy or pale or brown. Simon hoped that one day, perhaps tomorrow, he would get them sorted out. But meanwhile he was thankful the day was over.

Barnaby gave the left boot a final loving pat, and held the pair out at arm's length. ' What d'you think of *that* for a pair of fashionable boots? ' he demanded.

Simon gave up gazing at his sword, and turned his attention to the fashionable boots. 'Umm, they're very fine,' he said at last. 'How do you walk in them?'

'Why, it took a bit of practice, I'll admit,' said Barnaby airily. 'But I've got the knack of it now. Wait a moment, and I'll show you.' And he began, with many grimaces, to pull on his treasures. It took him some while to do so, but he managed it at last, and rising, began to walk up and down the cramped room with what was meant to be a careless swagger, but was actually a pigeon-toed waddle; for the turn-down tops of his boots were so wide that he could only get along with his legs almost as wide apart as though he was on horseback.

The sight was almost too much for Simon. He let out a stifled sound between a snort and a hiccup, and then recovered himself. 'They—they're splendid boots.'

'Yes, I think they're pretty good. Don't believe there's another pair like them in the Army,' said Barnaby, squinting sideways at his legs.

'I—I shouldn't think there would be,' agreed Simon.

'Ah, well, even in the Army one can observe the decencies, you know. It's different with the Ironsides, of course: they mostly pride themselves on dressing like a cross between a parson and a horse-thief.'

'Most of the officers of—of ours are old Ironsides, aren't they?' said Simon.

The other nodded, and sat down on the bed. 'The senior ones, anyhow. More than half of the men too.' He reached for the boot-jack and began to rid himself of his boots. 'The rest of us are Fairfax's men. Of course, between us, we're the cream of the Army.'

Simon sat silent for a few moments, watching him wrestling with his left boot. Then he said, 'You know, it was a tremendous piece of luck, my running into you like this.'

''Twas so,' agreed Barnaby, beginning on the other boot. 'You'd not have been in Fairfax's Horse tonight, if you hadn't. And—well, we *are* the cream of the Army. We're worthy of the General, and no one can say fairer than that.'

'What is he really like, the General?' asked Simon.

'How d'you mean?'

'Well—he seems queer somehow: that quiet slow way he has of speaking, when everything he *does* seems so quick; as if you were watching one man and listening to another,' fumbled Simon.

'Oh, there's nothing mysterious about that. The moment he slackens the bearing-rein, he starts stammering.'

'Stammering?'

'Like a July cuckoo,' said Barnaby, setting his boots tenderly in the corner.

Simon thought this over for a few moments; then he said, 'Yes, but what is he like?'

'Oh goodness!' the other said helplessly. 'How in the name of——'

The door opened and a young man, evidently the owner of the third bed, came in. Barnaby appealed to him. 'Fletcher, what's the Lord-General like? Carey wants to know.'

'Fiery Tom? Oh, he's all right,' said the new-comer, yawning. 'Lord, but I'm tired till my bones ache.'

'Why "Fiery Tom"?' asked Simon, made stubbornly persistent by his tiredness.

'Wait till you see him in action, then you'll know.' Cornet Fletcher turned to drag off his coat, but was checked by a shout from Barnaby.

'Hi! Don't go trampling over my best boots, you blear-eyed hippopotamus!'

'With all due respect, sir,' said Cornet Fletcher, continuing to take off his coat, 'curse your best boots! One can't move an inch in this dog-hole without falling over them!'

'If you don't like my boots,' said Barnaby reasonably, 'go and share with Bennet and Anderson.'

'Bennet's such a hell-fire red-hot militant Anabaptist. No stable-mate for a peaceable fellow like me.'

'There's that, of course.'

'And Anderson plays the recorder under the blankets.'

'*What?* Old Sober-sides? Gammon!' Boots and the General were instantly forgotten.

'Found him at it, when I went to rouse him out about that sick horse the other night.'

'It just shows you!' Barnaby said happily. 'I'd as soon have suspected Corporal Relf.'

Fletcher turned round on Simon. 'You've not met Corporal Zeal-for-the-Lord Relf yet, have you?—A pleasure in store!'

'Don't listen to him,' cut in Barnaby. 'The Corporal's all right. And anyhow, he's the cove who'll be teaching you your job.'

Discussing the matter of Lieutenant Anderson's recorder with unholy interest, they finished undressing and crawled into their blankets; Cornet Fletcher blowing out the guttering tallow dip before he did so. 'Good nights' were exchanged, slightly muffled by the bed-clothes, and silence descended with the blue darkness into the cramped inn chamber.

For a long time Simon lay awake, listening to the quiet breathing of the other two, and watching through the window the stars moving behind the dark head of the Garter tower. They were the same stars as those he saw through the little garret window at home; only at home they shone through the branches of the old warden pear tree that was a dome of snowy blossom in the spring. A sudden wave of homesickness flooded over him; the hard unfamiliar pallet, the breathing of the others in the alien darkness, the strangeness of everything, all brought back to him the desolation of his first night at Blundell's. He remembered the long bare dormitory and the smell of damp and candlesmitch, the confused rise and fall of many breathing in the dark, the emptiness of his stomach because he had not yet found how to get his full share of supper, his aching longing for Lovacott. But then, Amias had been there, so near that if he flung out an arm, he could touch him; and he and Amias had shared their homesickness as they had shared everything else.

He wondered where Amias was tonight. Quartered in some farm-house perhaps, or bivouacked under the stars . . . Serving with the Army of the King as he, Simon, was with the Army of Parliament. It seemed suddenly very odd, that if he reached out into the darkness, he would merely annoy Cornet Fletcher, because Amias would not be there.

## VI

## *The Empty Hoard*

URING that spring all Windsor was one great camp, humming with life and activity as more and more troops came in and were drafted into the re-formed regiments. All day and often half the night the cobbled streets rumbled to the arrival of the wagon-trains bringing stores and ammunition. For the first time an English army was being dressed in scarlet, and day by day the shifting crowds grew more colourful as the new uniforms arrived, and regiment after regiment appeared in good kersey breeches and red coats faced with blue or yellow or green according to their colonel's fancy. In the Commons Fields below the Castle, as far as Datchet Mead and beyond, the remnant of Essex's force, together with scattered regiments and new-joined men, were being nursed and hammered into an army; and the three men chiefly responsible, who seemed to be everywhere at once, needing neither food nor rest, were Sir Thomas Fairfax, the Commander-in-Chief, Sir Philip Skippon, the Chief of Staff, and Lieutenant-General Cromwell, who officially commanded nothing but the 6th Regiment of Horse.

Before long, these three became familiar figures to Simon, as they were to every man in the Army. The dark rather Don Quixote-seeming General, constantly appearing and disappearing between Windsor and Whitehall; grey-haired and stooping Sir Philip, a veteran of the Swedish Wars, known affectionately to his troops as Daddy Skippon or The Old Man; the thick-set ruddy Cavalry Colonel, with a laugh that seemed to shake the Castle Walls, a heavy farmer's walk that gave the impression of a pound or so of good East Anglian soil caked on each boot, and a reputation for wrestling whole nights in prayer. At first they were only figures, but very soon he began to learn things about them that brought them to life.

He learned how Fairfax had come by his scarred cheek at Marston Moor. 'You see the trouble with our revered Lord-General,' Barnaby told him, 'is that the moment he goes into action, he loses his helmet. It just flies straight off his old cock-loft like the lid off a pot when it boils over, and he goes stark staring mad. You wouldn't think it, to look at him, would you? No; well, it makes him a simply tremendous man to follow in a charge. He was leading a squadron of four hundred of us that day, and he lost his helmet as usual; and one of Prince Rupert's guards took a swipe at him, and there he was, with blood stream-ing down his face, as crazy as a March hare, still riding straight for the main body of Rupert's left wing, and yelling to us to follow—so we followed.'

He learned how Daddy Skippon had brought back the tattered remnant of Essex's Foot from Lostwithiel. An Infantry lieutenant, with a grim face old beyond his years, told him that story as they leaned over a gate together one off-duty evening, watching for the distant flicker of a roe-deer's passing among the glades of the Little Park. 'We were given our pass back to Portsmouth, and a lot of good that did us. We were starving and most of us were wounded, and the country folk were mostly for the King, all along the south coast. Leastwise, they were for the winning side; they harried us like wolves on our flanks, and we couldn't defend ourselves because we were disarmed. When any of our lads fell out, they killed them and left their bodies in the nearest ditch; and all the time it rained. Faith! How it rained! That meant fever, of course, especially for the wounded. If we'd had any other commander, I think we'd have lain down and died, rather than struggle on; but Daddy Skippon got us through somehow. Oh, it's no good asking how, for I don't know; he was our pillar of cloud by day and flame by night; he made us too afraid of him to give in; he comforted and encouraged us like a mother with a sick child, and he got us through—most of us, that is—to Portsmouth at last, under our own Colours, and with our drums beating.'

Of Cromwell, he heard many stories from many people (for already Old Noll was a legend in the Army), but chiefly from Corporal Zeal-for-the-Lord Relf, who had served under him from the days of that first little troop which Cromwell had called his 'Lovely Company' and which had grown into a double regiment and borne the proud nickname of Ironsides. Corporal Relf was a long lean man, with a harsh voice, a hollow cheek, and a brilliant eye; the word of the Old Testament was constantly in his mouth, and his right hand seemed empty when his sword was not in it. He was the type of man who had made Cromwell's Ironsides what they were, ranting heretics and red-hot Anabaptists, many of them, but men who ' knew what they were fighting for, and loved what they knew . Now the Ironsides had been split up to form the stiffening of the two Senior Cavalry Regiments in this new Model Army; and Corporal Relf of Disbrow's Troop was, as Barnaby had said, teaching Simon his job.

Simon, his Commission having duly arrived, was an eager pupil and learned quickly, he and Scarlet together. They learned to manœuvre with other horses and riders, and to know the trumpet-calls by which, from now on, they would live and take their orders. Scarlet was broken in to the noise of trumpets and kettle-drums, and trained to stand steady under gun-fire. Simon

64

mastered the correct handling of the Troop Standard and the use of the heavy Cavalry sword. Little by little, he learned to handle his section of the Troop; and this was made as easy as might be for him by his Corporal and his men, who looked on him kindly, and in his early and uncertain days dragged him through many a manœuvre in which, without their goodwill, he would have come to grief. And added to all this there were the ordinary routine duties of each day: 'Stables', 'Rounds', kit inspection, guard-mounting and the like.

At first life seemed strange and overful, but very soon the bewildering whirl of the days began to settle into a pattern; and in the pattern were many happy things that he would remember all his life. Sunday morning, and the drum-head service, with the Keep of Windsor Castle rising above the spring-flushed willows, and an ecstasy of lark-song soaring above the deep voice of the Army at its prayers. A squadron at the canter, and the quick music of trumpet and kettle-drum that made the horses all but dance. The comradeship of his men, and the slightly different comradeship of his brother officers.

They were an oddly assorted company, the officers of Fairfax's Horse: men of every type, from Barnaby Colebourne of the stylish boots to Captain Bennet who preached hell-fire and a God of Wrath, with his drawn sword in his hand, from Pastor Hugh Peter's makeshift pulpit on Sundays. But on the whole, they were friendly souls; and the only one of them with whom Simon could not get on at all was Cornet Denzil Wainwright, who was hurt in his dignity at being posted to the Third Troop, while the coveted cornetcy of the Second went to a raw West Countryman. Denzil, a townsman himself, considered Simon a bumpkin, and was at pains to let him and everybody else see that he did. He never missed a chance of showing up the mistakes which Simon, new to life in a Horse Regiment, frequently made; holding him up to sly malicious ridicule before the others; even, once or twice, before his men, which was an unforgivable thing to do. It was a process he had described to a friend as 'a little harmless boar-baiting', but for his victim it was not pleasant.

One morning about a month after Simon joined the Army, Denzil Wainwright was particularly objectionable on the way down to take early stables; flaunting his town airs and graces, pointedly calling him Hodge, and talking about cows in a way that made Simon, who was proud of the Lovacott herd, long to blacken his supercilious face for him. He took it all calmly enough, knowing that the pleasure of getting a rise out of him before the other cornets was exactly what Denzil wanted; but he was still fuming inwardly an hour later when he led his section out on patrol.

It was still very early as the party of horsemen came out into open country; the sun was not yet up, and the mist lying low in the water-meadows, but all the sky was full of sunshine, and the young leaves of the poplars caught the first light like flakes of gold tangled among the bare twigs. A most lovely morning in a most lovely part of England, and the beauty of it turned Simon's heart back to his own countryside, so different from this one of lush meadows and stately park-land trees—a countryside of little rounded hills and steep coombs; oakwoods that grew bent all one way by the west wind; sunk lanes where the foxgloves crested the high banks in summer, and little bleak fields hedged round with beech and thorn for a windbreak.

The sun began to rise, and at its coming the mist rose too, drawn upward by the warmth, so that for a while Simon and his men rode through a dim white world where tree and cottage and haystack seemed like phantoms, and even Corporal Relf, riding beside him, was dimmed by a veil of moisture. Then slowly the mist grew thinner; threads of blue appeared overhead, and stray glints of gold shot through the greyness, turning it to opal. A lark leapt up singing into the morning sky, and suddenly the mist was gone, only the mist-drops strung on every twig and grass-blade and silvering the manes of the horses sparkled with rainbow fires in the new sunshine.

The little company rode on, fetching a wide circle that took in several villages, where no one paid much heed to them, for these constant passings and re-passings of the Cavalry patrols had become familiar in the past few weeks. And some while after noon, coming to a pleasant river-side tavern, Simon called a halt to bait the horses and refresh his men. A stout man in a white apron bustled to the door as the troopers swung down from their

66

saddles, and Simon called to him. 'Bread and cheese, Landlord, and beer—lots of it—for me and my men.'

'Bread and cheese it is, General,' said the landlord cheerfully. 'And the best beer in Berkshire,' and he disappeared to attend to the matter.

The horses were picketed, and their nose-bags buckled on, and the troopers crowded into the dark tap-room, leaving two of their number to lounge before the door and keep an eye on their mounts. Simon wandered over to the window at the far end of the room, and stood looking out. The casement was open, and the scent of early wallflowers came in to him, and the murmur of a weir from somewhere beyond the willows at the foot of the garden. He swung round to find Corporal Relf at his shoulder, also looking out. 'I'm going into the garden,' he said. 'Bring me out some bread and cheese when it comes, Corporal, and send Perks and Wagstaff out their share.'

'Yes, sir.'

Simon flung a leg over the low sill and climbed out, carefully avoiding the wallflowers that grew beneath the window. There were new leaves everywhere, brilliant in the sunshine as tiny jets of emerald flame, and the untidy garden was a riot of daffodils and anemones; evidently someone here loved flowers like his mother, Simon thought, though unlike his mother, they did not care for weeding. He wandered down the sloping path into the realm of cabbages and currant bushes, drawn by the murmur of the weir; and parting the hazy willows, stepped down on to the river-bank. It was a backwater of the Thames, not the main stream, and the voice of the weir, whose foam-tumble curved across it a few yards farther up, was not loud and earth-shaking as that of an open river weir would be, but a soft wet thunder that was very pleasant to hear. Below where he stood, the water ran dark and smooth, and the curds of foam floated by, mingling with the flashing criss-cross web of gold that was the sunlight on the water. Simon was watching them, his shoulder propped against the bole of an ancient pollard willow, when steps sounded on the bank behind him, and Corporal Relf appeared with a large platter and a leather ale-jack.

'Food, sir.'

'Thanks, Corporal.' Simon took them from him. 'Ah, the best beer in Berkshire. This is a good place. Worth remembering another time.'

'Yes, sir,' said Corporal Relf, and even as he spoke his head whipped up, and he was watching something away down-stream. 'Kingfisher,' he said softly.

Simon was just in time to see the flash of living blue as it disappeared into the willows. 'That's the first kingfisher I've seen for months,' he said. And for the first time he realized that Corporal Relf was a countryman like himself, with a countryman's eye for things to which the townsman is blind; and suddenly there was a bond between them. 'There's plenty of bread and cheese for both of us, and we can get some more beer afterwards. Sit down, Corporal.'

'Sir?' said Corporal Relf.

'Sit down, Corporal Relf. I'm going to.' Simon suited the action to the word, and after a moment's hesitation, Zeal-for-the-Lord Relf folded up his long legs and did the same.

In a few moments they were settled very comfortably with the bread and cheese and black-jack between them.

'Are you a farmer?' Simon asked, after they had sat eating in silence for a short while.

'I had a small-holding, Spalding way—I and my brother.'

'Ye—es?' said Simon hopefully. After Denzil Wainwright, he wanted desperately to talk countryman's talk with a brother countryman; and as his Corporal showed no signs of carrying on the conversation, he added 'Tell me?...'

'There's not much to tell; 'twasn't a big plot, nor yet a rich one, but our father held it afore us, and his father afore him, and so on, way back I dunno how many generations. Maybe you know how 'tis with a plot of land—how it gets to be wove into a man's heartstrings, when it has bred him and his forebears.'

'Umm,' said Simon. 'I know.'

'What says the Good Book about every man sitting under his own vine and his own fig tree?—Not that the place was ever our own; we held it from Squire; father and son holding it from father and son.'

'Mixed farming?' asked Simon.

68

'No, bulb farming. Spalding be a great bulb district. That pheasant-eye there——' He nodded in the direction of a starry clump that had evidently strayed from the garden behind them and was growing in the long riverside grass. 'We used to grow a-many like that; tulips too, and daffy-down-dillies; all for the bulbs, you see. Folks mostly thinks of bulbs coming from the Low Countries, and so they did in the first place—a good many of 'em, anyways—but nowadays, when your mother buys jonquil bulbs for her garden, 'tis as like as not they come from Spalding.'

Having got started on the subject of his heart, he talked on for a while, about the little holding in the Fens that seemed to be the one thing in the world he really loved. About the business of bulb farming, the care needed in their storing, the difficulty of breeding certain flowers true to type; until it seemed to Simon that the man beside him was no longer Corporal Relf, the warrior-prophet of hell-fire that he had come to know, but a new friend, a peaceable man who grew things, and found joy in the flaming and feathering of a tulip petal.

'I suppose your brother is carrying on the holding until the war is over and you can go back to join him?' Simon asked presently.

There was no answer. And when he looked round the new Corporal Relf was gone, and the old one back again, with his dark face set like a stone. 'No, sir,' said Corporal Relf, in a grating voice. 'Henceforth, I am Ishmael. There is neither vineyard nor fig tree for me.'

In the appalled silence which followed his words, Simon heard very clearly above the murmur of the weir a distant splurge of laughter from the tavern behind them. 'I say, I—I'm sorry,' he blurted out at last. 'I wouldn't have said that if——'

Corporal Relf went on staring at the white flowers of the pheasant-eye beside his booted foot. 'Nay now, there's no call for that, sir,' he said harshly. 'Word-of-mouth don't make the matter no worse.'

Simon never afterwards knew quite how or why his Corporal came to be telling him the whole unhappy story, unless it was because of the kingfisher. He only knew that the other had laid

69

down the stub of his bread and cheese, and was talking, quickly and bitterly. ' 'Twas this way: we did pretty well with the bulbs, my brother and I—better nor ever our forebears did. We even managed to save a bit, and none of our forebears ever managed to do that. And we saved to the end that, if need be, we might one day buy the holding. Old Squire had no son nor any near kin to follow him, and well we knew that when his time came to be gathered to his fathers, we should see the Manor go to strangers, and maybe the holding ours no longer. For that end, we lived lean, and went without all else, wife and children included; all that could come later, we thought, when the holding was safe. We got all of thirty pounds together at last, saving and scraping, adding a bit each market-day, and hid it in the hole in the house-place wall. 'Twas a good hiding-place, and we used it for other things beside the money; we'd been at work for years breeding a double white hyacinth, and at last we had succeeded, and we hid the bulb there too, ready for planting time. But man is born to sorrow as the sparks fly upward, saith Job in his wisdom. 'Twas just after that the war broke, and Cromwell was gathering his men against Charles Stuart, that Man of Blood, and I joined him, that I also might smite the Amalekites. I hadn't been gone but a few weeks when word reached me that my brother was dead. Died of a marsh fever, he did; and when I got back to see to things, and went to the hoard in the wall—'twas empty. Neither silver piece nor hyacinth bulb was there.'

' Oh, what evil fortune!' said Simon, after another silence. ' What happened, Zeal-for-the-Lord?'

'I planted me vineyards; I made me gardens and orchards, and planted in them of all kinds of fruits—and behold, all was vanity and vexation of spirit, and there was no profit under the sun,' quoted Zeal-for-the-Lord moodily. ' What happened? Why, I went back to the Troop, and within a month old Squire died, and the Manor went to some gay young sprig as sold off up'ards of half the farms and holdings. Some of the farmers bought in their land. I couldn't.'

' But—would the thirty pounds have done it?' suggested Simon.

' No; but 'twould have been enough for a start, and I could

70

have paid the rest later. The white hyacinth would have brought in a goodish bit once 'twas on the market. New Squire weren't unreasonable.'

' There was no one you could have borrowed from? '

' If there had been, I'd have swallowed my pride, and borrowed,' said the Corporal. ' I loved the land well enough for that. But we aren't a rich folk with money to lend, we Fen farmers. James Gibberdyke, my neighbour, he'd have lent it me if he'd had it. A bit on the feckless side, James were, and had even less than most. But the staunches' friend any man could be wishful to have in time of distress. " A friend loveth at all times, and a brother is born for adversity," saith the Good Book, and that was James all over, and a deal closer to me than my own brother : for Aaron and me never had much in common, save the holding. Yet there was some as looked down on James for a ne'er-do-well, not knowing him as I do.' He drew his long legs under him and got up. ' And now, sir, 'tis about time you gave orders for the march.'

So Simon knew that the odd intimacy of the past half-hour was over. He got up obediently, finished the beer, and went back to the tavern with his Corporal marching at his heels.

# VII

# Into Battle

O N a summer morning some months later, two armies faced each other across a wide upland valley, a mile or so north-east of Naseby. The light west wind stirred and fretted the Colours of the opposing regiments, but save for the wind, it was very quiet; and as the waiting minutes lengthened, Simon, sitting his eager Scarlet in the ranks of the New Model, found himself thinking back over the events that had brought him there.

Six weeks ago, when Cromwell and a body of Horse had already been sent to keep the King shut up in Oxford, the New Model had marched west under orders from the Committee to relieve Taunton. Horse, Foot and Train, they had marched out under the grey Castle ramparts, with the camp-followers riding in the commissariat wagons or tagging along behind (for the New Model, like other armies of their day and long afterwards, were followed on Campaign by wives and sweethearts without whom it would have gone hard with the sick and wounded). There had been trouble about the rearguard before they were two days out: Fairfax's Foot had objected to taking their turn of rear-guard duty; they were the General's Own; why should they march in the rear with their mouths full of the dust of lesser regiments? They had chosen a spokesman and put their case to the General. Fairfax's reply was typical of him; he was sorry that his Regiment found themselves too grand for rearguard duty, but he himself did not; and he had dismounted and marched with them. There had been no more trouble with the rearguard after that; but plenty of another kind.

They had scarcely reached Taunton when they were recalled and ordered to besiege Oxford, from which the King had already escaped, slipping past Cromwell and heading north to join

Montrose on the Border. Cromwell had been sent off again, this time to see to the defence of Ely; the Army had grumbled and grown restive; the siege had dragged on, while the King and Montrose prepared to crush Lord Leven's force between them: and Simon, knowing that his father was in that threatened Army, had fretted more than most. But the orders of the Committee were not for questioning. Finally, when Charles, halting in his march, had sacked Leicester, and all the Eastern counties were in danger, Fiery Tom had taken matters into his own hands. He had called a council of war, raised the siege of Oxford and marched north, and sent orders to Cromwell to return at once and take command of the Horse.

That had been several days ago; and yesterday Cromwell had rejoined the main Army at Kislingbury, just as they were breaking camp in a chill mizzle-rain. Simon had seen him ride in with his six hundred troopers, red-eyed and mired to the combs of their helmets with hard riding, their horses leg-weary under them; and word had run like stubble-fire through the camp. 'Noll's back! Old Noll's come in!' The Foot had taken up the cry from the Horse, and the whole Army had cheered themselves hoarse as the weary company rode in, cheered until the voice of their cheering had seemed to beat against the sodden skies, bringing the rain down faster than ever.

Last night, the New Model had come up close on the heels of the Royalist Army, and bivouacked at Guilsborough, still in the driving rain. It had been creepingly cold, and in the black hour before dawn, when Chaplain Joshua Sprigg had offered up prayers for victory, and a meal of hard biscuit had been doled out to the troops, Simon had not wanted any. There had been a queer cringing in the pit of his stomach, of which he had been desperately ashamed, and the bare idea of food made him feel sick. He had not known what to do with his biscuit, for he could not give it to anyone else without owning to that shameful feeling, and had finally pushed it guiltily inside the breast of his sodden coat. Barnaby, who was beside him, had seen him do it, but most surprisingly had not laughed.

'Scared?' Barnaby had demanded in a low voice, close to his ear.

Simon had run his tongue over uncomfortably dry lips.

'Yes,' he said. ' Sorry.'

' Well, why shouldn't you be? It's your first taste of field action. I've been in action a good many times now, and I'm scared stiff.'

' No? ' said Simon, with a gleam of hope.

' Bless you!—yes; and I'm not the only one. This is the worst part though, the part that makes your innards crawl; you'll be as right as a trivet when we get going; we all shall. And look here, Simon——' Barnaby sounded suddenly embarrassed, almost apologetic.

' Yes? '

' It doesn't matter a straw *being* scared, you know. It's only when you let it interfere with the job in hand that it starts being something to be ashamed of.'

Somehow that had helped quite a lot, and Simon had fished out his biscuit again, and eaten it with a determined effort, though it turned to sawdust in his mouth. After that there had been no more time to bother about anything save the business in hand. Still in drizzling rain, the camp had broken up and begun to move, column after column swinging away into the darkness. But when the grey dawn came, there had been a bar of sodden primrose low in the west. It had broadened and spread, changing to aquamarine, to clear-washed blue; and by the time they reached Naseby and the baggage-train was left behind, the rain had stopped, and the spirits of the wet chilled Army had lifted to the reborn sunshine of the June morning.

And Barnaby had been right. The waiting in the dark had been the worst part. Simon no longer had to be ashamed for his queasiness; he was filled with a queer eager expectancy, and nothing worse, as he sat his fidgeting mount between the troopers of his Standard Escort, awaiting the order to advance. On either side of him, and behind, were ranged the Regiments of the Right Wing, under Lieutenant-General Cromwell, holding as their natural heritage the place of chief danger and chief honour. To their left were the Foot Regiments of the Centre, under Daddy Skippon; and beyond, Ireton's command of the Left Wing. The dragoons were out of sight along the curve of the hill; but a good part of the main battle line was clear to Simon, and a thrill of pride leapt in him as he looked down the great line; seeing the Foot bravely scarlet between the buff and steel of the Cavalry Wings, the Colours and Standards lifting and flowing out on the light wind, brilliant as strange flowers in the sunshine that flashed here and there on the serried ranks of pikes, or a musket barrel or a steel cap.

As the waiting time lengthened, Simon began to notice little things with a crystal sharpness that he had never known before. Small details and oddities never noticed until now, about the backs of the Regiment's officers out in front. The warmth of the sun on the back of his hand as he held the slender painted Standard-lance. The Standard itself, as he looked up at it, billowing against the sky with quick wind-ripples running through it as through standing wheat. Feathery wind-clouds flecked the blue above it, and a buzzard circled and circled on motionless wings. It was very quiet, up here in this country of rolling downs and shallow vales at the very heart of England. Simon could hear the quietness of it, through the sharp alien sounds of the waiting battle line; a quiet made up of country sounds, familiar and beloved; the mewing of the wheeling buzzard, the soughing of the wind over the hill-crest before him, the distant whit-whit-whit of scythe on wet stone. Somewhere, someone was haymaking. There might be a war in the next field, but a fine day was a fine day, not to be wasted at harvest time. They would be haymaking at home now, up in Twimmaways, Tom and Diggory and the rest; and Polly bringing them out pasties and rough cider in the shady corner under the may-trees. In the old days Amias had always been there too, to help get in the hay. . . .

The quiet was ripped apart by the strident challenge of distant trumpets; and Simon tensed in the saddle, as the scouts appeared, falling back over the crest of the hill. Parliamentary trumpets blared in reply, and next instant the whole of Ireton's Wing had swung forward over the skyline. Drums took up the challenge, and the Foot were moving forward, and the Right Wing with them, up and over the crest. And now for the first time, Simon saw the King's Army. He looked instinctively for the Royal

Standard, and did not find it, for the King was with his reserves. But if the Lions and Lilies were not yet to be seen, there were other Standards in plenty: those of Sir Marmaduke Langdale on the Left wing, of Sir Jacob Astley in the centre and Prince Rupert on the right, and the flash and flutter of lesser Colours thick between them. For an instant Simon wondered if Amias was carrying one of them, and then there was no more time for wondering. The Royalist Right Wing was already advancing up the near hillside, led by the red-cloaked figure of the Prince himself, and a spearhead of his own wild young Cavalry. Ireton's troops swept down to meet them, and the two wings rolled together with a formless crash that was more a sense of shock than an actual sound; and from both sides rose a shout that spread all down the lines: 'Queen Mary! Queen Mary!' cried the Royalists. 'God our Strength!' answered the New Model men, and the two war cries seemed to beat against each other in the air above the swaying battle line.

Cromwell was holding his wing in check, while the oncoming Royalist left drew near. Simon watched them, across the valley and coming uphill at a canter, the sun bright on their naked blades, the tossing plumes, the streaming Standards over all. Nearer and nearer yet! Simon's Standard hand was clenched so tightly on the lance that the knuckles shone white as bare bone. Would the order to charge never come? What is he waiting for?—Now! *Now* or it will be too late!

The enemy were half-way up the slope when at last Cromwell loosed Walley's Regiment down against them. The squadrons swung forward at the trot, their ranks curving a little, then straightening again. Simon saw them check to fire their pistols at point-blank range, and then fall on with the sword. Langdale's Horse met them valiantly, and instantly a desperate struggle was in progress, and Walley's reserves were charging down to join it.

Away to the left, a confused roar was swelling and growing ragged with the raggedness that means a running fight. But for Simon there was only the conflict directly below him; and there, the enemy were giving ground! And suddenly, above the ragged musketry and the roar of battle, the trumpets of Fairfax's Horse were yelping.

'Charge!'

'This is it! This is *us*!' The kettle-drums began to roll; Simon touched his heel to Scarlet's flank, and felt the horse gather and slip forward under him as the long ranks quickened into life. 'Oh, God of Battles, strengthen now our arms!' his heart lifted in wild excitement. This was the real thing, the charge that had been practised so often in the meadows at Windsor. He felt his knees touch against those of the men on either side of him, as they moved forward and down at the trot. The ranks curved and grew ragged, then closed again. The ground before the Right Wing was mostly rabbit warren, hummocky and patched with gorse. Gruelling ground to charge on; but Cromwell had known that when the battle line was formed, and trusted them to get through somehow.

Forward and down at the trot—look out for rabbit holes and try to keep station—can't fail Old Noll.

So with rolling kettle-drums and wind-whipped Standards, the Right Wing charged home. 'God our Strength!' Simon heard his own voice above the tumult, shouting at the full force of his lungs, as, following Barnaby, he drove straight into the reeling mass of the Royalist Cavalry.

But Walley's charge had done its work, and already the Royalist Wing was crumbling. Now came this new charge, and before it, despite a valiant resistance, they began to fall back. Soon there was no longer a solid battle line, only a chain of skirmishes. Simon found himself and his Standard Escort cleaving into them, with the Troop thundering at Scarlet's heels. 'God our Strength! Follow the Standard!' All around him were battling figures, upreared horses' heads, and a raving, roaring turmoil that seemed to engulf him like a sea. There was a thick mingled smell in his nostrils, of burned powder and blood and sweating horses. He ploughed on holding the Standard aloft, and found, with a vague surprise, that the press was thinning out. The Royalists were falling back faster now. Langdale's Horse was just about finished. Simon ranged up beside Barnaby, who yelled to him, 'Done it, by the Lord Harry!' before they were thrust apart once more.

Then quite suddenly the first stage of the battle was over.

Walley had been left to finish with Langdale's Horse, and Cromwell was leading his remaining regiments against the King's
reserves. Simon was riding hard, close behind the Lieutenant-
General himself. Corporal Relf, almost at his elbow, was
shouting whole verses from Isaiah as a kind of battle hymn.

He saw the Royal Standard now. It swelled brilliant on his
sight. But the shock of the charge-home never came. Some-

thing had happened to the King's reserves; they were falling into confusion, streaming away northward. Simon could not know that when the King would have led his troops in a counter-charge, Lord Cornworth had seized his bridle, crying, ' Will you go upon your death, sire?' He could not know of the strange confusion of orders that had caused the reserves to turn tail, sweeping the King with them into headlong flight. He only knew that the Royal Standard was in retreat, the Royalist chivalry gone like a dissolving dream.

Cromwell swung his squadrons back to the main business of the day.

Things had gone ill with the Left Wing; indeed they had come almost to complete disaster. Ireton had been wounded and taken captive near the outset, and Prince Rupert and his wild riders had broken clear through and charged away over the skyline, driving the remnant before them.

Daddy Skippon also was wounded, and though refusing to leave the field, was out of action to all intents and purposes; and the Foot, lacking their leader, and with their left flank exposed by Ireton's break, began to crumble too. The Left Centre gave ground and could not be rallied, and the Royalists broke through and flung themselves against the three veteran regiments of Pride, Hammond and Rainsborough, in the reserve. Only the superb steadiness of those three saved the day; that, and the flaming example of Fairfax himself, who had by that time lost his helmet and most of his staff, and was fighting like any berserk trooper at the head of a valiant company who had somehow gathered to his reeling Standard.

The fight was still raging when Cromwell brought his flying squadrons down against the exposed flank of the Royalist Foot. At the same time, Colonel Okey's Dragoons came against their other flank; and the remnant of Ireton's Wing, which had by now rallied, led by Ireton himself, who had escaped within half an hour of being captured, took them in the rear. The Royalists fought gallantly, dying where they stood. Prince Rupert, who had allowed his charge to carry him as far as the baggage lines at Naseby and been driven off by the musket-fire of the Escort, returned with his blown horses to find the battle hopelessly lost.

Having been away too long, he did the best thing he could, joining the King and forming a new Cavalry line, north of the old one. But the heart was gone from the Royalist troops; and when Fairfax, also re-forming, charged once more with terrible cavalry-wings outspread, Simon saw again that oddly pitiful sight of a battle line crumbling as a sand-wall crumbles before the incoming tide.

'They run! God our Strength! They run!' The triumphant shout spread through the victorious army; and the pursuit broke forward, and swept yelling after them.

In the forefront of the chase, Simon was riding hard. He felt the wind of his going whip back the Standard on its lance, and send Scarlet's mane spraying over his bridle-hand, as the horse leapt forward, snorting, in answer to the spur and the urging voice; he heard the hooves of his Troop drumming at full gallop over the downland turf behind him. But suddenly the exultation was gone. Simon had always disliked hunting anything, and hard-pressed fox or beaten army, it made no difference. He hated it now.

Behind them, in the wide upland valley that had so lately been a battle-field, the prisoners were being rounded up, and the Royalist baggage-wagons brought in to serve the wounded, and the camp-followers were busy. It was not yet noon of a day that was still lovely, and the June sun shone warmly, gently, on the dead of two English armies, who lay tumbled uncouthly among the thyme and the little white honey-clover of the downland turf, here at the heart of England. High overhead, the buzzard still wheeled, mewing, on motionless wings; and on every side the coloured counties fell away in shallow vales and hazy woodland, and little fields where the hay harvest was in full swing.

## VIII

## ‘ Mine Own Familiar Friend ’

AFTER fourteen miles of hard riding, Cromwell called off the pursuit. The Regiments turned aside and came, towards evening, down into a village in a hollow of the green Leicestershire hills : troopers who, now that the excitement of the chase was over, were utterly spent, on horses suddenly foundering. They descended upon the sleepy place like a swarm of bees on to an apple-branch, and dropped from their saddles in the fields all round it, too tired even to notice the presence of the gaping villagers.

Simon’s one desire, having dismounted in the corner of a hay-field under some ancient elms, was to lie down flat on his back and stare up into the green many-layered heights of the trees, and never do anything again. But there were others in worse case than himself; Scarlet’s bright coat was sweat-darkened almost to black, his flanks heaved distressfully, and the white foam dropped from his muzzle. Simon drew a consoling hand down the moist neck, then went hurriedly to the aid of one of his own troopers, who, having ridden with the best of them, was now swaying where he stood, with an arm that dripped red.

'Hi! Corporal Relf!'

The Corporal swung round from mustering his men. 'Sir?'

'Anyone found where the 'pothecary's shop is yet? Clerk's hit.'

A village sage answered him. 'Up the far end o' the village. They'm taking the wounded up along there now. I see'd 'em when I come by. Terrible gory, some of 'em be, to be sure. You been fighting, I reckon?'

'Yiss, we been fighting,' Simon agreed. Then, to a trooper standing near, 'Saundry, take Clerk up to have his arm seen to.'

'Sir.' Trooper Saundry got his shoulder under his comrade's sound arm, saying encouragingly, 'Hold up, Laddie.' And the two of them began a wavering progress towards the tumbledown cottage that marked the beginning of the village street.

'Sir.' ·It was the troop trumpeter this time.

'Yes?'

'The Major wants you, sir.'

'Right.' Simon turned and, leading Scarlet with him, crossed to where Major Disbrow had that moment dismounted from his weary horse. 'You sent for me, sir?'

'I did. Have you done anything about quartering your section?'

'Not yet, sir. I only arrived a few seconds ago.'

'It's your responsibility. Go and see to it now.'

Simon hesitated, and the little whipcord Major added testily, 'Well, what's the trouble?'

'Anywhere, sir?'

'Anywhere, my good boy, that is not bought up already, by officers quicker off the mark.'

'Very good, sir.' Simon saluted and stepped back, flushing.

Several of his troopers glanced at each other, for they had mostly suffered at different times from the Major's barbed tongue, and knew that he was always somewhat short in the temper immediately after being in action. And they made a great show of efficiency on their young officer's behalf, as they remounted and prepared to follow him.

82

The whole village was by this time thick with troops and their officers, all on the same quest; but after one or two fruitless efforts, Simon, or rather his Corporal, found vacant quarters in the shape of a small sturdy farm-house down a side lane behind the church.

The farmer, a square man with a truculent blue eye, proved difficult at first, when confronted by a young Parliament officer demanding shelter for himself and thirty-odd troopers. ' On-christian, I calls it!' he said bluntly. 'Making war on your lawful King, and trapesing about over the standing hay, and a-sitting yourselves down on respectable folks, fritting the maids and firing the farm over our heads as like as not!'

' Look here,' Simon said, after he had heard him out, ' we won't frit your maids nor fire your farm, but I'm afraid you have no choice but to give us the shelter of your barns and outhouses for the night; we shall need food too, and fodder for the horses; all that will be paid for, of course.' He grinned suddenly. ' I'm sorry about the standing hay.'

' What do the likes of *you* know about standing hay?' demanded the farmer.

' I know that I shouldn't like horses trampling through mine,' said Simon frankly.

' Farmer yourself, maybe?' said the farmer with deep suspicion. ' Yes.'

' Parliament'll pay, ye said?'

' Yes. Now will you come and show us our quarters—or send someone else to do it?'

Still grumbling, the man accompanied Simon out to the knot of weary horsemen waiting in charge of Corporal Relf, and led them round to the yard at the back.

In obedience to the age-old law of Cavalry, that the horse must be tended before the man seeks his own food and rest, the troopers set to work. The horses were unsaddled, rubbed down and walked to and fro until cool; then fed from the bins reluctantly opened to them by the farmer, watered at the mossy stone trough, and picketed in the home paddock.

Normally, Scarlet was the care of one of Simon's troopers, but this evening was no time to be putting extra work on any man. Besides, Scarlet had carried his master valiantly today, and

83

tonight his master wanted to do everything for him, by way of saying thank you. So, working beside his troopers, Simon unsaddled the weary sorrel and rubbed him down with straw, groomed, fed and watered him, pouring, all the while, soft proud endearments into his twitching ear.

He had just finished, and was standing to watch the picket lines pegged, when a hand came down on his shoulder, and he swung round to find his Lieutenant standing beside him.

'Sir?' said Simon.

'Just a social call. We're quartered up yonder, and I bethought me I'd best come and see how you was getting on. Any wounded?'

'Clerk shot through the arm. He's up at the 'pothecary's now. Three others wounded—or killed—back there.' He jerked his head in the direction of Naseby.

Barnaby nodded; and for a moment they stood looking over the quiet countryside. 'Well, you've had your baptism of fire,' he said.

'Yes, Scarlet too.' Simon drew his hand again and again down Scarlet's arched neck, while the horse slobbered lovingly against his breast. 'And we've put a spoke in Charles' wheel as sure as unicorns,' he added absently.

'As sure as *what*?'

Simon flushed. 'Unicorns. Short for "As sure as unicorns lay eggs". It's just a catch-phrase that a friend and I used when we were little lads. I'd almost forgotten it—and then it slipped out.'

Barnaby nodded. 'Friend out for Parliament too?'

'Out for the King,' Simon said briefly.

Barnaby glanced at him. 'Not all beer and skittles, this war, is it?' he said.

'No.'

There was a silence. Then, 'Leaves blowing back for rain,' said Barnaby. 'You all right? Managed enough fodder for the horses? I'll be getting back to my own lads, then.' He swung away between the elm trees, and Simon watched him go, thinking how different Barnaby in time of action was from Barnaby of the preposterous boots.

84

Long after the soft June gloaming had smudged away the outlines of barn and rick and hedgerow, the village continued to hum like a disturbed bee-skep. Cromwell and his staff had taken possession of the Happy Return Inn, and every farm and cottage in the village and for miles around was full of troopers, every paddock full of picketed horses. Men came and went, on guard duty or the business of the Lieutenant-General; officers making the rounds of their men and horse-lines. Small blind-weary clumps of stragglers kept coming in too. The apothecary and his shock-headed prentice were still at work. But the villagers for the most part kept their own firesides, grimly determined to see that at least the plague of troopers which had descended on them did not fire their houses, nor unearth their life's savings from up the chimney or under the mattress.

In the smoke-blackened kitchen of the farm behind the church, Simon and his section had eaten the supper of beans and cold bacon hastily prepared for them by the farm-wife and her maids. They were in complete possession, for the square and truculent farmer had shown his disapproval of Parliament and all its works by sending the maids to bed and the farm-hands to their quarters over the stables, and withdrawing himself, his wife and his wall-eyed sheep-dog to the seldom-used parlour. Those of the men who were not now on guard duty lounged on benches and butter-casks, or sat on the floor, with their backs propped against their comrades' knees, many of them three parts asleep.

Simon was sitting on a settle beside the fire, his sword-belt loosened and his steel cap on the polished seat beside him. The low flames curled like fantastic flower-petals among the red-hollowed logs; blue fringed with saffron, saffron with a heart of emerald green, emerald tipped with Royal scarlet. Simon watched them until, finding himself nodding forward, he woke up with a start and looked round at his men. There had been a great coming and going throughout evening, but for the moment all was quiet. Somebody had produced a greasy pack of cards (' The Devil's Picture Book ' was strictly forbidden by the authorities, but there were a good many packs cherished, none the less, in the ranks of the New Model), and four of the men were playing Post and Pair, their heads bent together round a dribbling candle in a brass pricket. Trooper Wagstaff, who always liked to have his hands occupied, was carving his name on the broad window-sill, and Simon supposed he ought to stop him, but somehow could not bestir himself to do so. Trooper Clerk, his arm having been dressed, was sleeping peacefully with his head in a corner and his mouth open. Several more were talking and dozing in alternate snatches. Corporal Zeal-for-the-Lord Relf sat in the corner of the opposite settle, his worn Bible open in his hand, his lips moving as he read, leaning forward to catch the firelight on the page. From time to time he raised his head, as though know-ing the words by heart, and stared straight before him with those burning fanatic's eyes of his, his lips still moving.

They had not the look of a victorious army, Simon thought; they were too tired. He was beginning to nod forward again when the outer door opened with a crash, and a stout red-faced trooper appeared against the background of the twilit lane.

'Captain Vanderhorst's compliments,' he said, addressing the room at large, with a cheerful grin, 'and could he be obleeged with the loan of a little corn? Six more stragglers just come in, and quartered in the vicarage, and the Reverend Gentleman ain't got no more.'

Simon struggled free of the sleep that seemed to enfold him like a blanket. 'I expect so. Corporal Relf, see to it, will you?'

Corporal Relf got up, stowing the Bible back into the breast of his coat; and in that same instant a joyful roar burst from the man in the doorway, and he tramped forward, holding out a hand like a mottled ham. 'Zeal! Zeal-for-the-Lord, or I'm a cross-eyed infidel!'

Corporal Relf swung round at the sound of his voice, and his dark face lit suddenly in reply. 'Jonnie! Why, Jonnie, what do you do here?'

'Come in with Old Noll, two days agone. Been garrisoning Ely, I have. My, but it's good to see you! Us heard you was killed at Gainsborough, two years back.'

'The Lord of Hosts in His mercy protected me,' said Zeal-for-the-Lord. 'The shield of His Power was stretched over me.' Then he recollected himself, and turned quickly to Simon. 'I beg your pardon, sir; I'll see about the corn.'

'I'll see about the corn,' Simon said. 'It isn't every day you come back from the dead. Give your gossip some ale.' He called out several of the watching troopers, sent one of them to inform the farmer that corn for six more horses was being taken from his bins and that he had better put it down in the reckoning, and set off with the others for the stable yard.

When he returned to the firelit kitchen, Corporal Relf and his crony were deep in talk of old scenes and old friends.

'I was up Spalding way in the spring, buying fodder for the garrison,' the stranger was saying loquaciously, and seemingly giving Zeal-for-the-Lord little chance to do the talking. 'And who should I run into but James Gibberdyke; so I went back with him for a meal. Most unwonted prosperous, he seemed too.'

Simon, back in his corner, could not help but hear every word, for the man's voice was loud, and a lull had fallen over the drowsy troopers.

'Barn re-thatched, and a new suit, and I dunno what-all! A aunt of his had died, seemingly, and left him a bit of money. Ah, I'll tell you another surprising thing about James. He'd got a most beauteous thing growing in his bulb-plot; been working on it for years, he said, to get it perfect—and you wouldn't think James was the sort for experimenting, would you? A double white hyacinth, 'twas, as sure as I stand here! A double white——'

A hoarse cry broke from Corporal Relf, and Simon, looking up quickly, saw him stagger back against the wall, as though from a blow between the eyes.

'Why, whatever be the matter, neighbour?' demanded the other. 'What be there in a double white hyacinth to——'

But Corporal Relf had pulled himself together before the astonished stares of his troopers. He shook his head, and after a moment answered, 'Nothing. Nothing in the world, Jonnie. 'Twas an old wound that ketches me sometimes, after a hard day.'

'Well, if it ketches you like that, you did ought to get it seen to,' said Jonnie severely.

'I will, Jonnie, I will. Go on with what you were saying.'

'I was saying as James Gibberdyke had growed this double white hyacinth. Going to put it on the market, come this autumn, and 'twill make a tidy bit o' money for him, I shouldn't wonder. We talked a good bit about you, Zeal—thinkin', both of us, that you'd been killed at Gainsborough; and James were saying what a hidjus sad thing 'twas. Very upset about it, James were.'

'That was—mighty good of James,' said Corporal Relf, heavily.

'Ah, but wait till he knows the joyful news!'

The old Ironside lifted his head, until it seemed to be looking into some dark prospect beyond the other's square figure. 'Yes, wait till he knows,' he said.

'Be you sure you're all right now? Powerful queer you do look, to be sure.'

'Quite all right. 'Tis time you was getting back to your Captain, Jonnie; you'll be riding the Wooden Horse, else.'

'Aye, mebbe so,' Jonnie agreed. 'Be seeing you again by and by, I reckon. And do 'ee take my advice and have that wound seen to! 'Twill most like turn to gout if 'tis left!' And still talking, he got himself as far as the door, then turned back, remembering his errand.

'The corn has gone off to Captain Vanderhorst,' Simon forestalled him.

The man saluted, beaming like a jovial red sun. 'Thank 'ee kindly, sir,' he said, and was gone.

A while later, Simon was returning from a last look at the horse-lines before turning in. It was a very still night, the wind having dropped quite away; the stars were swollen and soft with moisture in the summer sky, and the cool air sweet with the scent of elder flowers and new-mown hay; but Simon did not notice these things, for his mind was full of that story of a double white hyacinth. Corporal Relf had seemed quite himself again, when he had accompanied him a few minutes ago, on rounds; and yet——

The warm light of fire and candles still streamed from the uncurtained window of the farm kitchen, casting a golden stain over the garden plot; and on the edge of the stain, faintly outlined against the crowding shadows beyond, stood a tall figure; a wild, agonized figure with quivering fists up-thrust towards the stars. As Simon hesitated, uncertain what to do, his Corporal's voice reached him in a kind of shudderng whisper, 'Mine own familiar friend, in whom I trusted. Mine own familiar friend——'

Next morning, when the section mustered, Corporal Relf was missing. His mount was still in the horse-lines; his equipment, including his sword and one pistol, was ranged neatly on his sleeping-place in the big barn. But the other pistol had gone with him, wherever it was that he had gone. Simon, his heart suddenly sick within him, ordered a strict search of the farm-yard and nearby fields, knowing, as he gave the order, that it was quite useless.  The search did have one result, for it produced a shepherd who had passed a man heading eastward across the hills, some time in the night; he couldn't say when, not for sure.  A tall man, talking to himself; talk that sounded as if it came out of the Good Book—a surly sort of chap, who hadn't seemed to notice when the shepherd bade him good night in passing.

When Simon had heard the shepherd's story, he left his senior trooper in charge, and went to report the matter to Lieutenant Colebourne, whom he found watching his horses watered at the stream.

Lieutenant Colebourne cocked an inquiring eyebrow at his cornet, and then, seeing his face, sobered abruptly.  'What's wrong?' he demanded.

'I have to report Corporal Relf missing, sir,' Simon said.

'*Missing?*'

'Some time in the night.'

'But—you're not serious?  Relf isn't the man to—here, wait a moment.'  He gave orders to his Corporal for seeing the horses watered, and then moved away, with Simon at his side.  'You've searched the farm buildings?' he asked, when they were out of earshot.

Simon nodded.

'This is a queer business, Simon.  Relf isn't the sort who deserts.  Have you any idea what possessed him?'

'Yes, I have.'  Staring moodily down at the brown trout-stream, Simon told the whole story as he knew it.

When he had finished there was a long pause; and then Barnaby said, 'So you think he's gone off on private revenge?'

'Vengeance, he would call it,' Simon said.  'It was his friend, you see.'

'Yes, I see.  But the Lord-General isn't fond of deserters, whatever their reasons for deserting.  If he's caught, the Lord have mercy on him, for Fairfax will have none.'

'If only I'd done something about it last night; but—devil take it!—what *could* I do?'  Simon's voice was desperate.  'He's old enough to be my father, and he looked—like a man on the rack.  I thought the only thing to do was to leave him alone.'

'It *was* the only thing,' Barnaby said.  'Bar putting him in irons, there's nothing the likes of you or I could say or do that would turn Corporal Relf from anything he'd set his mind to.' He kicked thoughtfully for a moment at a tussock of grass, then shrugged, and turned back towards the place where the horses were now being led up from watering. 'I'll report to Major Disbrow. Get back to your own men now. Muster for the march in an hour.'

# IX

## *Sentence of the Court Martial*

AT Naseby, the New Model seemed to be settled in for several days. The whole place had become a vast camp, with Fairfax and his staff in the Manor House, and his troops quartered under every roof for miles around, including that of the church. The largest farm had been turned into a field hospital, where the army surgeons worked day and night among the Royalist and Parliamentary wounded lying side by side. The whole Royalist baggage-train had been captured, and was now parked with that of the New Model in the fields below the village; and there were five thousand prisoners to be dealt with, as well as horses, guns and several hundred camp-followers. And in the Manor House library, Fairfax himself, with Daddy Skippon, swathed in bandages but indomitable, beside him, went through Charles Stuart's private papers which had been captured with the baggage-train—papers that told a disturbing story of a King who had appealed to France, Lorraine and the Low Countries for help against his own countrymen.

Into this great camp, Cromwell and his weary troops returned before evening of the day following the battle. Quarters had been kept free against their coming, and they dropped thankfully into them, finding the prospect of a few days respite unbelievably good. From Cromwell himself to the latest joined trooper, their spirits kicked upward to match the boisterous mood of the camp, and for the first time they felt that they had accomplished something. But for Simon there was no mood of exultancy, even now. He had had his baptism of fire, and come through it without disgrace; he had done his bit to ease the threat of that hard-pressed Northern army; but he had lost Corporal Relf. Barnaby had reported the matter to Major Disbrow, and there was nothing more to be done. He tried to put Zeal-for-the-Lord out of his mind; but it was no use. Always before his inner eye was a picture of his Corporal, walking into the night, with a pistol in his belt for the man who had been his friend.

On the evening of the second day, as Simon returned from guard-mounting, he was met by a drummer of Fairfax's Foot, who saluted and asked, ' Cornet Carey, sir? '

' Yes, I am Cornet Carey.'

' The Lord-General's compliments, sir, and he'd be obliged if you will wait on him as soon as may be.'

' Right,' Simon said, and set off for the Manor House at a smart pace.

Sir Thomas Fairfax was punctiliously polite to his officers, and always sent his compliments and ' would be obliged '; but that did not mean that one dawdled in answering the summons: not if one was wise. As he strode along, his hands automatically making sure that the narrow crimson scarf about his middle was properly tied, his uniform coat as it should be, and his sword hanging at the correct angle, Simon was wondering what was the reason for the summons. He had not, so far as he knew, committed any dereliction of duty. Most likely, he decided, it meant that Corporal Relf had been rounded up; and he remembered with a sinking heart Barnaby's words: 'If he's caught, the Lord have mercy on him, for Fairfax will have none.' And yet, whatever his punishment, it would surely be better for Corporal Relf to be caught, before he could use that pistol. Not for James Gibberdyke's sake, who deserved to be pistolled if ever a man did, Simon thought savagely, but for the Corporal's own.

He had no time to think farther, for at that moment he reached the Manor House. For a few minutes, while news of his arrival was passed on to the Commander-in-Chief, he waited in a panelled hall full of the usual coming and going of soldiery, where captured Royalist drums and Colours had been stacked against one wall in a kind of rough trophy. He examined them as well as he could in the fading light, the piled drums with their banners still upon them, the Colours and Standards against the polished panelling, some bright and new, some ragged and battle-worn; the proud emblems of regiments that were now scattered in defeat. One of them, he knew—for the story had gone round the Army—had

93

been captured by Fiery Tom with his own band, and he wondered which one it was.

The door behind him opened, and an orderly came out and stood aside for him to enter; and he walked into a long room in which were many books and beautifully engraved celestial globes on stands. By the confused light that comes of candles being lit before the daylight is quite gone, he saw the usual writing-table scattered with papers. But for once, Sir Thomas was not working. He was sitting in a wing chair beside the empty hearth, supporting in one hand the silver bowl of a long-stemmed pipe, his head tipped back against the gilded leather squab, to look up at the only other occupant of the room. This was a loose-limbed greying-sandy Scot in a stained doublet, who stood with one elbow on the mantle, industriously poking bits of candlewick out of a pair of snuffers with the blunt end of a lancet. David Morrison was the Commander-in-Chief's personal friend as well as his regimental surgeon, but evidently it was as a doctor that he had been speaking the moment before, for as Simon entered, he heard Fairfax's slow pleasant voice answering through a cloud of tobacco smoke, 'Be hanged to you, Davy. How *can* I rest it? I've got a campaign on my hands.' An instant later he laid aside his pipe and sat up. 'Good evening, Cornet Carey.'

'You sent for me, sir.'

'I did.'

As Simon squared his shoulders and advanced, the Scottish doctor set down the snuffers with a click, and returned the lancet to his pocket. 'Ye'll no be wanting me for a wee while, I'm thinking.'

'Then don't be thinking, man. There is nothing in what I have to say to Cornet Carey that will not do for your ears.'

'Ah, weel . . .' The surgeon turned and crossed to the window, taking a book at random from one of the shelves as he passed.

Fairfax turned back to Simon. 'I sent for you to tell you that one of the patrols have picked up your missing Corporal, and brought him into camp a short while ago.'

'Yes, sir,' said Simon.

94

' And to ask you if you have any idea why he deserted.'

' I—I think I have, sir.'

Fairfax leaned forward, his eye on his young officer's face. ' The position is this: Corporal Relf will go before a Court Martial tomorrow, to answer for his conduct, and it may be that his reason for deserting will be better kept until then; but if you feel at liberty to tell it to me, I should be very glad. I am not fond of moving completely in the dark.'

Simon was silent for a long moment. It was a difficult decision to make. But though revenge was not, he supposed, a very good reason for deserting, he could not help feeling that it was likely to find more favour with Fiery Tom than the more usual ones. ' Well, sir,' he said at last, ' I don't know for certain; it's really only guesswork——' Once again, he told the whole story.

Fairfax heard him out, without moving. ' Not a pleasant story,' he said when it was finished. ' None the less, the pursuit of a private revenge is scarcely an excuse for deserting in time of war.'

' No, sir; but he's a fearsome good Corporal; and it was his friend. That was what made it so bad.'

' He has chosen the wrong time to commit a breach of military discipline.'

' The wrong time, sir?' Simon's voice was bewildered.

' Carey, I believe seamen will tell you that when a ship is newly launched, she is only so many pieces of timber and metal; and it is not until she has been at sea long enough for these separate parts to settle into one whole, that the ship herself is born. This Army is at present in a like case. It has not yet found itself, and whether or not it ever does so, depends on many things, one of which is discipline.' Simon found the clear dark eyes of the Commander-in-Chief looking very straightly into his own. ' There have been several cases of desertion in the past forty-eight hours; several more of looting and wilful damage. That is to be expected after a battle; but in this New Model Army of ours, *it must not happen again*.'

Over by the window, old David Morrison was softly whistling his one tune. Simon had once asked him what it was, and been told, 'Och, you will be meaning "The Flowers of the Forest"? It iss a lament for Flodden; for the King and the flower of the Clans lying dead among the broom and the bell-heather, and the peat hearths left desolate.' Now, as he found himself listening to the slow-falling cadences, they seemed to hold all the heartache of the world.

'As his officer, you will be called to testify to your Corporal's past conduct and character,' Fairfax was saying.

'Yes, sir—and he's a really good man,' Simon said again, eagerly.

The Lord-General's dark face lit for an instant with his rare smile. 'Tell the officers of the Court Martial that—— Oh, and, Carey, you are of course at liberty to visit the prisoner.'

'Thank you, sir. Where shall I find him?'

'In the village lock-up. Good night.'

'Good night, sir.'

Half an hour later, Simon was with his Corporal in the village lock-up. Viewed from the outside, it was a charming place, deep-thatched and dripping with Traveller's Joy; but inside, it was less pleasant: the walls damp-stained with leprous patches, the straw sodden. There was a thick smell of dirt and decay, and even as Simon entered and the door was fastened behind him, a rat scampered over his feet and disappeared into the brown shadows.

He found Zeal-for-the-Lord leaning against the blotched wall, reading his Bible by the light of a guttering tallow-dip stuck on the ledge of the high window-hole. He was clad in shirt and breeches, just as he had been taken, his skin showing through the torn linen at one shoulder, and a trickle of dried blood dark at the corner of his mouth. But there was nothing about him of that wild, agonized figure glimpsed in the farm garden, two nights ago. Indeed, he had an almost peaceful look as he read to the end of the verse, and closing the book, thrust it into the breast of his shirt.

'Evening, sir,' said Corporal Relf, in exactly his usual tone.

'I came as soon as I heard,' Simon said breathlessly. 'I've just been with the Lord-General. You're going up for Court Martial in the morning.'

' I guessed as much.'

The other's calmness suddenly exasperated Simon, and he jerked out, ' Zeal, you *fool*, why did you do it? '

' You know that, sir.'

Their eyes met steadily in the jumping light of the dip.

Then Simon said, ' Yes, I know.'

' Have you told Sir Thomas? '

' Yes. I thought that at least your reason for deserting would seem to him a better one than the usual white feather.'

' And did it? '

' Yes—but that's not saying much.'

' There could be no better reason in this world or the next,' said Zeal-for-the-Lord with absolute conviction. ' I have no fear for tomorrow. The justice of my cause is my shield against the workers of iniquity.' And in that certainty he remained unshakable, despite all Simon's efforts to bring him to his senses; while time dragged by, and outside, the steps of the sentry came and went, came and went.

' If you said that you repented of your conduct, and no longer felt any desire for revenge now that you had had time to think, can't you see that that would help to make a good impression? ' Simon demanded at last. But he knew what the answer would be.

' The words of the liar are abomination in the sight of the Lord,' said Corporal Relf. ' I repent of nothing, who am an avenging sword in the hand of the Almighty, for the smiting of the evil-doer ! '

' No, I didn't think you did,' Simon said miserably, staring at the sodden floor. Then he looked up. ' I must be going now, Zeal. I'll see you in the morning.'

' Aye, in the morning, sir.'

Suddenly they gripped hands; and then Simon went out into the soft June dusk, and the sentry re-secured the loop-holed door behind him.

Next morning, in the long dining-room of the Manor House, Corporal Zeal-for-the-Lord Relf was tried by Regimental Court Martial for the crime of desertion in time of war. Ever afterwards, Simon remembered the scene: the grave faces of the

97

captains seated in order of seniority down the long, leather-covered table, with Major Disbrow, in his place as President of the Court, at the head; the few lieutenants and cornets who were present, standing, like himself, bareheaded behind their betters; the prisoner, decently scarlet-coated once more, standing between his guards like a disdainful prophet. And from the panelled walls, portraits of women in farthingales and men in silk and steel looked down on the unfamiliar scene.

The disposition had been read, and Major Disbrow had begun to interrogate the prisoner. In answer to a quick fire of questions, Corporal Relf told his story once more, his replies as quick and clipped as the questions. Evidently he was keeping a strong hold on himself. Witnesses were called: the officer of the patrol who had brought him in; Simon himself, to testify to the prisoner's character and previous conduct. He heard his own voice: ' A most reliable man—strong sense of duty—great provocation— couldn't wish for a better Corporal.' He was doing his best for Corporal Relf, fighting for him to the last steps of Cæsar's throne; but he could not alter facts, and the facts were deadly.

And now the time had come for the Court to be cleared. Prisoner, witnesses and onlookers passed out into the hall, and the door closed behind them; and when they returned, Simon knew, it would be to hear Corporal Relf condemned and sentenced. Behind the closed door, now, Major Disbrow would be turning to the junior captain present, asking ' Guilty or innocent, Captain Mostyn?'

And there was only one answer to that question. ' Guilty.'

' Guilty.' Simon seemed to hear the word falling inexorably as the strokes of a clock striking for an execution. Suddenly the crowded hall began to press inward, stifling him until he could hardly breathe. It was as though he, and not Zeal, was the prisoner. Close beside him the house door stood open to the summer day, and scarcely realizing what he was doing, he turned and made for the open air, and having reached it, stood leaning against the house wall, breathing quickly as though he had been running.

' Captain Marjory?'

' Guilty.'

This time he really did hear it. He looked up with a start, narrowing his eyes in the sunlight, and saw what he had not noticed from inside the makeshift court-room; that one of the mullioned windows was a little open. And he was standing almost directly under it. He supposed he ought to move away, but he did not: he remained where he was, flattened against the wall and listening with strained intensity to the murmur of voices beyond the window.

Ralf Marjory was the senior captain, his verdict the last to be given, and they were discussing the sentence now; and Simon seemed to hear above the voices of the Court, the words of one of the Articles of War, read to the assembled Companies every pay day. 'No man shall depart a mile out of the camp without licence, under pain of death.' That sentence was rare, in the Ironside Regiments, he knew, for among them disgrace was held a worse punishment than death, and a deserter was usually flogged and turned adrift as a renegade. And yet, there *had* been disorders among the newer regiments since they left Windsor, and Cromwell's 'Lovely Company' must be all the more above reproach in consequence. Simon knew by now the value of example.

The Court Martial was having difficulty in reaching a decision, and the argument dragged on. A plot of heliotrope grew under the window, murmurous with bees, and their droning seemed to make a fine web of sound through which Simon heard voice answering voice. There was a surprising amount of sympathy, especially among the younger captains, for a man who had been wronged, and deserted to avenge the wrong. The Ironsides were not of a forgiving nature; and Simon found his hopes rising a little as he listened. For what seemed a long while, Corporal Relf's fate hung in the balance. Then Captain Mostyn's voice sounded, raising a new difficulty. 'If we turn him adrift, he'll go straight off after this revenge of his.'

'Is yon any concern of ours?' It was Ralf Marjory who spoke. Simon knew his voice by the Yorkshire burr.

'I think it is the concern of this Court to decide whether or not to let murder loose against one of God's creatures.'

'Hang him, then; it's all one to me.'

'You cannot hang a man because you don't know what to do with him,' snapped Captain Bennet. 'That is rank injustice, and injustice stinks in the nostrils of the Almighty.'

Major Disbrow's voice, in cool contrast to the heated tones that had begun to rise around the table, now put in the President's word. 'Gentlemen, there is a third possible course.'

There followed an instant of absolute silence. Only the bees zoomed among the mauve spikes of the heliotrope. Then the cool voice went on. 'I suggest that the more usual sentence be given, with this difference: that instead of being turned off as a renegade, the prisoner be degraded from the rank of Corporal and transferred from the Regiment he has disgraced, to the Pioneers.'

Another moment of silence, while this sunk in. The Pioneers, save for a few brilliant officers, were the scum of the New Model. Many of them were foreign mercenaries who would fight for anyone who paid them; and to them too fell all the most unpleasant jobs in the Army. It was not at all uncommon for men from prouder regiments to be transferred to them as a punishment, for which reason they were strongly guarded against escape. It meant almost as much disgrace as being turned off altogether, but on the other hand, it did give to a man so disgraced the chance to redeem himself by good service.

Simon scarcely breathed during the discussion of details which followed. He could not see the show of hands when the vote was taken, and Major Disbrow's coolly spoken 'Thank you, gentlemen,' told him nothing, save that the Court's deliberations were over. He could only hope, desperately, sickeningly, as he turned back to the crowded hall. The inner door was already opening, and he was just in time to file back with the rest into the court-room, and take up his place among the other cornets, before Corporal Relf was brought back, marching between his guards, with head up and eyes staring woodenly in front of him as though he were on parade.

He came to a halt; and Major Disbrow rose to pronounce sentence.

'Prisoner, this Court Martial finds you guilty of the heinous crime of desertion in time of war, and sentences you to receive one hundred lashes at the pikes, in the presence of your old Regiment.  It further decrees that after your sentence has been carried out, you shall be transferred from the aforesaid Regiment, to serve henceforth as a private in the Pioneers.'

Even as relief flooded over Simon, he saw Zeal-for-the-Lord go very white, and then flush crimson.  He never knew what his old Corporal had really expected, but assuredly it was not this.  He took one forward step, against the grasp of his guards, and the hold he had kept upon himself up to now broke and was swept away.

' Unjust!  Unjust!' he cried.  ' Woe to them that decree unrighteous decrees!'

' The decree of this Court Martial is not only just, but uncommonly merciful.'  Major Disbrow's voice cut across his railing like a whip-lash.  ' May I remind you that you are a tried and condemned deserter?'

' Was I not justified in my deserting?  I who am an instrument of Vengeance in the hand of the Lord, against one that is marked for the Burning Pit?'  The guards each held an arm of him now, but he tore himself free, and the torrent of his words poured on.  ' What saith the Good Book concerning Vengeance? " Eye for eye, tooth for tooth, hand for hand, foot for foot "——'

Again Major Disbrow's voice cut across his.  ' I also can quote from the Good Book.  " Vengeance is mine, saith the Lord." Take him away, guards.'

The guards had a good grip on him this time; they were two to one, and if he was a powerful man, so were they.  His arms were twisted behind him, and he was half thrown as they wrenched him round; but even after the door had crashed shut behind him, the men in the dining-room heard his voice, rising to a great sobbing cry: ' Burning for burning, wound for wound, stripe for——'

Another door crashed, and the raving voice was stilled.

Three hours later, before the whole Regiment drawn up in a hollow square to witness it, the sentence was carried out.  The sun had gone in, and a little chill wind stirred the silken folds of the Standards, as Corporal Relf was marched past his old troop, to the triangle of pikes where the farrier sergeants stood ready to carry out the sentence, with Major Disbrow and the surgeon beside them. Simon, standing rigidly in his place, saw the red coat with its proud blue facings dragged over Zeal-for-the-Lord's head, in the small terrible ceremony by which a man was degraded from his rank. He saw the tall figure stripped to the waist, and lashed to the triangle; saw the first farrier step forward with the terrible cat-o'-nine tails in his hand.

Simon had seen men flogged before, and hated the sight, but it had never before been a man of his own troop, and it had not sickened him as it did now. He shut his eyes and clenched his teeth; and in his self-made shell of darkness he heard the hiss and shock of every stroke, that seemed to fall on something quick and flinching within himself. But he heard no cry, until at last old David Morrison stepped forward with upraised hand to stop the punishment, eleven strokes before the end; and he opened his eyes to see the unconscious figure taken down from the triangle. It looked more like a puppet than a living man, a limp puppet from which the sawdust had drained away. But sawdust is not crimson.

A few minutes later, Zeal-for-the-Lord had been carried off to have his back dressed with brine, and Simon marched his men away, and having done so, went down in a hurry to the ditch beyond the regimental horse-lines. There, his shame hidden by the thick-growing willow-herb and fools-parsley, he was very sick indeed.

Zeal-for-the-Lord never served in the Pioneers. He went out through the field-hospital window in the early hours of the following morning, with his back like raw meat, and took to the wild. This time no patrol rounded him up.

Two days later, when the Army broke camp and marched south, no one saw the man who stood among the oak woods crowning a nearby hill, to watch them go. A tall wild figure with eyes of dark flame in a face the colour of cold ash, who stood motionless as the oak trunks around him, gazing down along the valley road until the last dust of the rearguard had settled on to the whitened hedgerows, and the distant lilt of fifes and drums was gone into the hum of bees among the clover bloom. Then he shook savage fists after them, and with a strange broken cry, turned and plunged away into the green woodland shadows, startling the pigeons as he went.

# X

## The Campaign in the West

THE Battle of Naseby had lost the Midlands to the King; and while he clung uncertainly with his broken troops to the Welsh Border, Fairfax marched the New Model south to deal with General Lord Goring, who was still besieging Taunton. The Royalist General, getting word of his advance, raised the siege and took up new positions along the valleys of the Yeo and the Parrot, and through the first hot days of July the two Generals manœuvred like chess-players looking for an opening. But that was a game at which My Lord Goring was no match for Fairfax and Cromwell. And on the morning of 10 July the New Model was across the Yeo and had come up with the main Royalist Army, half a mile or so from the little market town of Langport, astride the road to Bridgwater and the West.

It was a close heavy day, with thunder in the air, and the thick veiled sunshine that often comes before a storm. Simon, heading for the rearguard with a message from the Commander-in-Chief for Colonel Hammond, who had taken over command of the Foot while Daddy Skippon was laid low, wiped his forehead below the burning rim of his steel cap, and saw the heat dancing like a midge-cloud over the low green country. The troops were deploying for action. Horse moving up to the Van. Foot massing in the Rear. On the slightly rising ground in the centre, as Simon rode by, the great thirty-pounder culverin were already massed, and the eight-horse gun teams being led off, and a moment later he had to rein aside as the light guns—the drakes and sakers—went by with a shout and the crack of a whiplash; little deadly guns, each with two horses harnessed to the limbers of the grey gun-carriages, and their crew clinging on behind. After them went an ammunition wagon, lurching over the boggy ground, the heavy draft-horses straining into their collars, the driver leaning forward to encourage them, as perhaps he had done not long since, when he and his team were hauling timber or carting hay on some quiet farm of the Blackmoor Vale.

When, his message safely delivered, Simon re-passed one of the batteries a few minutes later, the limbers had been cast off and the horses led aside, powder and ball were in place behind each gun, and the crews standing ready for action. He edged Scarlet between a dyke and an ammunition wagon returning empty, skirted the flank of the massing Cavalry, and reached the place where Fairfax sat his black charger with his staff around him.

'Message delivered, sir,' he reported; and being given leave to rejoin his own Troop, wheeled his mount, looking for his Troop Standard among the many that hung limp in the heavy air above the squadrons. He found it without much trouble and edged Scarlet into place among the sliding horses that were being got into line.

Barnaby called back to him over his shoulder, 'Going to be a storm, by the looks of it.'

'By the feel of it too,' Simon said, wiping his forehead again. 'You could fry an egg in my skull,' and turned in the saddle to take the Standard with due formality from his new Corporal. The man was an Essex schoolmaster's son, a steady and dependable soul: and Simon liked him well enough, but he knew that there would never be between him and his new Corporal the real working friendship that had been between him and his old one.

As he settled the Standard lance in position, the heavy stillness that hung over the land trembled to a distant mutter of thunder, and then settled down again. Simon saw the shallow dip of marsh before them, the reed-beds and the standing water utterly still in the sultry air; and drawn up on the crest of the farther rise, the Royalist Army, guarding the road to Langport. There could be no broad advance here, for the only way across the marshy valley was one road fording the stream, with Lord Goring's troops massed at the head of it. A battle without a battle line. Simon wondered what it would be like. But he had little time to spare for wondering in the next few minutes, for Scarlet, made fidgety by the thunder in the air, was shivering and sidling, tossing his head and flinging this way and that; and ham-

pered as he was by the Standard, Simon had all he could do to
keep him from falling foul of the horses on either side.

Then suddenly the stillness was gone, as, with a roar like the
breaking storm, the guns went into action. First the deep
thunder of the culverin boomed and echoed away over the fens;
then the sharper crack of the drakes and sakers. A moment's
ringing silence, and then again the roar of the culverin, blending
raggedly into the saker's yapping, and swelling until earth and
heaven seemed to hum like a giant gong.

From the opposite side of the valley, the Royalist artillery had
opened up in answer, but Goring had sent many of his guns to
Bridgwater in readiness for a siege, as the New Model scouts had
reported; and the King's troops could not make an equal return
for the bombardment that was harassing them so sorely.

Simon's ears were so dulled by the guns that he scarcely heard
the trumpets when they sounded the charge. But away on the
right, Major Bethel's Troop swung forward into the Langport
road, followed by Captain Evanson's and Captain Groves's.
Simon knew them by their Standards carrying the gold and crimson of the Second Regiment, and a wave of cheering ran through
the Army as they went down the narrow way. The light guns were
firing steadily, holding the enemy back from the lane-head and
covering the advance of the Parliamentary Horse. Major Bethel's
Troops were through the ford now, and the squadrons of Walley's
Regiment were going down towards it. The guns fell silent, and
another cheer broke from the watching ranks, as the leading Troop
drew out of the lane where the high ground gave firmer foothold,
and charged the enemy on the ridge, driving them back to gain
space for Evanson's and Groves's to draw out beside them. Next
instant the trumpets of Fairfax's Horse sang through the din of
battle, and the General's Troop swung forward after the rest,
with Major Disbrow's at their heels and Captain Mostyn's last
of all.

As he followed Barnaby, Simon felt the familiar quick expectancy that always came to him in the moment of going into action,
and with the Standard of Disbrow's Troop held aloft, and the
troopers of his Standard Escort on either side of him, he headed
downhill to the ford. The General's Troop were already half-way

up the slope beyond as Simon and his Troop splashed through. As they did so, a puff of hot wind stirred the reeds, lightning flickered for an instant in the still water above the ford, and a low peal of thunder rumbled across the marsh. Then they were across, and Mostyn's men were threshing and splashing after them, as they headed for the crest of the ridge. Bethel's and Walley's squadrons, after being once forced back, had spread out across the solid turf of the higher slope, and were charging again; and with a wild yell, and a slipping and scrambling of hooves on the steep verge, Disbrow's were out of the lane after them. Following his Lieutenant, Simon swung Scarlet in a sharp curve, out over the verge and ditch, and up against the Royalists, his Standard Escort pressing at his flanks, the Standard whipping out on the wind of his going, and the solid phalanx of Ironside troopers drumming up behind with drawn swords on which the lightning flickered.

In place of the roar of the barrage, there was now the pealing thunder, distant still, but drawing nearer, the rattle of musketry and the shouting of close conflict. The Parliamentary Foot, pressing up behind the Horse, were spreading out to face the Foot of the King's Army; already the skirmishing parties were met and falling back, and the pikes were going into action.

Simon never remembered very much of that fight. It was a wild flurry of charge and counter-charge, a great yelling and the scream of smitten horses, a whirling of clumped Cavalry that split and re-formed and split again, while overhead the lightning danced in a sky the colour of a day-old bruise, and the thunder boomed and crackled along the marshes. Presently they had cleared the ridge, pressing the Royalists back over the teazle fields beyond, despite all their resistance. Royalist Horse and Foot were no longer separate forces, but a confused and reeling mass being slowly forced back and back into the home-fields of Langport.

On the rising ground at the very edge of the little town, Goring's forces made one last desperate stand; and Simon, charging at the head of a clump of troopers, had one of his Escort shot beside him. In the gap, a Royalist dragoon sprang forward with clubbed musket, his other hand grabbing at the Standard

lance.   Simon wrenched Scarlet round and up, up until the fore-
hooves of the big sorrel were lashing the air and the man's hold
was broken, while with his free hand—for he had shifted the
Standard to his left—he whipped the long dag from its holster, and
fired.   The Royalist's musket arm dropped to his side, and clutching at it he reeled back into the *mêlée*.   Simon thrust on grimly,
into a sea of battling figures and clubbed muskets, while his
troopers closed up behind him, yelling like triumphant fiends.

Within the hour Fairfax's Army was hunting the beaten troops
of Lord Goring through the narrow streets of Langport, where red
flame leapt from roof to roof, and flakes of burning thatch
dropped like petals of fire upon pursued and pursuers alike.
Simon never knew whether it was lightning, or misguided zeal, or
some accident of battle that had done the mischief; he only knew
that as they rode through, the streets were filled with dismay, and
the whole town seemed burning.   But already, as they gained the
open country, the rain was beginning to fall, straight heavy
thunder-rain that hissed and splattered on the hard ground,

lozenging the road with wet, and raising the unforgettable smell of summer rain on parched earth. The flames they had left behind them would soon be quenched.

My Lord Goring got away to Dunster Castle, and two days later was back in Barnstaple with the remnant of his men, while Fairfax sat down in front of Bridgwater, which fell before the month was out. Cromwell had meanwhile gone off to subdue the riots which were breaking out in Dorset, taking with him, amongst others, several Troops and Companies of Fairfax's Regiments. Disbrow's Troop, however, was not one of them; and so, still under the command of Fiery Tom, Simon saw the fall of Bath and Sherbourne in the golden harvest weather; and then sat down before Bristol, which Prince Rupert, who had taken over the command from Hopton, was holding with only three thousand Horse and Foot.

Cromwell had rejoined the main Army by that time, and there was a general assault on 20 September, a desperate affair which ended the siege, and the Prince was forced to yield. Simon saw the Royalist Garrison march out with full honours of war, Colours flying, drums beating, every musketeer with slow-match lit and bullet in mouth; and the Prince himself, riding at their head, a man with a pale masterful face, and the first autumn rain dark on the shoulders of his scarlet cloak.

Early in October, Simon and the New Model crossed the Devon border, and headed for Tiverton, in rain that was already turning the lanes to mud channels. Tiverton was ill-prepared for a siege; and Fairfax took the outer defences without much trouble, and pitched his headquarters at Blundell's School, while he made plans for taking the Castle.

It was a wild autumn afternoon when Simon rode with his Regiment into the town, where they were to take up their quarters; shrivelled golden leaves whirling down before every gust of wind, the bitter blue reek of bonfires, the last ragged marigolds and Michaelmas daisies falling into brown rain-sodden ruin in small town gardens. Tiverton had always been staunch for Parliament, and despite the fighting which had wrecked several houses only a few hours before, the townsfolk turned out almost under the walls of the Royalist-held castle, to cheer for the New Model troops as they rode in.

It seemed very strange to Simon, this return to a place he knew so well; he looked about him eagerly, as he rode up the familiar street. Everything was much as he remembered, and everywhere he saw familiar faces in the crowds thronging the way: Mr Yeo the Chandler, a little stouter than of old; Nick Veryard of the Hand-in-Glove standing in his doorway. The Hand-in-Glove's windows were all broken, but Nick Veryard was quite unchanged. The butcher's wife, who, way back at the beginning of the troubles, had thrown all the sheep's horns in the shop at Lord Bath when he came to read the King's Summons to Arms in the Market Place. Old Mother Tidball, who sold gingerbread and peppermint lozenges to the Blundell's boys, and had been a great friend of Simon's. But none of them knew him.

It was not surprising, for Simon the inky schoolboy with a cudgel under one arm was very far removed from Simon the Cornet of Parliamentary Horse, in worn buff and steel, with a season's hard campaigning behind him. He knew that, yet it made him feel rather like a ghost. Also the old familiar scenes made him think of Amias, who had been a part of them; Amias in the far-off days before the King came between them. Amias would have loved this triumphal entry into a town, under the walls of an enemy fortress, Simon thought; it would have appealed to his sense of the dramatic. And suddenly his heart ached and Tiverton put on the face of an unfriendly stranger.

The Castle fell two days later, almost by accident. A stray shot from the bombardment cut the main drawbridge chain, so that it came down with a crash; and the Governor, in consternation, gave up the struggle at the first assault that poured over it.

For the next month, Tiverton and the villages round about became the headquarters of the New Model Army. It was pleasant for weary men, after the stress of the last few months, to sleep in quarters again, and eat hot meals. There was even leisure for amusements. Cock-fighting and bull-baiting were forbidden; but there was always wrestling and cudgel-play, and the inns and taverns where you could meet friends and spend a cheerful evening. For the officers there was a little rough shooting and coursing over the land of the neighbouring gentry, who were mostly for Parliament, while the troops, not having been invited, went poaching every moonless night. Lieutenant Colebourne brought forth his beloved boots from the baggage-train, and waddled about Tiverton in them like a self-satisfied duck. The Commander-in-Chief disappeared from view for a while to have an old and troublesome wound in his shoulder re-dressed; and Lady Fairfax arrived from London, a little thing, as fair as Fiery Tom was dark, but with a valiant carriage of her small plain head that was what one might expect from a young woman who had travelled across England at war, to be near her husband.

There was still fighting, of course, outpost skirmishes for the most part, but the wet autumn that turned the roads and tracks to quagmires put a stop to anything more serious. So for a while the two armies remained bogged down, each in their own territory, the New Model around Tiverton, and Lord Goring's forces spread over the country between Exeter and the South Coast. By this time the Royalist Army in the West was beginning to be in a bad way. It was made up mostly of Devon and Cornish levies without much heart for their business, a fair sprinkling of wild Irish, and the rogues of every nation; but there was still a hard core of veteran fighting men; and the Royalist force was larger than that of Parliament. It looked as though the struggle, when it came, would be a hard one, and whichever way it ended, it would be the last struggle of the war, for the armies elsewhere did not amount to much, and the King was once again shut up in Oxford.

Midway through November, Sir Richard Grenville—that black disgrace of a proud name, hated for his cruelty almost as much by his own men as by his enemies, and certainly as much of a menace to his own cause as to the cause of Parliament—who had been encamped at Okehampton to guard the way to Plymouth, suddenly withdrew his three regiments without orders into Cornwall. And Simon, returning to quarters from an afternoon's shooting, with a brace of mallard swinging from his hand, was mournfully told by his superior officer, ' We're through with the fleshpots for a while.'

' What? ' said Simon.

'Marching south at dawn.  General advance on Exeter.'

Advance they did, save for a few regiments left in Tiverton; and before the end of the month, despite the state of the roads, they had taken up their new positions.  Fairfax made his head-quarters at Ottery St Mary, a brigade under Sir Hardress Waller was stationed at Crediton, and regiments at Powderham and other points held the city secure on the west.  On the east, Great Ful-ford was taken and occupied by Colonel Okey's dragoons; Eggsford House followed, and then Ashton; and Fairfax had a complete ring of fortified points round Exeter.

But strung between these great houses were others that must be occupied before the City could be quite enclosed; big farms and lesser manor houses for the most part.  Sometimes it was simply a matter of moving into an undefended homestead, with, or if needs be without, the leave of its master; but others were Royalist outposts from which the troops must be driven out at the pike's point; and for some, a battle of attack and counter-attack lasted for days.

One of these small manor houses was Okeham Paine, a low-set grey house, at the curve of a shallow valley, down which its garden and demesne sloped to a cluster of cottages and a bridge. Because of its position, commanding the road to Exeter, the place had been fortified and garrisoned by Royalist Foot, and because of its position, it was needful that the troops of Parliament should occupy it as soon as might be.

The attack was ordered, and in the pitch darkness of the mid-December night, the attacking force set out from Broad Clyst. It was made up of two dragoon companies, a troop of Waller's Horse, an officer and two privates of the Pioneers in charge of the powder-keg for blowing up the main door, and Disbrow's Troop of the General's Own.  None too many for the job, but men were short, for fever, bred in the Ottery Marshes, was rife in the Army, and there were no men to be spared for the taking of one small fortress.

It had been snowing off and on for days past, and the thick fall muffled their hoof-beats, so that the column moved in eerie silence, save for the occasional jingle of a bridle-rein.  It was very dark, with a loaded sky that seemed to press upon the tree-tops, and a

III

chill, moaning wind blew the snow-scurries in their faces as they rode. Like a cavalcade of ghosts they passed, by lanes and bridle-paths and over untracked open land, following the scouts who had covered the ground in advance; and like a cavalcade of ghosts they came at last down through a belt of hanging oakwoods, to the verge of open land above Okeham Paine. Here, where the snowy pasture glimmered white between the trees ahead, they dismounted. The troopers, like the dragoons, linked their mounts together by slipping each bridle over the head of the next horse, every tenth bridle being taken by a man who was to remain behind. Then, as a whispered order passed along the lines from the senior dragoon captain, who was in command, they started forward again on foot, still following the scouts, down the wood-shore.

It was snowing hard again; all the better, for the drifting flurries would help to conceal their advance, while the moaning wind covered any chance sound. The dragoons, usually armed with matchlocks, as befitted Mounted Foot, carried flintlock cavalry pistols tonight, that no glimmer of a slow-match should betray them in the darkness; and the jingling spurs had been stripped from the heels of the troopers for the same reason.

At the lower end of the wood, where the oaks gave place to birch and hazel, the whole party halted. There were no whispered orders now, for they had their orders in advance; and in utter silence they divided, Waller's and one company of dragoons melting off to the right, Disbrow's and the other to the left, towards the place where a long hawthorn windbreak led down towards the home paddocks. After a short distance a stream sunk between deep banks came looping almost to the roots of the windbreak. The dragoons dropped down one by one, and disappeared along the stream side, any movement in the snowy darkness hidden by the willow and alder scrub. Disbrow's stole on, the advance-guard scouting ahead, the rest following after a space, in single file, with the Pioneers and their powder keg bringing up the rear. Simon only knew when they reached the first guard-point by a faint scuffle and a grunt far ahead that might well have been made by a rooting badger; and a little farther on he saw the dark shapes of the sentries, lying where they had been dragged aside from the way.    To judge by the number of them, the watch had been doubled.

The windbreak grew thin here, where newly-planted thorn saplings gave poor cover, and it was a case of crawling from now on.    On the edge of the home paddock they came upon another sentry post, and here the guard were on the alert, and there was a scuffle and the beginning of a cry followed by the crack of a musket-stock on somebody's head; then a long prickling silence in which the men, crouching in the black gloom of the paddock trees, waited with straining ears for any sound of an alarm. None came.    Evidently the sentry's quickly silenced cry had been blanketed by the falling snow, or, if it had been heard, had been taken for the cry of some night bird.    The attackers crept on.

They encountered no further sentry-posts, and in a few minutes more they were in their places along the eastern verge of the garden.    A long wait followed.    Crouching under a yew hedge, Simon was filled with a tingling expectancy.    There was shelter from the wind here, and behind and on every side of him he fancied he could catch the faint breathing of hidden men. Away in front of him the whitened lawn dipped and rose to the dark bulk of the house itself.    The windows had been barricaded against assault, but here and there a spangle of yellow light shining through a loophole told where men were wakeful and standing to arms.    A little scurry of snow fell from the yew branches on to Simon's shoulder, and the chill of the ground on which he crouched seemed to strike upward, a sodden creeping cold, through all his body.    But still the waiting-time crawled. Surely, surely the other companies must be in place by now! They had farther to go, but they could not have run into any trouble, for there had been no outcry, no sound of shots.

Simon did not dare to shift from one chilled knee to the other, lest the movement should bring down a heavier fall from the yew branch, and so catch the notice of the sentries who must be on duty at the house.    The snow had stopped, he realized, and the loophole lights shone clear.

Then a faint glow sprang up for an instant in the darkness of the bushes opposite, carefully screened from the house.    Walley's

Troop was in position, and signalling the fact by the smuggler's method of a shielded lantern. From the far end of Disbrow's sector, Simon knew, the same glow would be signalling across the corner of the kitchen garden, to the remaining company of dragoons.

So far, everything had gone without a hitch. The next move was for the dragoons behind the house; and almost at once, they made it. There was the sudden, sharp challenge of a sentry, followed by a pistol-shot, and then a whole volley; and a swelling uproar as if hell had broken loose in the kitchen garden. The dragoons were staging an attack in force, to draw the enemy's fire. In the house and outbuildings drums were beating the alarm; and the golden spangles of the loopholes darkened one by one. Under his yew hedge, Simon drew himself together like a runner before the start of a race, waiting—waiting, while the defenders had their attention fully taken up by the mock attack in the rear. Then the voice of the dragoon Captain, raised in a staccato yell, gave the word of command, and like a dark wave the hidden men broke from cover, cheering as they did so. From all sides of the garden the attack swarmed in. Simon was up and running for the house, his long pistol in his hand. He was half-way across the lawn when fire spurted from the darkened loop-holes, and the rattle of musketry rose above the uproar on the far side of the house and the drums beating to quarters. He flung himself down like the rest, but in the pitch dark, firing was wild and most unlikely to do much harm, and an instant later he was up and racing forward again. The ranks grew thicker as the circle narrowed; one section was heading for the stables and outbuildings, another swerving left round the house to make common cause with the dragoons in the kitchen garden. Simon and his Troop, following Lieutenant Colebourne, held straight on to make a direct assault against the front of the house; and with them went the Pioneers who were to blast in the door.

Next instant, as it seemed to Simon, the darkness exploded into a fitful red glare in which the flashes of discharged weapons were myriad points of flame. There was shooting enough now on both sides. The rooms beyond the barricaded windows were in darkness, that the light might not silhouette the men at the loopholes; and they had flung down firebrands among the attackers to make them a possible target; but these quickly fizzled out in the snow, save a few which the dragoons had caught up and were using to fire the barricades, ripping out the blazing wood as it scorched and twisted. Again and again Fairfax's troops were driven back, again and again they rallied and pressed forward once more. The fight was swirling like an angry flood through stable yard and outbuildings; and crouched against the stout main door, out of the line of fire, three dark shapes made hasty but careful preparations with powder and fuse. Inside the house the Royalists stood to their posts, the marksmen firing steadily while their comrades loaded for them; but this was to be a hand-to-hand fight in the long run, and as the shutters and barricades went down, window after window became the centre of its own fierce struggle, where battling figures reeled to and fro with clubbed muskets; and the fitful red light flashed on leaping sword blades.

In the midst of one such *mêlée*, Simon was slowly but surely forcing his way inward. He had emptied both pistols, and was fighting now with his sword, his men pressing at his heels. It was a cut-and-thrust affair of random blows, like a fight in a dream, and in the course of it he had lost his steel cap, but would not have noticed it if he had lost everything except his sword; for suddenly the press against him was slackening, the defenders of the window were giving way! And with a yell he and his men poured across the shattered sill.

'First in! By the Lord Harry!' His voice was drowned by the roar of an explosion, and he knew that the main door had gone.

It was a small room in which they found themselves, and the light of a burning shutter showed them a door in the opposite wall. Shouting in triumph, they hurled themselves against it. More and more men were crashing in behind them, as they burst it open and stormed through into a yellow radiance of candles that almost blinded them.

They were in the main hall of the house, lit by candles guttering wildly in sconces against the damaged walls; the place was reeking with the fumes of burned powder, which hung like swirling fog in the air, and a desperate struggle was going on for the splintered doorway. A great staircase curved out of the murky shadows, and half-way up it stood a woman in a dark gown, a tall woman, standing with arms spread as though to make a barrier, and looking down with no shred of fear on the wild scene below her. Simon saw all this in a confused flash, before a band of the defenders came charging down upon him, led by a slight figure whose wild red hair shone like flame in the guttering candlelight.

The two bands came together in a reeling clump of men and clubbed muskets and leaping steel; and as the two leaders sprang to meet at the foot of the stairs, and their blades rang against each other, Simon saw that the red-haired man was Amias.

Amias recognized him in the same instant, and laughed. ' Well met, brother sober-sides ! ' His eyes were full of the old dancing fire, and his blade—it was Balin, Simon knew instinctively—never wavered out of line. Simon said nothing. He pressed grimly forward, full of a queer cold feeling of unreality. This could not be really happening ! It was something so horrible, so much against the nature of decent things, that it simply was not possible. But it *was* possible !—It was happening !

There, at the foot of the wide staircase, Simon and Amias fought, forgetful of the struggling figures all around them; seeing nothing but each other's eyes filled with deadly purpose above their leaping blades; while the woman on the stairs, standing coldly remote from the turmoil below her, looked down upon them.

The whole affair lasted only a few moments, then the resistance about the door broke suddenly, and the dragoons came flooding in. The *mêlée* in the hall was forced towards the stairs, and Simon, springing back from a lunge that had ripped his sleeve, glimpsed for a split second the menacing outline of an up-swung musket-stock above his head. It came whistling down, and he staggered sideways, not realizing that he had been hit. There was a wild sea-roaring in his ears, and something hot trickled down his forehead and cheek; for an instant he saw Amias's face, with a look on it that he did not understand. He saw it very clearly, but as though from a long way off, and then the floor tilted under him and he plunged downward into a great darkness.

## XI

## *Susanna*

A GREAT while later, as it seemed, Simon began to float up through the darkness, rather as one might float up through murky water towards the light and air above. Indeed, it was so like that, that he had a vague idea he had been swimming with Amias in the pool below the oak woods at home, and had somehow got stuck at the bottom. He kicked out strongly to come to the surface, but the nearing light beat on his head like a hammer, and he must have swallowed a lot of the muddy river water to make him feel so sick. . . .

Some sort of frightful upheaval took place inside him, and somebody said, ' There, he'll be better after that.' And the dark waters closed over him once more.

But he did not sink as deeply as before, and it was not so long before he began to come up again. This time there was a kind of wavering leaf of light far ahead and, little by little, a blurred halo began to spread round it, a golden glow, very comforting, like the glow of candle-light in a window when one has been out a long time in the darkness and the cold. And suddenly Simon knew that that was exactly what it was; a candle, or two candles, he was not sure which, for sometimes there was only one flame, and sometimes two, with a possible third. It seemed to waver about, growing sometimes very large and blurred, sometimes very small and sharp. Then, as his sight began to clear, he saw that it was only one candle, and that it was held aloft in the hand of a woman who was regarding him fixedly by its light. A tall woman in a grey gown, with her hair showing smoothly dark under the edge of her white Puritan coif. He seemed to remember that he had seen her somewhere, a long while ago, but where?

Next instant a small clear picture sprang out of the darkness in his head, and he saw her standing in the curve of a wide staircase, looking down with a kind of rigid calm on the fighting men below her. Memory of at any rate part of the night's work flooded back to him, and with a choking cry he tried to struggle to his elbow. The world tilted and swam, and the hammer in his head nearly deafened him, and next instant the woman was beside him, with her free hand in the middle of his chest, pushing him firmly back on to soft pillows. 'Lie still,' she commanded. 'God has seen fit to preserve your life, and will you undo His work?'

'W-where—what——' stammered Simon, finding the words thick and heavy on his tongue.

'No, you are not a prisoner, if that is what troubles you. This house is once more in the hands of Parliament, and the Men of Blood have been driven forth from it.'

Simon gasped with relief. 'What—happened after——' he began.

'After you fell beneath the musket-stock of the man of wrath? The Royalist Captain cried quarter, his position being hopeless and many of his men slain; he and his troops were ordered out and, praise the Lord, General Fairfax's men entered into possession. This house has been too long an abode of the wicked; but now, righteousness is again within its walls.'

Simon squinted at her, trying to get her face into focus and not quite succeeding; trying to understand what she said, and scarcely succeeding in that either, for his dazed mind was straining after other things he wanted to know. 'How long have—I been here?' he mumbled at last.

'A night and a day. It is ten of the clock now.'

'And is—my Troop still here?—Disbrow's Troop?'

'Only the dragoons are left. The rest have marched back to where they came from.' The tall woman had set down the candle, and now she began to measure something from a flask into a glass she took from the table beside the bed.

Simon ploughed on. 'Were there—many wounded?'

'Upward of a score, beside the Men of Blood. The Army surgeon came this morning and took them in to Crediton in two baggage-wagons, but you, he said, the jolting would most likely kill, if he were to move you for two or three days.' She turned to him, the glass in her hand. It was big and globed, and caught the light like a bubble. 'Now I have answered enough questions, and you must sleep. Are you thirsty?'

'Very thirsty.'

Simon found that she had slipped an arm under his head and raised him against her shoulder. 'Drink this. Not too fast, now.' He gulped the cool herb-smelling brew, while she held him with unexpected gentleness, taking the glass from his mouth when he drank too quickly, exactly as though he were a small child. When the glass was empty, she laid him back on his pillows. 'Now you will sleep; and I shall sit here for a while at the foot of the bed. And in the morning, by God's mercy, you will feel better.'

She moved the candle so that it would not shine on his face, wrapped herself in a dark cloak, and drawing a tall-backed chair to the foot of the bed, sat down and opened a book which hung from her girdle. Simon, watching her as she read, was reminded of Zeal-for-the-Lord. It was a friendly memory, and in a few minutes he was asleep.

When he next woke, the small room in which he lay was filled with the grey light of a winter's morning, and there was a small rhythmic clicking sound in his ears that he did not understand. There was a good deal that he did not understand; what was the matter with his head? for instance. He edged a hand free of the bed-clothes, and put it up, clumsily, to find out: bandages, and a thick pad over his left temple that hurt horribly when he pushed at it with fumbling fingers. Then it all came back: the assault, the red spurts of fire, and the fight milling through the candle-lit hall. And this time the picture was complete, and he remembered Amias.

He drew a deep shuddering breath that was almost a whimper, and found that there was a woman bending over him; not the tall woman of last night, but a little stout one with broken veins in her cheeks like a withered apple.

'There now, lie still, my poor dear soul,' said she. 'Lie still and give thanks to the Lord who gave you a thick skull—if so be as the lengthening of one's days in this vale of tears be a matter for thanksgiving, which I doubts. And I'll get you nice broth that has been keeping warm for you beside the hearth this half-hour or more.'

Simon protested weakly, but his protests were of no avail The little fat woman fetched the broth from its place beside the low fire, and Simon drank it because he had not the strength to rebel.

' 'Tis as sinful to repine at good broth, as 'tis to bewail the lack of it,' said she, as she ruthlessly tipped the last spoonful into his mouth. ' Broth when you don't want it, and no broth when you do; that be the way of life in this wicked world.' And she went back to her chair beside the bed-foot, and took up again the knitting with which she had been busy when Simon awoke.

'Click-click-click,' went her needles. Faintly, from the outside world, came the sound of the dragoons at morning stables. Left to himself, Simon lay very still, with his face turned towards the whitewashed wall. Amias. What had become of Amias? Where was he now? Living or dead? Captive or free? And weren't there enough men in the two armies, without himself and Amias needing to draw swords on each other? Why did it have to be Amias in the hall that night? Why? Why?

But despite his utter misery and the questions that dinned themselves over and over in his throbbing head, he was presently asleep once more; and the next time he woke, an hour or two later, the tall woman was beside him again. Before he went to sleep he had meant to ask her about Amias, but now he found that he could not. It was queer, stupid, but the words stuck in his throat, and he couldn't speak about Amias; not to her, at all events.

When she saw that he was awake, she put down on the table the bandage linen that she had been holding. ' Good morning to you, friend,' she said. ' I have come to dress your head.'

' Yes, ma'am,' said Simon, dutifully.

She began to undo the bandages; her hands were quick and sure, not fumbling, as the hands of people who are afraid of hurting so often do, but going straight ahead with the work. ' It is an ugly wound,' said she, when she had uncovered it. ' Eight stitches scarce seem enough to me, but the chirurgeon should know his own trade. I must clip away some more of this hair. Am I hurting you?'

' A bit. But you're a very good surgeon, ma'am.'

' I have had enough practice,' said she, clipping. ' We had many wounded here during the first siege of Exeter. Men of both armies, and I tended the goats with the sheep, bidding them repent of their evil ways, as I did so, and leave off following after the Man of Blood, Charles Stuart.'

She finished her task, and re-bandaged Simon's head. Then, dropping to her knees beside him, and bidding him repeat the words after her, folded her hands and gave thanks to Almighty God, who had spread the shelter of His wings over His unworthy servant, saving him from being cut down with all his manifold sins still upon his head and consigned to the fiery furnace. Simon did as she bade him, very devoutly. He was perfectly conscious of his own shortcomings, and because he was rather a humble-minded person, it never occurred to him to wonder how the tall woman came to be so sure of them.

When she left him, he went to sleep again, and slept off and on through most of that day, save when he was woken up to drink more broth or warm milk with herbs in it. But even in his deepest sleep the throbbing of his head was still with him, and so was Amias's face, white and set, and bright-eyed above his leaping sword blade. The mistress of the house and her little round henchwoman seemed to come and go about him a good deal; and towards evening the dragoon Captain looked in on him, and in reply to his anxious questions, told him that Scarlet, with the other horses whose riders had been killed or wounded, had been taken back to Broad Clyst. But about Amias, Simon found that he could not ask him. Once, waking suddenly from an uneasy doze, he thought he caught sight of a girl's face—a little white pointed face, all eyes, like a changeling's—peering at him from the darkness of the open doorway; but it was gone so quickly that it might have been only the ravelled end of a dream.

Next day the surgeon came; not old Davey Morrison, but a younger stouter man, kindly but harassed, with heavy hands that hurt Simon a good deal when he examined the wound. 'Yes, yes, we shall be able to take him off your hands quite safely to-morrow, Mistress Killigrew,' he said, when he had felt Simon's pulse and peered into his eyes.

'In my opinion, he had better stay until the day after,' said the mistress of the house.

'No need—not the least need in the world, I assure you, ma'am. A thick skull and a strong constitution.'

Mrs Killigrew drew herself to her full height, which made her taller than the surgeon, and faced him across Simon's bed. 'This young man has been set in my charge by Providence,' said she. 'The Lord has seen fit to deliver him alive out of the fighting in my hall; and do you think that I shall allow the Lord's work to be undone by a meddling and probably inefficient army surgeon who orders his untimely remove from under my roof?'

The surgeon, not liking to be called meddling and probably inefficient, began to splutter. 'May I remind you, ma'am, that this house has been taken over by the forces of Parliament?'

'I am aware that the ground floor and outbuildings have been so taken over, but this room happens to be in the part of the house reserved to the use of myself and my family, and if you come upstairs after your patient tomorrow, I warn you that you will find the door locked against you, and myself, my maids and my daughter on guard before it,' said Mrs Killigrew, with the air of one speaking what she knows to be the final word.

The indignant surgeon also knew that it was the final word. He snatched at the last shreds of his dignity, and bowed. 'I must accept your ruling, since I can scarcely order an attack on a party of wilful women, and have Cornet Carey taken by force. I will arrange for a wagon passing this way the day after tomorrow to pick him up.'

After he had gone, Mrs Killigrew came back, carrying under her arm a huge Family Bible with brass clasps. She made no reference to what had just taken place, but told him, 'At some time in every day it is my custom to read a chapter from the Scriptures. This afternoon I shall read it here in this room, that your spirit may be refreshed thereby.'

Someone else had stolen in behind her, and now stood, with demurely folded hands and downcast eyes, just within the door; a girl of about the same age as Mouse, or perhaps a little younger, with a white face, and pale reddish hair strained back under her coif, and Simon knew that the girl he had seen peering at him yesterday had not been a dream, after all.

'This is my daughter Susanna. You have not seen her before, for she has been repenting her sins, locked in her own room these two days past,' said Mrs Killigrew.

The pale girl raised her eyes suddenly, and Simon found them fixed upon him; enormous dark eyes that seemed to shadow all her face, filled with an agonized appeal.

'No, I have not seen Mistress Susanna before,' he said.

But Mrs Killigrew was not listening.

'However, since she has come to a proper state of repentance, we will say no more of the matter,' she said. 'Draw up that stool, child.'

She seated herself in the straight-backed chair, while Susanna, with one quick look of gratitude at Simon, pulled up a small joint-stool and settled herself at her mother's feet, folding her hands in her lap and once more gazing downward.

Mrs Killigrew opened the great Bible, lifted out the pressed moss-rose bud that marked her place, and began to read. It so chanced that she had reached the first chapter of the second book of Samuel: the chapter which holds David's lament for Jonathan. Mrs Killigrew had a beautiful voice, deep and throbbing; and as she read, the little whitewashed room seemed to fill with the tearing pain of the King's lament for his dead friend.

'"How are the mighty fallen in the midst of the battle! O Jonathan, thou was slain in thine high places.

'"I am distressed for thee, my brother Jonathan: very pleasant hast thou been to me: thy love to me was wonderful, passing the love of woman.

'"How are the mighty fallen, and the weapons of war perished!"'

To Simon, sick with anxiety, it seemed like an ill omen that she should have reached that particular chapter. The beauty of it hurt him intolerably, making his stomach ache with misery, and he lay rigid, with his hands clenched under the blankets, hating every moment of it, until she had made an end. He only just remembered to thank her politely, when she closed the great book and rose to her feet.

'I am glad to find that you appreciate the Scripture,' she replied. 'It is not every young person of whom one can say the same. Come, Susanna.'

And she went from the room, with the pale girl moving soundlessly behind her.

Presently, when the shadows had begun to gather in the corners of his room, Susanna returned to mend the fire and bring him a candle. She stole in as silently as before, and having done what she came to do, was stealing out again without a word, when Simon, desperately needing someone to talk to, called to her.

'Mistress Susanna.'

She turned and came to his bedside. 'Is there something you want—a drink?' It was the first time Simon had heard her speak. Her voice was husky, rather like a boy's, and he liked it.

'No, I don't want a drink,' he said. 'But, I say—what did you do, that you had to repent of for two whole days locked in your room?'

Susanna never raised her eyes nor unfolded her hands. 'I went down into the stable yard to listen to a strolling fiddler that the soldiers had there,' she said, and added with bated breath, 'it was on the Sabbath too.'

'Oh!' said Simon. 'How did you come to be out of your room yesterday?'

'Old Jinny forgot to re-lock the door after she took away my supper plate. Thank you for not telling Mother,' and almost before he realized what she was about, she had stolen from the room.

Simon gazed after her with surprised and puzzled eyes. Who would have thought that such a spiritless-seeming little creature had it in her to steal off to listen to a strolling fiddler on the Sabbath.

Next day, the last of those he was to spend at Okeham Paine, Simon saw quite a lot of Susanna Killigrew, for it was her mother's still-room day. But she stole in and out of his room like a sad little grey ghost, with her eyes cast always on the ground; and he had to work hard to get an occasional word out of her when the apple-cheeked Jinny was not there. Little by little, in answer to determined questioning, she told him that her father was confined to bed with the gout; that she was the youngest of three, but her sisters were both married; that her mother did not mind having troops quartered there—Parliament troops, that was—though she had been anxious on the night of the assault, when it had looked as if the house might be fired, and all the maids were frightened and Father threatening to get up, gout or no gout. But all the while she never raised her eyes nor volunteered a remark of her own accord; and by the time her mother appeared, late in the afternoon, with the great brass-bound Bible, Simon had given the pale girl up as a bad job.

The reading went on just as the day before, but when she had finished and closed the book, Mrs Killigrew did not at once get up to go, as she had done yesterday. Instead, she began to question Simon about his home and his family. It was as though, having nursed him, she felt a little responsible for him, and wanted to make sure that he had a good Puritan background to keep him from slipping into evil ways when he was no longer in her care.

Simon answered her questions, about his father with Lord Leven in the north, about his mother and Mouse, about his schooling, about Lovacott. His answers seemed to satisfy her on the

125

whole, and she sat talking with him while the time drew on to sunset, and the world was flushing pink.

Presently, as she rose to go, she noticed Simon's uniform coat lying across the press, where it had been put by Susanna after having the rent in the sleeve mended. She picked it up to examine the mend, shaking her head as she did so, over the brilliant hue. 'An ungodly colour!' she said. 'My mind misgave me when first I heard our troops were being put into scarlet; bedizening themselves like the Men of Wrath, who walk abroad in purple and fine raiment.'

'It's a good cheerful colour,' Simon protested, 'and it makes it easier to tell friend from foe, when you have all your men dressed alike.'

'They could be dressed alike in good hodden-grey. Scarlet is no fit colour for God-fearing men,' said Mrs Killigrew, firmly.

But Susanna, who had sat ever since she entered the room, with hands folded and eyes downcast as usual, most unexpectedly rallied to Simon's banner. '*I* think it is a very valiant colour —and it's beautiful.'

'That, Susanna, is sinful folly,' said her mother. 'Valour is of the spirit, and not the raiment; and the only true beauty is the beauty of righteousness. Now go and fetch Cornet Carey's broth; I must be away to your father.'

Susanna followed her mother from the room; dutifully as ever, with downcast eyes and hands folded before her. In a few minutes she was back, carrying the bowl of broth carefully in both hands. 'I am to wait for the bowl,' she said, as she gave it to Simon. Then she drifted across to the window, and stood looking out. 'You wouldn't think God would make pink sunsets like this one, if He didn't like bright colours, would you?' she said rather wistfully, after a while.

Simon looked up from his broth, and saw something as surprising and as lovely as the moment in a fairy-tale when the bewitched Princess is freed from the spell that bound her. For Susanna, standing in the full glow of the sunset, was no longer the little white waif she had been the moment before. The pink light streaming in upon her flushed her pale skin and made her hair under the prim coif flame red-gold, so that you felt you

126

could warm your hands at it.   But it was not that alone which
made the change : it was something inside Susanna, shining out
to meet and mingle with the radiance of the winter sunset, that
made her suddenly beautiful.

'The sun is going down like a scarlet lantern behind the trees,
and all the sky is singing,' she said.   'Look!   If I hold the curtain
back, you can share it too.'

But Simon did not look at the sunset; he was too busy looking
at Susanna, his broth forgotten and dribbling gently over the side
of the tilted bowl on to his sheet, seeing for the first time the
girl who had run to listen to a strolling fiddler on the Sabbath.
Suddenly he knew that he could ask this Susanna the question he
had not been able to ask her mother.   He did not really hope that
it would be the least use asking, but still—'Susanna,' he said,
dropping the formal 'Mistress' for the first time, 'when the
Royalists were here, there was one of them called Hannaford;
Amias Hannaford.   Do you know the one I mean?'

She thought for a moment, still holding aside the curtain.
Then she nodded.   'Yes, a tall one, with red hair that grew like
a horse's crest.   I heard him called Hannaford.'

'That's the one.   Do—do you know what happened to him?'
Susanna shook her head.   'No, I don't.'

'Oh.'   Simon's voice was full and heavy.   He looked down
at his dribbling broth bowl, and righted it, very carefully.

'I do know that the Royalist garrison were given a pass to
Exeter,' said Susanna's voice above him, 'because I heard Father
and Mother talking about it.   Mother said Sir Thomas Fairfax
was being too gentle in his dealings with the enemy in these
parts; and Father said that was maybe because of the Cornish
Levies—and the General having orders to—to pacify the West
Country as well as conquer it.'

Simon had the oddest feeling that she was talking on like this
to give him time to have his own voice under control.   But
that was ridiculous, because she couldn't know about him and
Amias; and when he looked up, she was still gazing out of the
window, with the same winged and shining look upon her . . .
'So I expect he's safely in Exeter by now,' she was saying.

'Yes—yes, I expect so.'

Susanna let the curtain fall back into place, and came across to him. 'Is he a very special friend?' she asked.

'M'm.'

'I'm so sorry,' said Susanna, softly. 'Poor boy! I'm so sorry.'

Simon was not sure whether it was himself or Amias that she meant, or both of them; but her sympathy comforted him, and made him feel less desperately alone.

The sunset light was beginning to fade, and the little room, which had been pink as the inside of a shell, was turning grey. Mrs Killigrew's step came down the passage, and instantly Susanna folded her hands and cast down her eyes, while Simon began guiltily to sup up the remains of his broth. The footsteps passed without stopping, but neither of them spoke again until Simon gave her back the empty bowl. When he looked up at her, he saw that her little changeling's face was white and pinched, just as it had been before. But quite suddenly, they had begun to be friends; and they smiled at each other, because they both knew it.

'I must go now,' Susanna said, but at the door she hesitated and looked back. 'You know my name,' she said, 'but I don't know yours—your Christian name, I mean.'

'It's Simon.'

'Can I call you Simon?'

'Well, of course you can. I call you Susanna.'

'Yes, but that's different. You are properly grown up.'

'I shall be seventeen in February.'

'And I shall be fourteen on Christmas Eve.'

'You are just the sort of person who would have a birthday on Christmas Eve,' Simon told her, gravely, and she evidently took it as a compliment, for she gave him a quick glimmering smile. Then she slipped out like a little grey ghost.

She must have been kept busy at other tasks all evening, for Simon did not see her again until next morning when he was being carried downstairs in a blanket, by two dragoons; and then it was only a glimpse he caught of a pointed, rather piteous face with enormous shadowy eyes, peering down for an instant over the carved balusters. He had no chance to do more than grin foolishly and make violent signals with his free eyebrow, before a turn in the stairs hid her from view. Then Mrs Killigrew had joined them, and was giving orders to someone about his bundle of equipment.

He was glad to be returning to his own kind, but he had an unhappy sense of leaving something behind, forsaken, and the first faint stirring of a determination to go back for it, one day.

XII

# Tidings of Old Friends

THE next few hours seemed to Simon like whole days and nights of misery. A space had been left for him and his bundle in the back of the wagon, and lying there on a pile of old sacks, between the footboard and the piled salt-beef casks with which the wagon was loaded, he was jolted along the Crediton road. More snow had fallen since the night of the assault; and the glimpses he caught of it when the rear apron of the tilt flapped aside, snow piled in drifts along the hedges and beaten into icy ruts and hummocks in the roadway, explained why the speed of the wagon so often dropped from a walking pace to that of a crawling baby. The wagon heaved and jolted through the ruts, swaying like a ship in a gale, so that Simon felt more sick and dizzy with every mile that spooled out behind the wheels, and his wounded head began to burn and throb as if there was a

130

forge fire inside it, and somebody was plying the bellows. Once, the wagoner stopped at a wayside tavern for a drop of something to keep out the cold; and sent his boy back to see if Simon was all right and if he would take a drop of anything likewise. But by that time Simon was feeling too wretched to want anything, save to be left alone; and presently the wagoner returned to his place, and Simon heard him cracking his whip and shouting to his team. Slowly, they lumbered forward again.

Gradually, he sank into a sort of doze, in which the noises all around him, the starting and squeaking of the timbers, the cease-less flapping of the tilt, the rumbling of wheels and clip-clop of horses hooves on the frozen snow, the shouts of the wagoner and his boy, all blended together into an uneasy dream that went on, and on, and on.

But at last he found that the wagon had stopped; and somebody let down the foot-board and said, 'Here 'e be, Corporal, so safe as a bagged gamecock.'

He opened his eyes, and saw several men who he judged by their tawny coats to belong to the Artillery Escort, then shut them again very tight, because the world was swimming un-pleasantly.

'Looks in pretty poor fettle to me,' said another voice; and a third retorted, 'So'd you be, if you'd just done a day's trip in a 'orrible equipage like that, with yer 'ead busted open. Take his feet and don't stand there gabbing.'

Simon felt himself lifted out. He had a confused idea that he was being carried indoors, for the bitter cleanness of the open air had changed to a smelly cold fug, and the footsteps of the men carrying him sounded hollow, as though they were in a big building. Then he was set down on what felt like straw, and somebody was unwinding his blankets and putting him to bed as though he had been a baby; someone with large hard hands and a caressing voice, who called him her lamb, her poor honey. He opened one eye cautiously, and found that it was Mother Trimble, the wife of one of the sergeants. Mother Trimble was a veteran of many battles, for she had followed her man through the Swedish Campaigns, and now she was one of the oldest and most respected of the camp-followers, and a well-known figure throughout the

Army.  She was an immensely fat woman, and very dirty, but love flowed from her towards anything that was sick or sorry, and the people she tended generally thought ever afterwards that she was beautiful.

'Hullo, Mother Trimble,' he mumbled.  'Nice to see you again.'

Mother Trimble beamed at him, her begrimed face lit with a gigantic tenderness.  'Hark to the pretty dear,' said she.  'Do 'ee go to sleep now, my lamb.  Sleep be what you needs, sure-ly.'

And Simon obediently went to sleep.

Space was limited in Crediton, for by this time upwards of half the New Model Army was centred in or around the town, and every house, every barn and church and market-hall was bulging with quartered men.  There were a fair number of wounded, for although there had been no large-scale action since the fall of Tiverton, the scattered fighting had been constant, as one by one the great houses around Exeter were taken, and the City more closely encircled.  And besides those of the New Model, there were a good many wounded Royalist prisoners. Fever was still rife in the Army too, and sick and wounded, Royalist and Parliamentarian alike, had been housed in the grouped barns and outhouses of a couple of farms close behind the church. It was in one of these barns that Simon found himself when he awoke.

He was wrapped in blankets and lying on a straw pallet, and when he turned his head carefully he could see other blanket-wrapped figures lying side by side all down the long building which reminded him of the nave of a church.  It was night time, and he saw them faintly, by the light of a lantern a long way off, which was moving slowly nearer, sometimes stopping by one of the figures, and then advancing again.  A soldier was carrying the lantern.  Simon caught the gleam of scarlet; and there was another man beside him, one of the surgeons making his night rounds.  He lay watching, until the yellow light flooded into his eyes, and the surgeon was bending over him.

'When was he brought in?' asked the surgeon of a frowsy woman who appeared out of the shadows.

'This afternoon as ever was, your honour,' said she. 'And so pale as a larded fowl when they carried him in; give me quite a turn it did, and me with my weak inside——'

'Yes, never mind that; has his head been seen to?'

Nobody, including Simon, seemed to know the answer to this, until a voice with a strong Cockney accent informed them sleepily from the next pallet, 'Muvver Trimble cast 'er peepers over it, s'arternoon.'

'Might as well leave it alone, then,' said the surgeon. 'All right, carry on, Corporal.' The lantern moved on to the owner of the Cockney voice, and almost at once, Simon was asleep once more.

It was towards evening of the next day when Lieutenant Colebourne appeared in the entrance of the great barn, where the double doors were always kept ajar, partly to let in a little air and partly because it was too much trouble to keep on opening and shutting them. He looked along the rows of pallets, then spoke to a Sergeant of Fortescue's, who was lounging against one of the roof-trees with a wounded foot stuck straight out in front of him. The man turned and pointed to where Simon lay, and Barnaby came swaggering down the barn to join him.

Simon, who had been watching a beetle in the straw of his neighbour's bed, looked up to see his visitor standing over him, and let out a pleased croak.

Barnaby folded up beside him, and slid into a comfortable position with his knees under his chin. 'Been beating up a couple of deserters. Not ours, thanks be! So here I am,' he said. 'How's the old cock-loft?'

'It's mending,' Simon told him. 'But it still feels twice its usual size.'

'Aren't you a pest!' remarked Barnaby amiably. 'Now here am I left without a cornet until you get it mended.'

'I'm really sorry.'

'Yes, so you ought to be. How long are they going to keep you in this flea-pit?'

'Another ten days or so, the surgeon says.'

Barnaby nodded. 'Well, I daresay I shall survive—oh, and while I think of it, I've got that sorrel of yours safely; and a more

134

ill-tempered fidgety brute than he's been ever since we brought him back, I never met!'

'He's never been parted from me since he was broken,' Simon explained. 'And when he was a colt, and I was away at school, he was at home in his own paddock, among people he knew as well as me.'

'I don't see that he need behave like a fine lady with the vapours, even so,' said Barnaby. 'Anyhow, he'll be doing pack duty up to Tiverton tomorrow; that ought to bring down his airs and graces a bit.'

'Tiverton?' Simon said quickly.

'Yes, didn't you know? Fiery Tom is moving his head-quarters back there. The men are dying like flies in those blazing swamps round Ottery, and its more than time we pulled out.'

Simon felt as if he had been weeks away from the Regiment, instead of only four days. It was queer, he thought, how quickly things moved when you were not there to move with them. They talked on for a while, and then he made up his mind.

'Barnaby,' he said, 'Barnaby, listen——'

'What's the trouble?'

'Did you happen to notice a red-headed Royalist among the garrison that night—in the hall when you broke in?'

'The one who looked as though we all smelt?' inquired Barnaby.

'Yes, that would be him. What—happened to him?'

'He marched off with the rest of the garrison after their Commanding Officer surrendered. They had the usual pass into Exeter.'

'You're sure?'

'Course I'm sure. I saw him go, with his nose akimbo.'

Sheer relief flooded over Simon, and suddenly, joyously, he laughed. 'Yes, he would! He'd go just like that.'

Barnaby was looking at him with rather puzzled eyes. 'Friend of yours?—It wouldn't be your fellow unicorn, would it?'

Simon mumbled something incoherently.

135

'Yes, but look here! When we broke in, you were——'
Barnaby checked, and then asked in a rush: 'What's the food like
in this place?'

'Pretty good; the charitably minded housewives of the town
bring us all sorts of extras in covered baskets,' Simon said quickly.

Presently Lieutenant Colebourne scrambled to his feet. 'I
must be marching. Get your head well soon, there's a good lad.'

'I will,' Simon promised, and watched him swaggering away
down the barn and out into the fading light of the winter afternoon. He felt light and clean with relief; later, the memory of
that night at Okeham Paine would begin to hurt unbearably again,
but for the moment, it was enough that Amias was all right, after
all. Suddenly he was very hungry, and the greasy smell beginning to waft from the camp kitchen seemed to him glorious.

Upwards of a fortnight later Simon had news of another friend.
It was the last night of his stay in hospital, and he was very thankful to be going back to his troop in the morning. Life had not
been exactly dull, with the constant coming and going of army
chaplains and surgeons, and the charitably minded of the town
with covered baskets; the food had been rather more interesting
than the food on active service, and the women of the camp had for
the most part been kindly. Still, he was thankful to be getting
out of it. It was the nights he hated; the long nights when men
tossed and muttered in pain and the dawn seemed to have lost
its way in the tangle of dragging hours. Anyhow, by this time
tomorrow he would be back with the Regiment, back to the
horse-lines and the familiar routine, and the trumpets sounding
for watch-setting.

He stretched his stockinged feet luxuriously to the makeshift
hearth, and looked about him at his companions. There were
five of them gathered round the fire that night, all who were well
enough to leave their beds, and they were a motley company,
huddled close for warmth, with blankets drawn over their
unfastened uniforms, like so many Redskin braves around their
council fire. A cuirassier of Cromwell's Horse, a man of true
Ironside mould, such as Zeal-for-the-Lord had been, though as
unlike him in body as might well be, being square and ruddy as
the other was lean and dark. A grizzled Lieutenant of the Artil-

136

lery Escort, with a hand badly mangled by the accidental explosion of a powder-keg. A long-faced pikeman with a merry eye, who had got into the New Model by way of the London train-bands. The fifth was a Royalist officer captured in an outpost skirmish and found to be suffering from neglected fever; a man older than the rest, except perhaps the Escort Lieutenant, with the face of a scholar rather than a fighting man, whose doublet showed gold-laced but very tattered beneath the brown folds of the blanket wrapped around his shoulders.

Usually the Royalist sick and wounded were housed in a smaller barn to themselves, but after the capture of Eggsford House on the eighteenth it had become too crowded, and the overflow had been put in here. They were accepted quite peaceably, for the fighting men of the two armies had very little real bitterness against each other; and Captain Weston sat quite naturally and comfortably with the men of the New Model, round their makeshift fire.

Looking round at them as they sat talking idly, Simon thought, ' What a funny crew we are, to keep Christmas night in company,' for it was Christmas night. Parliament had declared that 25 December should no longer be celebrated as a ' Pagan Festival ' but be kept only as an ordinary Sabbath. But Christmas night, Simon thought, remained Christmas night, and no Parliament on earth could stop it—might as well try to stop the spring. There had never been wild Yule-tide merry-makings at Lovacott, but there had been cake and cider for the mummers, and the singing of old carols and the telling of old stories round the fire on which the Ashen Faggot was burning, and people had called out the Season's Greetings to each other on the way home from church. And in the great hall at Lovacott, the kissing branch had hung like a crown of light from the rafters. Simon's father had not really approved of the kissing branch, but he had suffered it to hang there every Christmas, because it had hung there in his father's day, and his grandfather's, and so on, back to Christmases before Agincourt was fought; sparkling and glowing in the light of its own candles, and making a link with all those other Careys who had gathered under it. Susanna Killigrew would like the Lovacott kissing branch, Simon decided suddenly; there was something inside her that was kin to the warmth and the joyousness of it.

The great barn was settling into its night-time aspect. The horn lanterns shed their uncertain light on the double row of pallets, where some of the men were already asleep, while others amused themselves with greasy cards, or tried to read their Bibles, or talked half under their breath. A low moaning wind had risen with the dusk, and came eddying in through the small high window and the ragged chimney-hole in the roof, driving the smoke down in occasional stinging clouds, setting the flames of the lanterns jumping, and filling the long building with swirling icy draughts. Sometimes two men laughed quietly over a shared joke, or the rattle of the forbidden dice sounded sharply in a dice-box; and all the time there was the heavy breathing of the man on the nearest pallet who had been filled with opium for the pain of a smashed leg, and was deep in a drugged sleep. A queer Christmas night, and Simon, sitting silent beside the fire, while his elders and betters discussed the new high-explosive shells which were beginning to be used, knew that he would remember it always when Christmas time came round again.

Outside, a sentry went by; Simon heard his footsteps on the beaten snow as he passed the barn door, and caught the air of an old Carol that he was whistling cheerfully out of tune. No, you couldn't stop Christmas by an Act of Parliament.

> As Joseph was a-walking,
> He heard an angel sing;
> This night there shall be born
> On earth our Heavenly King.

The familiar words sang themselves over in Simon's head:

> He neither shall be born
> In housen nor in hall,
> Nor in the place of Paradise,
> But in an ox's stall.

He found that he had taken up the air and was whistling it under his breath; and he broke off, half expecting that the cuirassier would berate him for the ungodly tune. But hardship or pain shared has a way of making folk tolerant one with another, and the cuirassier said nothing. It was the pikeman who spoke, breaking a silence which had fallen on them when the subject of explosive shells was talked out.

'Cove sounds cheerful,' said he, cocking an eye towards the doorway. 'Of all the company a fellow can have on sentry-go, commend me to a good loud whistle, specially after dark. Psalm tune or pot-house ditty, it makes no odds, s'long as it's loud enough.'

'That may be, friend,' said the cuirassier, 'but if your ears are full of your own whistling, how are you going to hear your enemy?'

'Why now, there's drawbacks, I grant you.' The pikeman grinned. 'But it keeps yer courage up, now don't it?'

'Whistling in the dark.' This time it was the Royalist who spoke. 'There is a lot in it. It is in the silence that a man's nerves start jumping; I have found that often enough, on outpost duty.' He held out his hands to the fire, as though he was suddenly cold. 'I believe most savage tribes sing before battle, or drum their spears on their shields—anything to make a noise; not to strike terror into the enemy, as is so often supposed, but to strengthen their own courage. It is a very comforting thing, noise of one's own making.'

The Escort Lieutenant sat forward, his face thoughtful in the firelight, his sound hand curved about the bowl of his short clay pipe. 'Maybe that is why it is our English custom to fight shouting; though oddly enough the Scots do not, as I know, for I served with Lord Levan in Sweden. They are brave fighters, the Scots, but I've ay noticed that men charge best when they're yelling like demons.'

The talk meandered on, drawing farther and farther from the original subject under discussion, until, from whistling on sentry-go, it became an argument about those things which best kept up a man's heart—or an army's—in time of hardship or danger. The Escort Lieutenant was inclined to think that a strong personal trust in one's leader was among the greatest of these, and talked of the retreat from Lostwithiel. 'If it hadn't been for the Old Man, we'd have lain down and died rather than struggle on,' he said, much as the Infantry Lieutenant had done, that evening at

Windsor. 'There was only one of the Old Man, and upwards of five thousand of us, but somehow he forced his will on every man of us, individually—and he brought us through. He was something for us to hang on to, and we hung on.'

Meanwhile, the cuirassier and the pikeman were arguing keenly, the cuirassier declaring again and again that faith in the righteousness of his cause was the best thing any man could have for the strengthening of his arm in the hour of battle, while the pikeman staunchly maintained that the hope of loot was even better.

The Escort Lieutenant listened to them, puffing steadily at his pipe. 'Mind you,' he put in, with a cocked eyebrow, when the argument began to wax hot, 'the hope of getting one's own back isn't far behind when it comes to supporting someone under difficulties. I've known a man dragged safely through the smallpox, when he'd been given up by the apothecary, simply by his determination to recover in order to be revenged on an old enemy who had stolen his Sabbath hat.'

A grin ran round the group; but the cuirassier said gravely: 'Aye, a just vengeance is a powerful strengthener to a man's arm.'

The Royalist leaned forward into the firelight which lit his thin scholarly face. 'The lust for revenge may be all that, but it has an odd trick of destroying its owner in the end,' he said. 'I have seen it at work, not long since. It was not a pretty sight.'

The others looked at him expectantly; for the fire was warm and their pallets not inviting, and they were in the mood for any sort of anecdote. 'And did it destroy its owner in the end?' asked the Escort Lieutenant.

'It may have done, by now,' said Captain Weston. 'It was in the late summer that I last saw the man I have in mind. I was serving under Prince Rupert in Bristol, when he came in to join the Army. He was a renegade from your ranks, by the way: a tall black-browed fellow who talked like an Old Testament prophet. He actually served in my Company for a while, and I got to know something of him; not that there was anything wonderful in that; the whole Army was in a fair way to knowing his story. That was the strange thing about him; he told his story to all and sundry, and yet he was not a babbler by nature.

It was as though he wanted someone to hear it, and be afraid. It was a coldly calculated attempt to make someone suffer the torment of a rabbit with a stoat on its trail.' He broke off for a few moments as though sorting the story out in his mind; and when he went on again, Simon, who had already a suspicion of the truth, found that he was listening to Zeal-for-the-Lord's story of a false friend and a double hyacinth.

'. . . He was caught by a patrol.' The Royalist had almost come to the end of that part of the story which Simon knew. 'He was tried by Court Martial for desertion, and sentenced to be flogged and degraded to the Pioneers. It seems that you are more tender with your deserters than we are. And from the Pioneers he escaped and went once more after his revenge. He reached his old home, and found that the man who had been his friend was gone. The new Lord of the Manor had come out to join Prince Rupert, and many of the tenantry had followed him, this man amongst them, not because he wanted to, but because he had no choice. In the hope of finding his enemy and filled with a bitter sense of his wrongs—for remember, he felt his own revenge was so righteous that the sentence of the Court Martial seemed to him a mad injustice—he followed, and joined himself to us at Bristol. And as I have said, he told his story to all who would listen, so that it should come to his enemy's ears and he should know what was loose on his trail.' Captain Weston paused again. 'How the story ended—if it has ended yet—I do not know. After Bristol fell, my Company was split up, and I did not see him again.'

'Poor devil!' said the Escort Lieutenant.

'Aye, poor devil. If you had had the man under your eye, as I have done, you would have good cause to say so. He was bitter as gall against the Parliament Forces; but he hated the Army of the King. He took some pains not to show that; but I happen to be something of a student of men, and I saw plainly enough. And most of all, he hated himself, because in joining our ranks he had broken faith with the things he still believed to be right. He had paid away his self-respect, and though he clung all the more fiercely to his revenge in consequence, maybe it was dear at the price.'

'You seem to have taken a most uncommon amount of interest in this unhappy wretch,' said the cuirassier.

'Did I not say that I am a student of men? I find the study absorbing.'

'How did such a man come to be accepted into your ranks?' asked the Escort Lieutenant. 'Even to a less discerning eye than yours, he can't have seemed a very promising recruit.'

The Royalist made a small, hopeless gesture with the hand which hung lax across his kness. 'We need men,' he said; and suddenly his face was bleak and haggard in the firelight.

'If it come to be the fashion, slingin' yer hook and going off to get yer own back on coves wot helped theirselves out of yer pockets,' ruminated the pikeman, grinning at the Royalist, 'I'll wager there'd not be many of your coves this side o' the Channel tonight; and yer'd be able to walk across to Spain on the boats making the trip.'

There was an awkward silence; for a few weeks since, Lord Goring had deserted his command and fled to Spain with every penny of Royalist funds that he could lay hands on. Between the men around the fire there was a kind of unspoken truce; they did not use the slighting nicknames of Cavaliers and Roundheads, they did not speak of King Charles as the Man of Blood, nor of Fairfax and Cromwell as accursed rebels; and they felt that the pikeman's gibe was untimely.

'I may have my own opinion concerning My Lord Goring's conduct,' said Captain Weston, after a moment. 'But in my present rather unfortunate position you can scarcely expect me to discuss it.'

The pikeman, who was a friendly soul, grinned more broadly. 'No offence meant, yer know.'

'And none taken,' said Captain Weston.

Someone put another turf on the fire, and the talk wandered in a more cheerful direction; but Simon took no part in it. He sat, elbow on knees and chin on fists, staring into the warm up-leap of flames, and thinking about his old Corporal. But if the older men noticed his moodiness, they thought maybe the lad was homesick—Christmas time, even when it had been abolished, was apt to turn the heart homeward.

## XIII

## *Special Duty*

AFTER a wet autumn the winter had turned bitterly cold, and from early December the West Country was deep in snow. It was weather for hugging the home fireside and leaving the roads to the north-east winds and the deepening drifts; but neither army went completely into winter quarters, as they had done each year before. This year, the end of the struggle was coming, and King's men and Parliament's men knew it, and faced each other warily, like two wrestlers watching each other's first move. The New Model was encamped around Exeter and Tiverton; one part of the Royalist Army covered the country between Dart and Teign, while the other was strung from Oke-hampton to Tavistock, where the young Prince of Wales was quartered. North Devon had become a sort of Tom-Tiddler's ground, where the patrols of both armies skirmished and foraged and made life generally difficult and dangerous for the folk of the countryside.

Soon after Christmas the scouts began to bring in news of preparations for a strong Royalist attempt to relieve Exeter: Cornish train-bands were daily expected at Tavistock, five hundred of the Barnstaple garrison and all the troops that could be spared from the siege of Plymouth were to join them, and the Prince of Wales, with his own Guards, was to lead the whole lot to Totnes, where a magazine was being made for them with stores brought by sea from Cornwall. After that would come the relief of Exeter, and the beleaguered garrison would sally out to join forces with their comrades.

Fairfax and Cromwell bided their time while the Royalists gathered; and when the right moment came, they struck. The young Prince was on the very eve of marching, when news reached him that Cromwell had surprised the main body of his Horse under Lord Wentworth, and scattered them to the four winds. And at the same time, though word of this did not reach him until a day or two later, Fairfax and a Brigade of Horse and Foot, with the straining gun-teams in their midst, were heading across the moor in a snowstorm, to attack Dartmouth, which fell within a few days.

The whole Royalist plan for the relief of Exeter had become hopeless; the blockade had to withdraw from around Plymouth lest it should be cut off, and Tavistock was no longer safe for the Prince, who withdrew to Launceston, taking the Foot with him, and leaving only the remaining Horse to guard the Tamar. The Cornish train-bands began to desert, on the excuse that their first duty was to defend their own homes; and by mid-January the whole army was falling to pieces, while the generals fought among themselves.

Meanwhile, Simon was facing a stiff fight of his own. He had been so glad to rejoin his Troop; in a way it had been like coming home, and to outward seeming he had slipped back at once into his old place. But from the first, something had been wrong. If he had come in for active service just then, it might have been easier, but Fairfax's Horse did not form part of the Dartmouth expedition; and the slow, grinding business of the Exeter blockade did not help in the least. To begin with, he was desperately worried about his mother and Mouse, alone in Lovacott with his father still in the north. There had been no word from them for some while past, and knowing that his home countryside was overrun by Grenville's troopers, he could not get much comfort out of Barnaby's suggestion that in the present upheaval many letters must be sent that never reached the people they were meant for. Denzil Wainwright was being a pest too, never missing the least chance for making life difficult, goading him by every means in his power. In the months since he joined the Regiment, Simon had learned to bother about Denzil no more than if he had been a gnat; but now, quite suddenly, his carefully planted stings were maddening, and it was all Simon could do not to let him see when they reached their mark. Above all, and at the root of all the trouble, he could not forget about his encounter with Amias at Okeham Paine. Something in him had been hurt, that night, before ever his head was broken, and though his head mended, the deeper hurt remained raw and aching. Even his old joy of his Troop seemed dulled in him, and he carried out his duties doggedly, but with little pleasure in them.

That was an unhappy time for Simon, but it ended with a most surprising suddenness, when, one evening about three weeks after he rejoined his Troop, he received orders to report for special duty to Major Watson of the Scouts. Half an hour later, wondering very much what it was all about, he was standing in the low-ceiled back parlour of the Hand-in-Glove, breathing the warm throat-catching reek of tobacco-smoke and Hollands, and gazing inquiringly at the man who sat at a littered table before the fire.

Major Watson was a meagre man, who peered at the world through mild blue eyes behind fluttering sandy lashes; a most unlikely-looking individual to have charge of the bunch of brigands who made up the Intelligence Service of the New Model Army. Only his clipped voice gave the lie to his lamb-like appearance.

Having nodded amiably to Simon when he entered, he put the tips of his fingers together and blinked at him over the top of them; while Simon, knowing that he was being sized up, gazed levelly back.

'I could have wished for an older and more experienced man,' said the clipped voice at last. 'However, you have a good record. I am glad to see your head has not completely healed yet.'

'Sir?' said Simon in bewilderment.

'Cornet Carey, I understand that your home is in North Devon.'

'Yes, sir.'

'Where, exactly?'

Simon told him, and he listened with close attention, putting searching questions about distances and communications; then nodded above his joined finger-tips, as though satisfied with the answers.

'So. You have a good knowledge of your own countryside. That may be a help.'

'Am I to go home, then, sir?'

The Major regarded him consideringly for a few moments, then, as though making up his mind, abruptly parted his finger-tips and sat up. 'Yes. I am arranging that you shall be transferred for a few weeks to my—shall we say to my family? I am sending one of my men up to Torrington tomorrow, and you will ride with him. Officially, you will be going home on sick leave, and that is the reason that you will give in the Regiment; also I think you would be wise to give the same reason to your family. The less they know of the matter, the safer it will be for them.'

'And—the real reason, sir?' Simon asked quickly.

Major Watson blinked mildly at the young officer's eagerness. 'The house we have been using as a meeting-place and clearing-house for dispatches, in your part of the world, was occupied by the enemy, three days ago. Now we need another house—and another man; and you and Lovacott together have the needful requirements. The house, from what you tell me, is in a good strategic position, easy of access from the three main towns and the country between, and with good communications with the Exeter road behind it. You know the country, and your recent wound gives you a reason for your return home, which is above suspicion.'

'Yes, sir.'

'Your job, so long as nothing goes wrong, will be simple. You will act purely as a go-between. You will receive dispatches from the man you ride with tomorrow, or from others, and you will pass them on to a man who comes for them later, and who you will know by a password I shall give you presently; and while they are in your care, you will guard them as you never yet guarded anything in your life. Understood? Very well, then.

The details you will arrange for yourself, through Podbury, your travelling companion.'

'Yes, sir—is that all?' Simon said blankly.

'That is all for the moment. The job may not be as dull as it sounds, for if you run into Royalist soldiery you will have only your own wits to depend on; and Grenville's troopers are not likely to take the fact that you are on sick leave into account, if they once discover they have a Parliament Officer in their hands.'

Simon hesitated. 'Sir, may I ask you something?'

'You may certainly ask. I make no promise to answer.'

'Is something going to happen in North Devon?'

Major Watson shrugged. 'I make you a present of three facts, all of which are common knowledge: since Dartmouth has fallen, South Devon is in our hands. North Devon is still open and the three main towns are Royalist held. There is a Royalist Army—of a sort—across the Cornish border, which may yet be pulled together again. There are your facts; marshal them together, and perhaps you will find the answer to your question. It may of course be the wrong answer, but it is best to take no chances. Oh, and Cornet Carey, the password is "There's many a good cock come out of a tattered bag", to which the reply is, "And a good tune played on an old fiddle". You have that?'

Simon repeated it, and Major Watson nodded. 'The messages you receive will sometimes be by word of mouth, in which case you will take them down accurately and send them on in the usual way. Your signature will be the number 7, and under it the number of the man who brought in the information. We do not put names into writing in this game.'

'Yes, sir; the number 7. Can you give me any idea how long I shall be away from the Regiment, sir?'

'None whatever. But you will not leave your post for an hour, *whatever happens*, until you are recalled; or until battle actually joins, in which case it will probably not be possible to recall you, and you must make your own decision.'

Dinner was already begun in the long upper room of the castle which served the officers of both Fairfax's Regiments for a Mess when Simon slipped into his place far down the crowded

147

table; and he glanced about him with the eye of leave-taking, wondering what would have happened before he sat among these men again. They were discussing a piece of news that was fresher than the fall of Dartmouth, their faces alert in the candle-light that fell warmly on scarlet and blue, and the sober black of the surgeons and chaplains.

'Well, Lord Hopton will have his hands full, with that precious lot of lambs,' said a crop-headed captain of Foot.

'There's been no Royalist Commander-in-Chief since My Lord Goring sailed for foreign parts with his boots full of other folk's guineas,' put in Ralf Marjory, farther up the table. 'Perhaps that's why their army has fallen to bits.'

'Has anyone heard who is to command under him?' asked a late-comer.

Several voices answered him. 'Wentworth the Horse and Grenville the Foot.'

'Skellum Grenville! Phew! The Skellum will be more of a handful than all the rest combined. I wonder how Hopton will deal with him.'

Captain-Lieutenant Meredith leaned forward to help himself to more salt. 'In dealing with a rogue,' he said, 'Lord Hopton is at a disadvantage, being an honourable man.'

All down the table men were deep in the discussion, and Simon, left to himself, sat with his elbow on the table, staring down into the tawny depths of his beer mug, and thinking about his interview with Major Watson and the task that was ahead of him. Odd, to think that in two days' time he would be at home again; odd, that it really would not be a home-coming at all, but just going somewhere to do a job in the Army, and the somewhere happening to be Lovacott. There was a queer mingling of feelings inside him: relief that at last he would be able to see how things were with his womenfolk; interest and excitement at the prospect of this new kind of danger; and a queer distaste for the idea of bringing the hidden beastliness of war into Lovacott. And yet, for the very reason that Lovacott meant so much to him, standing for all the things that he was fighting for, the beloved place could not be grudged to the fight like a fine lady who must not be allowed to soil her hands. Deep in this confusion of thoughts and feelings, he did not notice that the air was thickening with tobacco smoke and men beginning to lounge up from the table and make for the fire that burned at one end of the room.

'Our friend Hodge would seem to find his thoughts deeply interesting,' said Denzil Wainwright's voice at his shoulder, and he looked up with a start, to see his tormentor beside him. 'Pleasant thoughts?' inquired Cornet Wainwright tenderly.

'Yes, thank you,' said Simon, with elaborate politeness.

'Were they of cows, may one inquire—or possibly turnips?'

Simon said nothing. He was aware of a small crowd gathering around them to look on with interest.

'Or could it be your worthy mother?'

Simon was staring into his beer-mug as though he had not heard. But his left hand, hidden under the table, was clenching and unclenching convulsively.

Denzil gave him a light poke. 'I'm talking to you.'

'I beg your pardon,' said Simon between shut teeth. 'I thought it was a blue-bottle buzzing.'

'Rude,' sighed Denzil. 'Also crude.' He lounged against the table. 'This is your part of the world, isn't it, Hodge?'

Simon did not look up. 'Farther north, Torrington way,' he said briefly.

'Ah, a case of "so near and yet so far", eh?'

'Not really. I'm going home tomorrow—on sick leave.'

There was an instant's surprised pause; and then, in a clear amused voice, raised a little for the whole room to hear, Denzil said, 'You're not such a fool as you look, Hodge.'

'Meaning?'

'It must have taken quite a lot of—shall we say intelligence?—yes, intelligence, to get sick leave out of that scratch on your head. I take it that when once you get back among the ancestral pigs and pastures, we shall not be counting you among our numbers again?'

Simon stopped staring into his beer-mug and got up deliberately. 'Look here, drop it, can't you?' he said, breathing quickly through widened nostrils; and the onlookers saw that he had gone very white.

'Drop what?—Oh, don't come trampling over me, you oaf!'

149

'*Drop it!*' Simon said again, his voice shaking with passion. And Denzil, hearing the tremor, and mistaking its cause, laughed.

At the sound of that laugh, a scarlet flame seemed to leap up in Simon, fanning out so that he saw Denzil's dark amused face through the fiery redness. He drove his fist into it, with the full weight of his body behind the blow, and saw it suddenly surprised and with a bloody mouth. There was a fierce joy in him, and he never heard the crash of splintering wood as a chair went over and was kicked aside; he never felt the blows that were landing true on his own face. All he knew was the savage exultation of battle as his own blows went home, every blow the avenging of an insult too long borne.

Presently the red flame began to sink and he found that he was leaning against the table and drawing his breath in whistling gasps, the centre of a crowd of staring faces.

'Phew!' Cornet Fletcher was saying admiringly. 'I never knew Carey had a temper like that!'

One of his eyes was rapidly closing, but out of the other he saw an overturned chair and a litter of pots and dishes that had been swept from the table; and beyond, Denzil Wainwright sagging against the wall in the midst of another group. Denzil's face seemed the most appalling mess, and Simon looked vaguely from it to his own broken knuckles, and back again. Chaplain Joshua Sprigg was saying something about lewd brawling and ungodly behaviour, but Simon was not listening; without the red flame, he felt suddenly cold and very tired. The crowd parted to let someone through, and he saw that it was David Morrison.

The old surgeon took him by the shoulders and turned him to the light of a branch of candles. 'Ach, these hot-headed bairns that canna' thole a fancied smutch on their honour!' said he, severely, shaking his head. 'No harm done, save a black eye; but ye may thank your Maker that ye have na' reopened that wound, ma laddie.' And he patted Simon's shoulder approvingly as he turned away.

'Major Disbrow's going to hear about this!' said Denzil, as he dabbed at his bleeding mouth. 'You went for me like a devil, Carey!'

Barnaby Colebourne, who was standing at his Cornet's side, swung round on him in cold contempt. 'Don't be a fool, Wainwright. You've been asking for trouble all this past year, and now you've got what you were asking for. And I shouldn't do any reporting, if I were you; too many of us can tell the truth about this evening's performance.'

There was a murmur of agreement; and Ralf Marjory, the senior captain present, who had been ostentatiously staring out of the window into the night, with his back turned to the whole proceedings, looked round for the first time. 'I suggest Cornet Wainwright puts his face to rights, and then turns in,' he said, but it was an order, not a suggestion.

'Sir,' said Denzil, pulling himself together with an obvious effort, and stalking rather groggily from the room. But in the doorway he turned and looked at Simon, a long, dark look. 'I swear I'll even the account with you for this!' he said, and lurched out into the gallery.

So next morning Simon rode northward, beside one of Major Watson's scouts. They were an ordinary-looking couple, with nothing about them to catch the notice of any Royalist they might encounter; farmers or well-to-do tradesmen, to judge by their comfortable homespun garments; though to be sure the face of Simon's companion, under the brim of his beaver, seemed somewhat leery for a farmer. As a matter of fact, he had been first a lawyer's clerk and then a fairground thimble-rigger before he joined the New Model.

Simon had pulled his slouch hat far down to cover the general state of his face, as well as the ill-healed scar on his temple, for a beefsteak applied last night to his eye had not had much effect; and he rode lazily, with his free hand thrust deep into the pocket of his russet riding-coat, in manner very different from the way he had learned to ride as an officer of Fairfax's Horse. His saddle felt unfamiliar after the hard Cavalry saddle he had grown used to, and he missed the light kiss of his sword against his left thigh. It had become so much a part of himself, his sword, and he had had to leave it behind, since a farmer going about his lawful business would be most unlikely to carry such a thing. But pistols were another matter; anyone going on a journey in these hazardous days might carry pistols, and Simon's were safe in their holsters at his saddle bow.

He had spent a rather worried night, for he realized that last evening's affair had not been quite in keeping with sick leave. But save that Barnaby had remarked in a slightly puzzled tone, ' I must say that for an invalid, you have an uncommon punishing left,' there had been no awkward developments, and as they turned into the familiar road, his heart lifted because he was going home, just as it used to lift when he rode that way on the first day of the school holidays.

It was not a pleasant journey, with the roads churned to quagmire and every stream coming down in green spate from the melting snows of Exmoor, and some miles short of South Molton they were thankful to turn aside for the night at a dirty hedge-tavern. Here they found two troopers of Grenville's, who seemed to have mislaid the rest of their regiment, though they assured the newcomers that they were not deserters. They all spent a very merry evening together, and Simon, watching Mr Podbury drinking rum with his feet on the table after cheating the younger of the Royalists out of one and ninepence at the dice, remembered with interest a rumour which had run through the Army a while before, that the scouts had demanded a rise of pay to recompense them for the danger to their immortal souls.

Simon slept in the stable with Scarlet that night, partly because the straw seemed less flea-ridden than the tavern beds, and partly because he did not trust Grenville's troopers where a horse was concerned. But nothing happened, and in the morning he and the scout took the road again.

Some miles short of Torrington they parted, after making certain careful arrangements. The scout held straight on towards the town, while Simon turned off into the maze of lanes and bridle-tracks that he knew like the lines of his own palm; and in the first fading of the winter day, he swung into the dearly familiar track that led home.

Horse and rider were both tired, but Scarlet pricked his ears and started forward to the sudden glorious memory of the home stable, and Simon lifted his head and gazed about him hungrily.

The muddied snow still lay drifted along the hedge-bottom, but already the withies were flushed with rising sap. Salutation was down to winter wheat, and as Scarlet's hoof-beats disturbed them, a flock of green plover rose from the bare plough-land, their pied wings pulsing and flickering against the dun woods beyond. Then the track rounded the spinney where the white owl lived, and Simon reined back an instant by the gate and looked across the home paddock to the warm and welcoming huddle of the house and outbuildings. Always, in the old days, he had paused like this when he arrived back from school, for his first glimpse of home. But this time surely there was something different about the steep lift of the orchard beyond; a bareness about the crest where the old cider trees had always stood against the sky.

However, he had no time to notice what the difference was; scarcely time to notice that it was there at all; for at that instant Tom appeared from among the farm buildings, carrying a huge forkful of hay. He halted at sight of the rider in the lane, and then dropped the fork and shot back towards the house. 'Missis!' Simon could hear him roaring. 'Maister Simon's back! 'Tis Maister Simon, my dear souls!'

'We're home, Scarlet!' Simon said, drawing a hand down the horse's neck, and urging him on up the lane, the difference in the orchard quite forgotten. 'We're home again, old lad.'

Late that night three very contented people were still sitting round the fire in the parlour, where the firelight was reflected dancingly in the sheeny depth of the panelling, and the wintry darkness was shut out by drawn curtains of faded damask that seemed to fold the little room in warmth and shelter as though they had been wings folded close around it.

All the excitement of home-coming, the joyful astonishment and the breathless questions and answers, the supper with Mrs Carey's storeroom raided in honour of the occasion, were over. There had been so much to say, so many things to tell, after almost a year of being apart; but for the moment they had talked themselves out, and now they were sitting quiet, with the dogs dozing at their feet.

Then Mouse, who was sitting on her heels before the fire, with one of Jillot's latest puppies asleep in her lap, looked up at Simon, and sighed. ' I wish you were in uniform,' she said. ' We heard that the soldiers of the New Model Army all wear scarlet—I should like to see you in scarlet, with your sword.'

' Why, a scarlet coat, or a buff one for that matter, would be likely to land one in trouble, in these parts nowadays.'

Mouse's eyes suddenly grew round and solemn. ' Oh, Simon, is it safe for you here? I hadn't thought——'

' Safe as houses,' Simon reassured her. ' Should I have been sent home on sick leave if it wasn't safe, you goose? The village won't talk, and if we should get Royalists round the place, how are they to know I didn't cut my head open falling off a haystack?'

' On to the edge of a scythe,' added his sister, with a sudden glint of laughter in her eyes that had been so startled the moment before. ' Yes, I see.'

' This Mistress Killigrew who tended you when you were wounded,' said his mother, looking up from the ancient damask cloth she was mending, ' what is she like?'

Simon considered. ' She's a good woman,' he said at last. ' But not comfortable. Now, *you* are comfortable as well as good, Mother; it makes a lot of difference.'

Mrs Carey smiled at him fondly. ' At all events, she seems to have been very kind to you. I shall write and thank her, when there's any likelihood of a letter getting through again.'

' Umm,' said Simon, and smiled back at her. He leaned down to put some more wood on the fire; then paused, looking at the lichened log in his hand. ' Hullo, have we had a tree blown down?'

There was a little silence, then Mrs Carey said, ' Not blown, my dear—cut. A party of Lord Goring's troopers passed this way in the early winter.'

Simon felt a small chill shock, and the sense of Sanctuary faded a little from the firelit room, and he heard the strident call of a hunting owl in the bitter darkness outside. ' Have they cut down much of the orchard? The Old Warden?'

' No, only the cider trees at the top. They were ordered on before they had time to start on the rest.'

' And the Spinney close at hand, with enough dead wood in

it to cook for an army after the autumn gales,' said Mouse, in a small grim voice, playing with the puppy's ears so hard that it woke and whimpered. 'Well, the green wood made them very poor fires; that's one consolation. Even now we can only burn what was left a bit at a time, when the fire is hot.'

'Have you had much trouble, these past months?' Simon asked.

Mrs Carey was beginning another darn. 'Not really. A few sheep stolen, and the granary fired by deserters—but we managed to put that out—and the apple trees. There are scars; but I doubt if you'll find many houses quite unscathed that lie in the path of the war.'

'No, I suppose not,' Simon said slowly. He looked at the log in his hand, with its delicate tracery of grey-green lichen; thinking of the autumn cider-making, and the beauty of white blossom in the springtime, that would not come again. It seemed so wanton, so stupid. He put the log gently on the fire, and watched it flower for the last time into petals of saffron flame that scented all the room with aromatic sweetness.

# XIV

# *Of Cocks and Fiddles*

ON the surface, the next few weeks were very peaceful ones
for Simon. There was plenty of work for him on the
demesne, with the lambing season in full swing, and the
farm men away at the war, and old Diggory, who had been laid
up with the rheumatics most of the winter, still in bed. And he
worked hard, beside Tom, and came in tired at nights, with a
deep quiet tiredness, and slept in his chair after supper, with weary
legs stretched to the fire.

But he never for an instant felt that he had come home. He
was no more than a passage-hawk: here under orders, to carry
out a certain task; and it was as though Lovacott, grown wise
with centuries of being lived in and loved, knew it, and did not
try to claim him. Presently, when the war was over, he could
come home, knowing that he had earned his heritage; and Lovacott would take him back. But that was not yet.

And underneath the quiet surface there was the job he had come
to do; and a certain secret coomb screened round by hazel and
crack willow through which the little stream, Jewel Water,
splashing down toward the parish boundary might have told a tale
of disreputable characters who came and went in the darkness, and
an occasional scrap of dirty paper passed from hand to hand or a
message taken down by the shielded light of a lantern. The turn
of the little-used chapel path above Lovacott Moor might have
told another, of a messenger waiting in the ditch, while his horse
grazed beside him, to whom the message would be passed on
before the following dawn. The lambing season was very useful
to Simon, for it gave him a good reason for his night-time comings
and goings; and if he chanced to meet anyone, he was looking
for a ewe who had strayed, as ewes often will at lambing time.

Upward of a fortnight went by in this way; the after-dark

visitors came and went, sometimes from as far away as the Cornish border, and several routine messages had passed through safely to Major Watson; but so far there had been no sign of a Royalist advance.

Then one evening Simon called in to see old Diggory, and found him downstairs for the first time, and sitting wrapped up and smoking his pipe by the fire in the little dark gatehouse kitchen.

'Good to see you down at last,' said Simon. 'You'll be out again soon, Diggory.'

'Oh, aye, now that the spring be coming,' said Diggory. 'And you, my dear—I reckon you'll be off back to your sojering any day now? Bain't much the matter with 'ee now, as I can see.'

Simon stooped to roll a fat tabby kitten on to its back. 'Any day now.'

'This 'ere war, now,' the old man said wistfully, after a few puffs at his pipe, 'do 'ee reckon 'tis going to last much longer? Maister bad for the crops a war be.'

'Not so much longer,' Simon said. 'There's a rough bit coming, though, before it's over.'

'So long as they keeps their 'oofs offen my winter wheat,' said Diggory.

And somehow the war was forgotten, and they were discussing the winter wheat and the lambing season, and what was to be done with the boggy bit down by the stream.

They were deep in plans for draining the boggy bit, when hurried footsteps came sludging down the lane, and the door flew open to reveal Jem Pascoe, the hurdle-maker, crimson-faced and obviously bursting with important tidings. 'Yer, neighbour Honeychurch, 'ave 'ee 'eard the noos?' he demanded; and then, seeing Simon, put up a grimy forefinger. 'Yer, young Maister, 'ave 'ee 'eard the noos?'

'Come in and shut thicky door, Jem Pascoe,' said Diggory, crushingly, 'or us'll all be froze afore 'ee can tell us.'

Jem Pascoe came in and shut the door. 'Oh, my dear souls! I been travelling that fast, my legs do be proper used up,' he said, and sank on to a stool, panting loudly.

'Niver mind 'bout your legs, Jem. What about thicky noos?'

'Well, I be coming to that, bain't I? Lord Hopton, it be, and a hugeous gurt army!'

'Where?' Simon was on his feet on the instant.

'In Torrington; leastways, a' will be by nightfall. Some on 'em's there a'ready, for I seed en with my own eyes, when I were visiting my sister's man this afternoon; every inn in the town be spilling over wi' 'em, so familiar as if they'd been there all their lives! Up from Launceston, 'tis said they'm come, and driving half the cattle in Cornwall wi 'em, to feed Exeter! Yiss!'

Old Diggory turned to Simon, and remarked very quietly between puffs at his pipe, 'Seems like this be the rough bit you said was coming.'

Simon nodded. He was thinking furiously, his eyes fixed on the pot of herbs which Phoebe always kept in the window; and as soon as Jem Pascoe had stumped off to spread his news through the village, he took his leave of Diggory, and went hurriedly out into the drizzling twilight.

His first thought was to go straight into Torrington and find out for himself the truth or otherwise of Jem's story; but after a moment he realized that he could not leave his post. The Torrington end of the job was Podbury. He went down to the agreed meeting-place beside the Jewel Water, but it was deserted, save for a fox who slunk off into the darkening coppice at his approach. There had not really been time for Podbury to get there, he supposed, as he went back to supper. In a few hours he would certainly come. Anyhow, careful plans had been laid for just such an emergency, and if the news was correct, the scout whose territory was the Cornish border would be well on his way to Tiverton by now with the first news of the Royalist advance.

The news had reached the household by the time he got back, and supper was a silent, uneasy meal. After it was finished they gathered in the firelit parlour as usual, and outside the curtained windows the waiting night was as silent as they. Simon had taken down his grandfather's rapier from its place above the mantel, and sat with the double sheath at his feet, polishing the long keen blade across his knees. He might have need of a sword soon, in place of his own left behind in Tiverton, and if so,

Balan would serve him as Balin served Amias.  But as he worked he was listening for sounds from the outside world, for it had been settled at the outset that, in case of need, any scout was to come up to the house on the excuse of having lost his way; and every instant he expected the sound of such an arrival.  But he heard only the white owl's eerie hunting cry, only the distant call of a vixen, and the whisper of the rain.  And his womenfolk tried to sew, stealing glances at him between every stitch.

At bedtime he returned Balan to its sheath and hung the worn crimson slings from the back of his chair, then strolled over to the door with pretended unconcern.  'Going to say good night to Scarlet.  Don't wait up for me.  I'll be taking a look at the lambing pens before I come in.'

But still there was no sign of Podbury in the secret hollow, and though he waited a long time, staring with anxious eyes into the rainy darkness, until he was chilled to the bone, the scout did not come.

He returned to the house at last, relit the candles in the parlour, and getting out writing materials, sat down at the table.  'Sir,' he wrote, 'I have heard this day that the Lion is come out of his thicket, and is now descended upon Torrington with both Horse and Foot, and with him a large herd of cattle for the feeding of Exeter.  More, I do not know, nor even if this be true, for no word has come to me out of the town, and I heard of it only by chance.'  He added the number seven, sanded and sealed the message, and stowed it in the breast of his doublet.  If no news came by dawn, he would send it south by the usual messenger.

He spent what was left of the night in a chair before the banked fire in the hall, with Jillot and her puppies in their flannel-lined box for company; and long before dawn he was out again, and heading back to the meeting-place.

As he came down into the coomb, something moved beside the stream; a tall shape of darkness against the lesser darkness of the hazel scrub: taller, it seemed to Simon, than any of the three scouts who came there.  He checked an instant, and then went on. Probably it was only a poacher.

'Is that Bill Darch?' he demanded.

The tall figure moved again.  'No.  Is that Cornet Carey?'

The voice was very quiet, but perfectly familiar, and Simon caught his breath sharply. 'Zeal-for-the-Lord! What in Heaven's name are you doing here?'

'There's many a good cock come out of a tattered bag,' said the dark shape, slowly.

There was an instant of utter silence, and then Simon said, 'And a good tune played on an old fiddle.'

'I have a dispatch for the Lord-General.'

A piece of limp paper changed hands, and Simon stowed it inside his doublet, with the message he had written himself, earlier that night. As he did so, he demanded with desperate urgency, 'What crazy game are you playing? Where is Podbury?'

'If Podbury be the name of him you were expecting—in Torrington lock-up, suspected of spying for the Parliament,' said Zeal-for-the-Lord briefly.

'What has happened, Zeal?'

'An ale-house brawl, that's what's happened. There was a good many such last night. What else can you expect from a godless rabble such as follow Lord Hopton? Your man got caught up in it; talking very wild, he was, and fought like a tiger when some of Webb's Dragoons went to take him. I was there.'

What an appalling mischance! Simon thought. But aloud he said only, 'What do we do now, Zeal?'

'You don't do nothing, sir; you're too well known in the town, and I reckon you've orders to stick fast at your post here. He'll be brought up for questioning in the morning, and I'll find means to get him away before they hang him. But he'll have to lie hid for a while in the town; he got mauled in resisting arrest—a wrenched knee amongst other things, and he'll never get past the guard in his present state without rousing suspicion.'

'Do you know of any such place—where he could be hid—I mean?' asked Simon, his thoughts racing ahead to odd holes and corners of the ruined castle, familiar from the days when he went to school in its shadow.

'There's one place in Torrington where they'll never think to look for him,' said Zeal, with a certain grim satisfaction.

'Where?'

' Above the powder store.'

Simon made no protest.  It was a hideously dangerous hiding-place, but its very danger made it completely safe from search.  Zeal was right: it was the one place where no sane man would think of looking.  ' Can you get him there? ' he demanded.

' Aye, with the Lord's help.'

' Zeal, how did you get hold of him—and the paper? '

' Told you he was talking pretty wild, didn't I?  I had my suspicions before ever the trouble started; and the Lord of Hosts granted that 'twas me as searched him.  Also there's a little barred squint at the back of the lock-up, as two men can talk through while the guard on the door knows nothing of it.  It weren't hard to convince him I was a friend, for he was knocked silly, and a man's apt to be either extry suspicious or so trusting as a new-born babe, in that condition.  He told me what must be done with the paper, and how to find this place.  Have you any orders for me, sir, beyond saving Podbury's neck for him? '

' Yes,' Simon said.  ' Tell me the exact strength of Hopton's force, what artillery he has with him, and what his plans are.'

' I don't know, sir, but I'll find out.'

' Good man!  Now that Podbury's out of the game, you've got to take over.  I shall be here at dusk each evening, and I'll wait until eight o'clock.  If you need to get hold of me in a hurry, come to the house; you'll see the light in the window from the top of the rise yonder.'

' Sir.'  The old Ironside turned on his heel, then checked and swung back, saying with an obvious effort, ' You don't ask how I come to be in—my present company.'

' I don't need to.  I was in hospital at Christmas with a certain Captain Weston, a Royalist prisoner.  He told me a queer story.'

' The ways of the Lord are unaccountable strange,' said Zeal heavily.  ' I have followed James Gibberdyke these many months, and never caught up with him until last evening.  That will show you what a scattered Army 'tis.  And now, he's dead.'

' You—had your revenge, then? ' Simon said, and the sickness rose in his throat.

' No, sir.  That was Podbury.'

' You mean, last night? '

'Aye. Telled you he resisted arrest, didn't I?

'Yes,' said Simon dully. 'Yes, you told me. Zeal, I would to Heaven it hadn't worked out like this—but at least I'm glad it wasn't you that killed him.'

Zeal-for-the-Lord was silent for a moment. Then he said, 'So am I. Queer, that, isn't it? Seems like the last few years have been wiped out. But just at first, a man feels a bit lonely and lost-like without his vengeance, when it was the closest thing he had. Good night, sir.'

'Good night,' Simon returned. There seemed nothing else to say.

As he cut back across the fields towards the place where, by now, the messenger should be awaiting him, Simon's mind and heart were so full of the encounter that was just over, and the strange trick of fate that had brought his old Corporal back from the unknown, that he did not notice a faint rustle behind him, which was not made by the wind. Nor did he turn his head to see the flitting figure that stole after him through the thinning darkness of the misty February dawn. He crossed the lane and turned into the chapel path that he had followed so often on his way to school. At the bend above Lovacott Moor, a horse was tethered under the dripping hawthorn trees, and a man loomed out into the path.

The scrap of paper changed hands with a few muttered words; the man remounted his horse, and Simon turned back down the bridle-path, his own dispatch still in the breast of his doublet, since it was not needed now. Behind him, as he went, he heard the soft drumming of hooves, growing fainter up the track.

A few moments later he had all but blundered into a figure that rose from the shadow of the hedge-tangle, right into his path; a grey shapeless figure that seemed oddly hazy.

His heart gave a sickening lurch, and instinctively he sprang forward and grappled with the thing; conscious of a queer relief when his hands caught heavy rain-wet cloth, instead of sinking into mist. Not a ghost then: a spy! He shifted his grip, and swung his captive out to face the growing light. As he did so, a breathless but laughing voice said, 'Simon, don't. Ow!' and he found that he was grasping Mouse. Mouse in her grey hooded cloak that blended ghost-wise into the grey dawn.

'Mouse!' he said furiously. 'What do you think you're doing?'

'Following you.' Mouse sounded quite unabashed.

Simon released her. 'I might have known it! You always were a Paul-pry!'

'I don't think you ought to say that, Simon, just because I was always interested in the things you and Amias did.'

'*Interested*!' snapped Simon. 'We never did a blessed thing that you didn't find out about!'

'But I never told anyone, did I?—Even when you dug a mine under the pigsty and the wall collapsed. I never told a soul how it came to happen.'

Simon did not answer for a moment. It was quite true: Mouse had always known their secrets, but their secrets had always been safe with her. 'No,' he admitted at last, 'you didn't. Look here, Mouse. How much do you know about all this?'

'I know you met someone down by the Jewel Water, and someone else just back here. But I couldn't get near enough either time, to hear what you said. You're passing messages through to General Fairfax, aren't you? Is that why you came home?'

'Perhaps,' said Simon. 'And if ever you kept a secret, you've got to keep this one, even from Mother.'

'Of course,' said Mouse.

They were walking back down the bridle-path by now, and after they had gone a little way, Simon asked, 'How did you guess?'

'Well, I thought it couldn't *always* be the lambs; not every time you went out in the night. Mother thought it was just that your head made you worry too much—as people do when they've been ill, you know; but somehow I didn't. And then last night the news came and everything was queer, and you didn't come to bed. I know that because I always keep my door open a little bit and I always hear you go by; and I listened and listened, but you never came. And then I found I'd been asleep, and I wondered if you *had* come to bed, after all, and I went to look, because I thought you might be having an adventure and leaving me out of it. And there was firelight in the hall, and when I looked over the balusters, there you were, looking as if you might be going out on an adventure at any moment; so I went back to my room and put on some clothes, and waited till you went out. Then I followed you.   It was quite simple.'

'Yes,' said Simon, ' yes, I suppose it was.'

They entered the garden close, and gaining the unbarred back door without disturbing the dogs, slipped inside.   Before going upstairs, Simon thrust the unused dispatch into the red embers of the fire, and watched it flame up and then crumble into ash.

At odd times during the days that followed, news reached Lovacott of what was going on in the outside world.   Lord Hopton was entrenching Torrington and barricading the roads into the town with felled trees.   It looked as if he meant to wait there while his supplies came up, and certainly it was the best place for the purpose in all North Devon : surrounded on three sides by the Castle Hill and the Commons, which fall almost sheer from the town to the Torridge far below.   His Foot was quartered in the town itself, and his Horse in the villages round. Heronscombe escaped having troops quartered on it, because it was too far out, but ragged foraging parties swooped on it at all hours of the day and night, so that it was little better off than Huntshaw or Weare Giffard.

Simon stayed very close to the house during those days, to be on hand in case of trouble, or of a message from Zeal or the remaining scout.   He kept clear of the foraging parties when he could, and when he could not, he pulled his hat low on his forehead and did his best to blend into the background.   He could not afford to catch the notice of the Royalists; and there was nothing that he could do, anyway, to prevent the constant streaming away into Torrington of cattle, fodder and even the preserves from his mother's storeroom, all carried off by hungry, hardfaced men of an Army that had become a rabble and ceased to care for its officers.   After those few days he found it easy to believe the common talk of the New Model, that of all the Army under his command, the only troops Lord Hopton could rely on for loyalty and discipline were his own small Company, and the Prince's Guard.

The second evening after his meeting with Zeal-for-the-Lord, Simon found his old Corporal waiting for him again in the hollow of the Jewel Water. The password was exchanged in low voices, and Simon asked: 'Have you found out what we wanted?'

'Aye, but I've had no chance to write it down.'

'That doesn't matter. 'Tisn't the first time I've had a word-of-mouth dispatch to deal with.' Simon was groping under a mass of brambles and alder scrub, and his voice was slightly muffled. A moment later he brought out a small shielded lantern, and striking flint and steel, kindled the candle-stub. The flame sank away to a blue spark, then rose again, guttering in the damp air. Simon closed the lantern, and producing a sheet of paper and a stick of sharpened lead from the breast of his doublet, squatted down to use his knee as a writing desk. 'Now—carry on, Zeal.'

'Four thousand Foot, five thousand Horse, mostly in poor condition,' began Zeal-for-the-Lord, in the manner of one reciting a lesson learned by heart. 'Of the Horse, six hundred are dragoons, and upward of five hundred cuirassiers. No Artillery, and so far, precious little Train at all. Lord Hopton's biding where he is until his reserves catch up with him; and that will be all of four days. He's desperate short of transport. I don't know nothing about the reserves, sir, save that there's no guns with them.'

'Never mind about the reserves,' Simon said, writing hard 'The other scout sees to them.' He finished the message, adding various other details that the old Ironside gave him, and signed it with the number 7. He hesitated over the second number, and finally left the place blank. 'Thank you, Corporal,' he said.

The word had slipped out from old habit, and he could not recall it. He looked up quickly, but the light from the shielded lantern did not reach as high as the other man's face.

Neither of them spoke again until Simon had doused the lantern and returned it to its hiding-place, and risen to his feet once more. Then he asked, 'What of Podbury?'

'Got him away yesterday, sir, on the way up to Lord Hopton's lodgings for questioning. There was only two of us guarding him, and the Lord sent a sleet-scurry at the right moment to hide our escape after I'd knocked t'other man out. Podbury's snug enough now above the stacked powder-kegs. Close quarters, but secluded, if you see what I mean. He's got supplies with him, drinking-water from the waterspout above the window, and all complete, and he can lie up there for a few days, till he's mended.'

'I see,' Simon said. 'But look here. If you laid out your fellow guard, they'll know you're on our side, and you can't clear off, because of Podbury. What's to be done?'

'I'll contrive somehow, sir,' Zeal said. 'If need be I'll take to the magazine myself. There's precious little discipline in the camp of the Amalekites, and it's easy enough to slip by the guards, while this sleety weather lasts.'

'I don't like it,' said Simon. 'It's not right that I should leave you to bear the brunt of this business—but the devil of it is that my orders are not to stir from Lovacott whatever happens.'

'Your action station is here, and mine is in Torrington, and us can't neither of us leave them,' agreed the other.

And a sudden jubilance swept over Simon, as he realized something that he had not thought of before. 'Zeal!' he said, 'Zeal! You see what this means?'

'Sir?'

'Why, man! You've earned your return to your old place! When Fiery Tom knows about this business——'

'No!' Zeal-for-the-Lord cut in harshly. 'There is no way back for me.'

'But there is! Don't you understand, Zeal?'

'I will have no man say, "He only turned to our Service again, that he might crawl back thereby, like a fawning cur to his old place".'

'Who would be fool enough to say that?' Simon demanded vehemently. He had not thought that Zeal was a man to care what others said of him. 'And if the whole Army said it, what would it matter, so long as you knew it wasn't true?'

Zeal's answer, when it came, was hoarse with intolerable pain. 'But I should *not* know it! If, through your good report, I was to—find the way back, I should never know it wasn't true!'

'It may become known in spite of you,' Simon said, and he

sounded angry, because suddenly he was desperately miserable. 'Podbury has a tongue in his head.'

'He only knows me by the name of Ishmael Watts,' said Zeal, with a touch of grim amusement. 'Watts was my mother's name.'

There was no need to ask where Ishmael had come from. "Henceforth I am Ishmael. There is neither vine nor fig-tree for me." Simon remembered the words, across the months from that spring morning beside the Thames backwater. 'I may send in a report,' he said stubbornly.

'But you won't, sir, because if you did that, you'd be destroying the last rags of my own respect that are left to me.'

There was a long, heavy silence. Simon was very sure that there was a kink somewhere in this line of thinking, but he could not see where it was. Corporal Relf had got crosswise with his own conscience, and no one, certainly not Simon, had the right to interfere with his own way of straightening the tangle.

'No,' he said at last, 'I shall not send in a report.'

A church clock in the distance chimed the hour of eight, and Zeal-for-the-Lord moved abruptly. 'I must be on my way back. Watch-setting is my best chance of getting through.'

'Yes,' Simon said.

'If I shouldn't see you again, sir——'

'Well?'

'I never had no son; I never had but one friend, and he's dead now. I'm glad you'll know who 'twas as got you the tally of Hopton's troops, and God willing, returned your scout to you with a whole neck.'

'So am I!' They gripped hands, quickly and silently. 'Good-bye, Zeal,' Simon said huskily, 'and—good-bye.'

He looked back once, as he crested the little rise, and saw by the light of the rising moon, which broke silvery through the clouds at that moment, the dark solitary figure of Zeal-for-the-Lord standing motionless beside the flash and flicker of the Jewel Water. He saw a dark arm raised in greeting and good-bye, and flung up his own arm in return. Then he went on downhill, towards the light in Lovacott windows.

XV

## The Royalist Officer

WHEN Simon reached the turn of the chapel path in the
darkness before the dawn, no horse was tethered beneath
the hawthorn trees, and no dim figure rose to meet him;
only the green plover cried over the moorland and the little bitter
wind soughed through the rushes. Evidently the messenger had
been delayed. He would be, today of all days, Simon thought,
as, after kicking his heels for the best part of an hour, he turned
back towards Lovacott. Well, when he did arrive he would
come up to the house, according to plan; and there was nothing
for Simon to do but keep the precious packet on him until the
messenger came for it. It was maddening to have the dispatch
that would tell so much to his own side delayed here, and getting
no nearer to Major Watson; and as he trudged back through the
grey mist that was coming up with the dawn, Simon was filled
with a fury of impatience to be astride Scarlet and away down the
Tiverton road, carrying the thing himself. But once again he
remembered the Major's clipped voice saying, 'You will not
leave your post *whatever* happens.'

If the messenger had not come within three hours, he decided
suddenly he would send Tom. He had no right to do so, he
knew, but Tom was a loyal man and no fool, and the dispatch
must go through somehow. Meanwhile, making the best of a
bad job, he set about the early morning work of the farm which
was already waking to life.

It was not a fortunate day. Tom wanted him to come and
look at Selina, the cart mare, who had gone lame; and there was
trouble at the lambing-pens, so that when at last he went in to
his breakfast he was carrying a motherless lamb that hung from
his hand, a limp and almost lifeless tassel of damp wool. He was
very late, and only Mouse was waiting for him beside the table
in the hall.

168

'Mother's gone out to see Grannie Pascoe; the soldiers frightened her yesterday, and the poor old thing is ill again,' she said, bending over the fire, before which a rather meagre dish of fried ham had been keeping hot.

'I see,' said Simon. 'Here's a lamb for you. Its mother is dead, and it is pretty weakly too.'

She turned and set the smoking dish on the table. 'Give it to me. There, that's right. Now get on with your breakfast, before it gets cold or another foraging party arrives. Oh, just reach me that old sack in the corner, first. No, Jillot, you go and 'tend to your own puppies; this is nothing to do with you.' Mouse had reared more than one motherless lamb, and before Simon had well begun on his breakfast, the little creature was settled in a nest of sacking in the warm chimney corner, and she had disappeared into the kitchen. A few minutes later she was back, carrying a pipkin of milk in one hand and the old cloam baby-bottle in the other.

'I didn't mean to be so long, but Meg says she's sure we're all going to be murdered,' she remarked composedly, as she settled the pipkin to warm in the hot ash. 'And Polly has just scat the biggest cream-pan, and *will* not stop crying.'

Simon paused with a piece of ham half-way to his mouth, and looked down at her where she sat before the fire, amid the soft grey folds of her outflung skirts. 'You're getting awfully like Mother,' he said. 'Nothing ever upsets her either. If one of us came home in two pieces, she'd just stick them together with that herbal paste of hers, and heat up some nice nourishing broth.'

Mouse was working on the limp lamb, and she looked up, laughing, but without stopping work. 'Well, you see, it isn't any use getting upset, is it?' she said. And then, very quietly, her lips scarcely moving, 'You've sent it off?'

Simon shook his head. 'He wasn't there,' he muttered. 'Have to keep it till he comes.'

'Where is it?'

Simon touched the breast of his doublet, then went on with his breakfast. It was a much smaller breakfast than he had been used to, for the Royalists had taken most of the winter's supply of

169

smoked bacon and as many of the hens as they could catch. Food was running short, and no one knew how long the present state of things would last. Simon was just finishing the last scrap when he had a sudden suspicion.

' Mouse,' he said, ' did you and Mother have as much breakfast as me? '

' We had all we wanted.'

' Truly? '

' Truly.'

Simon looked at her for a long moment, very searchingly. ' I don't believe you,' he said at last. ' I'll take care we all eat together in future.'

At that instant the lamb began to twitch its untidy sprawl of legs, and Mouse sat back on her heels to watch it. ' Look, it's going to be all right,' she said.

Simon pushed away his plate and sat with chin between fists, watching her. It was warm and very peaceful in the shadowy hall; the flames fluttered on the wide hearth, and Jillot sat among her squirming puppies, thumping her plumy tail from time to time; while from the outside world came the clatter of the maids in the dairy, and the crooning of the doves in the courtyard, whose wheelings and struttings filled the winter sunshine beyond the windows with the passing shadows of many wings. The war seemed a very long way away.

Simon sprawled sideways in his chair, and in doing so, noticed for the first time a sealed packet lying on the table. ' Hullo, what's this? '

Mouse had taken the pipkin from the fire, and was pouring the warm milk into the feeding bottle. ' Oh, Mother wrote to Mistress Killigrew last night while you were out. She said to give it to the carrier if he comes before she's back. She put in your message about begging to be remembered to Mistress Susanna.'

' Oh,' said Simon.

Mouse gathered the lamb on to her lap, and began coaxing it to feed, dipping her fingers into the warm milk and holding them to the little thing's mouth, making small sucking noises to encourage it.

'Simon,' she said after a few moments, 'what is Susanna Killigrew like? You've never really told us. Is she good but not comfortable, like her mother?'

'No,' Simon said, 'she's not a bit like her mother.'

'Then what *is* she like?'

Simon cudgelled his brain. He really wanted to answer Mouse's question, but he was no hand at describing people. 'She's a little pale wispy thing,' he said at last. 'But just once, she seemed as if—as if she had lit all her candles; and then she was quite different.' He smiled apologetically. 'I'm sorry, I can't do better than that. But I think you'd like her. Maybe if Mother strikes up a friendship with *her* mother, you'll be able to see for yourself one day—when the war is over.'

'When the war is over,' echoed Mouse; and she sighed. 'Everything is always " When the war is over ", and it has such a far-off sound, like "when my ship comes home".' She was still holding milky fingers to the lamb's muzzle as she spoke, and suddenly it sneezed; its sprawling legs woke into vague scramblings, and it began to suck. 'There!' she said. 'That's the way. Why couldn't you have done that before, silly-billy?' She dipped her fingers in the milk once more, and gave them to the lamb, then put the nozzle of the baby-bottle into its small sucking mouth. The lamb sprawled forward, half standing; its tail began to wag.

She was still feeding it a few minutes later, and Simon was still watching the two of them, when a sudden turmoil arose in the courtyard: Ship the cattle-dog baying his head off, Diggory's voice upraised in furious protest, and a heavy and confused trampling. The doves burst upward on drumming indignant wings. Simon got up quickly, and as he did so, Mouse set the lamb back in its nest of sacking, and rose quietly beside him, shaking out her grey skirts. Their eyes met for an instant. Another Royalist foraging party! Well, there had been plenty such in the last few days, and there was little more that they could take. Only this time there was no chance for Simon to avoid them, as he had mostly contrived to do before; no time to gain the stairs; and he felt the dispatch in the breast of his doublet burning a hole through the cloth. Still, there was no reason why they should suspect him, and certainly none why they should search him. With some show of annoyance at being disturbed at his breakfast, he swung round to the door, just as it burst open and several men crowded into the hall.

Then Jillot, who had been sitting on watchful guard among her puppies, growling softly in her throat, suddenly let out a pleased whine and abandoning her family went squirming and waggling forward to greet the tatterdemalion officer at their head.

The officer was Amias.

Amias, gaunt as a scarecrow and almost as ragged, with bruise-coloured shadows under his eyes that were partly weariness and partly dirt. The startled unbelief broke over Simon like a wave, and ebbed away, leaving a cold quiet hopelessness behind it. No use putting up any sort of pretence, then. He must find means to slip the dispatch to Mouse before they took him; that was all.

Then something clicked in his brain, and he saw the look in Amias's eyes. It had been as startled as his own in that first instant, but now it had changed to a clear hard warning.

And at the same moment, out of the tail of his eye, he saw Mouse gather her wide grey skirts and move forward. 'I beg your forgiveness that no one opened the door to you,' she said. 'We did not hear you knock.'

Amias turned to her, pulling off his battered beaver hat.

'*Touché,*' he said quickly. 'I apologize. The war has made us forget our manners, Mistress Mouse. Your father is—away from home?'

'My father is with Lord Leven's Army,' said Mouse steadily. 'And my mother is out. Unless you wish to wait for her return, will you tell me what it is that you want?—I suppose cattle and fodder, but there is not much left for the late-comers. We have been overrun with foraging parties, these last few days.'

'Alas, Mistress Mouse, even your enemies must eat now and then. But we are a search-party, not a foraging party.'

Simon, standing by like an onlooker at a play, was warned by some instinct to leave the acting to the other two, and take his cue from them, when the time came.

172

'Oh?' Mouse said. 'You want to search for something, or someone, here?'

'For a Parliament spy who escaped from his guard in Torrington, two days ago; and for one of our own men who is in league with him. We have orders to search all houses of known Parliament sympathies in these parts.'

'You won't find them here,' Mouse said. 'But we can't stop you pulling the house about our ears if you want to. Lovacott *has* Parliament sympathies.'

All this while the men of the search-party had been staring about them and muttering among themselves; and at this moment the sergeant, a bearded giant with a sullen honest face and uncomfortably keen eyes, who had been staring at Simon with a puzzled frown, turned and whispered something to his officer. Simon could only guess what it was, but Mouse, who was nearer, rounded on him, saying very clearly, 'That is my brother. He is——' she made a quick gesture touching her forehead, 'not quite 'zactly.'

'As mazed as ever?' asked Amias, with deep sympathy.

Simon had his cue now, and he was not sure whether he most wanted to laugh or to shake Mouse until her teeth rattled. Instead, he sat down on his heels, seeming to lose interest in the whole proceedings, and picking up the nearly empty baby-bottle, began feeding the already full lamb. It seemed somehow to fit in with the part allotted to him, but he hoped the lamb would not burst.

But the sergeant was not yet convinced. 'He looks sensible enough to me,' he growled, 'and he's had a woundy great gash on his head, what's more! 'Twouldn't surprise me if he was the knave we're looking for.'

'Be quiet, you numskull,' said Amias sharply. 'I've known him all my life. He's as mazed as a March hare.'

'Well, if you says so, sir, far be it for me to say contrariwise, but a gashed head be a gashed head, and apt to mean a cove's been fighting, and——'

'My brother fell off a hayrick just before Christmas, and cut his head on the edge of a scythe,' Mouse said. 'I trust that you are satisfied.'

' Well it looks to me a deal more like somebody laid it open wi'
a musket stock,' began the other stubbornly. ' I seen a many
heads laid open wi' a musket stock in my time, and——'
' We are *perfectly* satisfied,' Amias said, with a quelling look at
his sergeant. ' All right, take over, sergeant. Search the house
and outbuildings. I shall remain here in the hall.' He turned the
quelling look on to his men. ' And remember, I said search, not
loot and break up. If I hear the slightest sound of wanton
damage, you're for it, all of you. Understand?'

A mutter of agreement came from the men as they split up.
Several of them looked thoroughly ill-contented, but Simon
could not help noticing that Amias seemed to have his disreputable
band under better control than most of the King's troops he had
seen lately. Mouse had drawn back to the hearth again, and
stood there, very straight in her grey gown, her head up and a
queer brightness in her eyes. Amias crossed to the table and
perched on it, swinging one dusty foot and looking down at her.

' Mistress Mouse,' he said soulfully, ' pray believe me to be
truly desolated that we should meet now as foes, when we have
so often met in the past as friends.'

' I am sorry too,' said Mouse, with no softening in her voice.

But Simon, glancing up, could have sworn that the brightness
in her eyes was laughter. Suddenly it dawned on him that they
were enjoying themselves hugely, those two, like a pair of well-
matched fencers playing a bout with unbuttoned foils. That
Amias should find pleasure in playing with danger did not
surprise him in the least; but Mouse was a different matter. It
just showed how little you really knew of people.

' May I go to the maids? They will be frightened.' Mouse
was saying, as a scared squealing sounded from the kitchen
quarters.

Amias shook his head. ' I regret infinitely; but you and your
brother must remain here, and the maids in the kitchen. Only
my men may move about the house at the moment. You will
see that there is a guard on the doors.'

Simon caught the warning note in his voice, and out of the
tail of his eye saw the lounging soldier in the house-place doorway.

'So I see,' said Mouse coldly. 'We are your prisoners, it seems.' Then she turned to Simon, saying in a very sweet and gentle tone, 'Simon, you have fed that lamb enough. Put it back in its nest, dear, before it is sick.'

Simon obediently dumped the sprawling lamb back on to its sacking, from which it instantly staggered forth again, bleating shrilly. He let it go, and sat idly on his heels, watching it as it made unsteadily for Jillot, who had returned to her puppies under the table. Amias had suddenly bent sidewise and picked up the letter which Mrs Carey had left for the carrier.

'Cock and Pie! What a trick of chance!' said Amias, laughing. 'I was quartered in Okeham Paine, last autumn.'

There was an instant's silence, which seemed very long to Simon, who was wishing desperately that he had told Mouse about his encounter with Amias.

Then Mouse said, 'Were you? It is not really such a trick of chance; Mistress Killigrew is a very old friend of my mother's.'

Amias sniffed, the old insulting sniff, and laid the packet down. 'So? Well, everyone to their own choice of friends. But a most sour good woman. I was glad to be out of her house.'

'How did you come to leave it?' inquired Mouse, with a gleam in her eye.

'You know, you should be called Mistress Spit-cat, instead of Mistress Mouse,' drawled Amias. 'We left with colours flying, and the Psalm-smiters in possession behind us, if you want to know. And in recognition of the noble defence we put up we were provided with a pass into Exeter, so that we could be besieged in comfort, with the rest of the Garrison.'

'You don't seem to be besieged?' Mouse pointed out.

'No. The prospect did not appeal to us. We took a vote on it, and made tracks across the Moor to join the Prince at Tavistock.'

It was said to Mouse, but Simon knew that the message was for himself. Amias wanted to tell him how he came to be with Hopton's force, and what had happened since their last meeting; and this was his only way of doing it. The sentry on the door was craning his neck after a comrade in the courtyard, and for the moment no one was watching them; and Simon looked up full into the other's face. Amias's eyes were dancing, as he had expected them to be, but there was a kind of bitter brightness in them too; and he realized for the first time what it must be like to serve in a beaten Army, to belong heart and soul to a lost cause. For one long moment their gaze met, and Simon knew that the old friendship was strong as ever it had been, perhaps stronger.

Then Amias pushed off from his perch on the table, and, turning, crossed to the door. He did not come back to the two before the hearth, but stayed there in the doorway until his men had returned from their fruitless search with a grudging 'Nothing to report, sir,' from the sergeant. Then he bowed with a flourish to Mouse, clapped his battered beaver hat very much on the back of his head, and marched his band of brigands away.

Simon got up. He stood quiet in the chimney corner, hearing their voices and the ragged tramp of feet across the courtyard. It passed out through the gatehouse, and died away. The doves were settling again already. Only Ship had started baying once more, and the shrill scared chittering of Meg and Polly in the dairy went on—and on.

Then Mouse went down the hall with a whisk and rustle of skirts, and disappeared through the door into the kitchen quarters; and the frightened voices rose to a clamour and then grew quiet. Simon still stood in the chimney corner, quite unmoving, until, realizing that he still held the baby-bottle, he set it down on the table, arranging it with great care exactly half-way between the loaf and his mother's letter, and crossing to the window, stood looking out into the wintry garden.

Then Mouse came back. 'That was—queer, wasn't it, Simon,' she said, coming to join him.

'Ye—es.' He swung round from the window, and put both hands on her shoulders. 'What do you mean by telling that crew I wasn't quite 'zactly?' he demanded.

'Well, it seemed the best thing to do. I'm sorry if you didn't like it, Simon, but you weren't being very helpful, and I couldn't think of anything else. I was rather surprised, you see.'

'You didn't show it. Anyhow, thanks, Mouse.'

Mouse showed the unexpected dimple, just as she had been used to do when she was small, and anything she did found favour with the two boys. 'Do you know where they are, the men they were looking for?' she said.

'I can't tell you that, Mouse.'

'Not here, anywhere?'

177

'No, not here.'

'I was dreadfully afraid they might be.'

'You didn't show that either,' Simon said.

The dimple deepened, if that were possible, but she only said, after a few moments, 'You never told me that Amias was in the Okeham Paine garrison when you took the house.'

'Didn't I? I must have forgotten,' Simon said. He smiled at her, and turned back to the window. The night encounter at Okeham Paine did not matter any more! Suddenly he noticed that the buds were swelling on the quince tree, and the brown bed under the window jubilant with snowdrops. Suddenly, from beyond the war-scarred orchard, the first curlew of the year was calling. 'Listen!' he said. 'The curlews are coming up from the Estuary.'

A few moments later Tom stuck his head round the house-place door. 'There's a chap outside says a' has a message for 'ee, 'bout a litter of pigs,' he said, jerking a thumb over his shoulder. 'Proper disreputable character, if you asks *me*, and so I telled 'en, but a' says there's many a good cock come out of a tattered bag, and so I was to tell 'ee.'

Simon had only just finished with the man about the litter of pigs, when the carrier arrived. Mouse gave him Mrs Carey's letter, took in various packages he had brought, and when he was gone, returned to Simon, holding something in triumph.

'Look! This is one of those days when everything happens at once. Here's a letter from Father.'

There had been no word from Simon's father for a long time, and the arrival of his letter now seemed to set the crown on this oddly joyous morning. They put it on the table, and waited about, to make sure their mother got it the moment she returned and that they themselves were present to hear what was in it.

They had not long to wait before she came in, slipping the grey cloak from her shoulders, and glancing about her.

'Meg says the King's men have been ransacking the house,' she said, a little wearily. 'What have they taken this time?'

'Nothing this time,' Simon told her. 'They were hunting somebody, but with any luck he's away by now. Look, Mother, here's a letter from Father at last.'

Mrs Carey cast her cloak on the side chest, and went quickly to pick up the long-hoped-for packet. Her face had grown soft and sparkling as she broke the seal and opened the crackling sheet. Then quite suddenly the sparkle was gone; she gave a little cry, and put one hand on a chair back as though to steady herself.

Simon had rounded the table to her in an instant. 'What's wrong, Mother?'

She looked up, her face grown small and pinched. 'Father—he's been wounded.'

'Badly?' Simon asked, but he knew it must be badly, or his mother would not look like that.

'Yes,' said Mrs Carey. 'Yes.' She looked from Simon's anxious face to Mouse's, then down again at the letter in her hand and began to read aloud, quite steadily. "I would have written before but that I have been laid by, nursing sundry wounds gained when my Troop was ambushed on patrol some three weeks ago. A small affair, but 'twas well done. The Royalists mined a bridge by which we were to pass, and fired the charges when our foremost Horse were actually upon it, myself included. A brilliant piece of timing. We beat them off, though hardly, and ourselves suffered fewer losses than might be expected : five men killed and a round dozen wounded. The affair has cost me a leg. My left. That leg was always unlucky—I broke it climbing after an eyas when I was a boy. Hector was killed under me, but save as an old friend, he is no loss to me, since I shall not ride again. The surgeons here in Newark have done their work well, and, save for sundry rents in my left side which are slow to heal, such as is left of me begins already to grow strong once more, but it may be some time before I can come home to you, for the war continues, and the Army authorities have other matters to attend to than the transporting of one crippled soldier. In the meantime, it is useless to bid you not to worry, but worry as little as may be, beloved, and——"' Mrs Carey faltered for an instant in her reading : ' " and the Lord of Hosts give you courage, as I pray He may do me, for I——"' she broke off, and finished the last few lines in silence, while the other two watched her. Then she refolded the sheet and stood for a few moments, very still, looking down at it.

'If only he was not alone. It—must be harder to bear—all alone.'

'He'll be all right,' said Mouse, in a small clear voice of utter conviction. 'You can trust Father; he'll be all right.' It seemed a queer thing to say, but Simon knew what she meant, though he could not have put it into words.

He slipped a hand under his mother's elbow. 'Come and sit down for a little while.'

But Mrs Carey shook her head. 'No, my dear, I won't sit down. I want to tidy my store cupboards this morning, and I think I'll go and do it now.' And putting the letter very gently into her hanging pocket, she went. Mouse followed her, and Simon watched them go, and then, deciding that it would be best to leave his womenfolk to themselves for a bit, went and hung over the orchard gate, and thought. He had a good deal to think about. Over the hill-crest the curlews were still crying, and the snowdrops in the half-frozen borders had not lost their joyousness. Life looked good, for Simon, only—what must it look like for Father, now?

# XVI

## ' *Emanuel, God With Us !* '

THREE days later, Simon had gone down after the midday meal to see that all was well in the lambing-pens. Sanctuary was very full of new life, and the air shrill with the babble of newborn lambs and the song of a triumphant blackbird in the topmost branch of the budding spinney; and Simon, turning to look for the singer, saw a tall, fantastic figure with a fiddle under one arm, leaning on the gate into the lane.

He flung up his arm in greeting, and whistling Ship to heel, headed for the gate where the other waited for him very peacefully, leaning on the top bar. 'Pentecost! What are you doing up this way?'

'Come looking for you,' Pentecost Fiddler said. There were a few pale dog-violets stuck in his battered hat, and he stooped to fondle Ship's woolly head.

'But how did you know I was here? I haven't exactly shouted it from the tree-tops, like the blackbird yonder.'

'There's precious little happens a'twixt Beaford and Hartland that I don't know about,' said Pentecost, simply. 'And I've got some news for 'ee.'

'Yes?'

'Parlyment troops gathering in Stevenstone Park.'

Simon, who had opened the gate and joined the fiddler in the lane, closed it behind him and dropped the iron pin into place, because it had been inbred in him, as in all countrymen, that one does not leave field gates open, though the heavens fall.

'Horse or Foot?' he demanded as they turned towards the house. 'You're sure they *are* Parliament men? When did they get there, Pentecost?'

'Horse,' said Pentecost. 'But there'll be Foot to follow, or I'm a Don; and they're Parlyment all right, leastwise they drove

out Hopton's Dragoons that were holding the house. Not much above an hour gone, that were, and I come straight to tell you.'

'What were you doing in Stevenstone?' asked Simon, when they reached the gatehouse and came to a halt before it.

'Playing me fiddle.'

'To the Royalist Dragoons?'

'They pay,' said Pentecost, with his old mocking smile curling his long mouth. 'Sometimes they pay, anyhow.'

Simon laughed. 'You're a disgrace. Come in and have something to eat.'

'No. I'll be on my way back. You're off at once, I reckon?'

There was an instant's pause, while Simon made his decision. He had received no recall, but it was not at all likely that he would, and he could do no good by remaining here any longer. Major Watson had said that in such a case he was to make his own decision. 'Yes, I'll be off at once,' he said. 'Thanks for the news, Pentecost.'

The fiddler's mocking smile narrowed his eyes. He turned away, calling back over his shoulder, 'Good luck to 'ee. You're going to have fine weather for your battle, seemingly,' and he pointed up at the clear milky blueness of the February sky.

'Oh, aye; heron was flying downstream this morning,' Simon called after him. Then he turned into the courtyard, shouting for Tom to get Scarlet saddled up; and went indoors, to be met by his mother coming from the still-room with Mouse behind her.

'Was that Pentecost Fiddler I saw you talking to just now?' asked his mother.

'Yes, he came to tell me our Horse are gathering at Stevenstone. Tom is saddling Scarlet for me now, and I'll be off as soon as he's done,' Simon said, and ran upstairs without waiting for any reply.

A few moments later he came clattering down again, carrying his pistol-holsters in one hand and his spurred riding-boots in the other. Mouse and his mother were awaiting him in the hall, Mouse holding his grandfather's sword, and his mother in the act of setting a well-filled wallet on the chest by the door.

'You'll need some food, my dear,' she said.

'Thanks, Mother.' He sat down on the chest to pull his boots on. 'Oh, Jillot, go *away*!'

'There's Scarlet. Tom's bringing him round now,' said Mouse, who had gone to the door; then, as Simon got up, 'Here's your sword—stand still and I'll put it on for you.'

In an unbelievably short time he was ready to go, and had turned about beside Scarlet to take his leave of them. 'Good-bye, Mother, good-bye, Mouse.' He hugged them both, and his mother drew down his face and kissed him on the forehead.

'God speed you, Simon,' she said. 'We shall be praying, Mouse and I, for you, and for our Army's victory.'

'Yes, do,' Simon said eagerly. 'Pray for all you're worth; we shall need it. The Royalists haven't much discipline, but there are a lot of them, and they're in a strong position. Bless you, both of you.' He turned away, and taking the reins from Tom, swung into the saddle. 'If Father gets home before I do, give him my love and my duty; and tell him—and tell him I'm hidjus proud of him,' he called.

Scarlet, not having been out that day, was only too eager to start, and sprang forward as soon as he was given his head, sidling and prancing like an unbroken colt. Simon swung him out through the gatehouse, turning in the saddle to wave to the two in the doorway, who waved in return. Then he sent Scarlet at a canter up the wagon-way, and never looked back. The queer quiet-surfaced weeks were behind him, and he was riding out into the open storm again; and in time to the beat of Scarlet's flying hooves, his heart seemed to quicken into a jumping expectancy.

Up on the high moors, when he reached them, the light wind came soughing in from the sea, cold and thin, smelling of bog and wet moss and the thin February sunshine. From the edge of the ridge-road, the land dropped away, rising and falling in moor and coppice, brown plough and green fallow, to the ten-mile-

183

distant sea. And looking seaward, as he always did when he passed that way, Simon saw the whole sweep of the bay from Morte Point round to Hartland, and Lundy floating cloud-wise, dream-wise, where sea and sky came together. He wondered when he would see that sweep of coast again.

After half a mile he turned off down a by-lane, and the distant bay dropped away behind the skyline, and the moors were left behind. Presently he turned in between the granite gate-posts of Stevenstone Park, and instantly ran into a vedette of Ireton's Horse posted just inside. He reined in, as one of the two men wheeled across his track and demanded his business.

'I am an officer of Fairfax's Horse, returning to duty. But first I have to report to Major Watson. Can you tell me where I shall find him?'

The man looked him up and down, taking in the homespun doublet, and the ancient sword at his hip, and said doubtfully, 'That may be, sir; but you don't look much like it.'

'Look.' Simon pulled off his hat. 'I have been recovering from this gash, at my home near here, and now I am returning to duty. I was wounded at the assault on Okeham Paine, on December the twelfth. Now will you tell me where I can find Major Watson?'

The second man urged his horse a pace nearer. 'What was the watchword for that night, sir?'

'The Lord shall deliver Israel,' said Simon, 'and the sign, a white kerchief round the left arm.'

'He's all right, Jerry,' said the second man. 'I'd go straight up to the house, sir, if I was you, and ask again. He's bound to be about there somewheres.'

The two men reined back into the shadow of the oak spinney beside the gate, and Simon rode on. He had never been in Stevenstone before, for Lord Henry Rolle was an ardent Royalist, and even in the days before the war he had had no truck with the Puritan gentry of the country round. But the paths were clear to follow, and he had not gone far when he came upon two troops of Walley's Regiment, and a few yards farther on, rounding a dark mass of holly and ilex, he saw the great house before him, its mellow red brick warm as a ripe apricot against the darkness

184

of the trees, and the sloping turf round it alive with men and horses under the great oaks of the deer park. Evidently the Foot had begun to arrive, for their red coats flecked the wintry turf with colour, among the drab masses of the Horse. He rode on, followed here and there by a glance of curiosity or recognition; and asking his way again, first from a passing commissariat sergeant and then from a dragoon, finally ran Major Watson to earth in an outhouse, where he was questioning a prisoner about the town defence.

He raised his brows and blinked mildly at Simon when he appeared. 'Yes, Cornet Carey?'

'I had word an hour ago that you were here, sir,' Simon said hurriedly. 'So I came to report, and for your orders.'

'So I see. Well, you have done the job I sent you to do, and done it efficiently. I've no further use for you, and your report can wait a fitter season. Get along back to your Regiment.'

'Where shall I find them, sir?'

'Half a mile west of here, towards the townward gate.'

Simon collected Scarlet from the dragoon in whose charge he had left him and set out once more. He was thankful not to have to make his report until Podbury had had time to make his. Until that happened, he was not sure what to say; and it might even be that Zeal would change his mind and come in with the scout, after all. But he knew in his heart of hearts that that would not happen.

The General's Horse, when he found them, were bivouacked in the lea of a great curve of ilex, and looked as if they had been there for some time, for the horses were picketed and cropping contentedly at the grass which belonged by rights to Lord Rolle's deer; and each troop, gathered about its own Standard set upright in the ground, was checking equipment in readiness for action.

Simon picked out Disbrow's Troop easily enough, and dismounting, saluted his Lieutenant. 'Cornet Carey, reporting back for duty, sir.'

Barnaby Colebourne swung round on him. 'What the— Simon!'

'Reporting back for duty, sir,' Simon repeated.

185

A broad smile spread on the other's face. 'This beats cock-fighting! I hoped you'd turn up, but——' Then he too looked Simon up and down. 'You look like Guido Fawkes, or Don Quixote! You can't go into action like that; you'll be cut to pieces, or shot by one of our own men, and I wouldn't blame them.'

Simon grinned. 'It can't be helped.'

'Yes, it can, though. Nothing is going to happen for hours yet, and you'll have plenty of time. Trooper Wagstaff was hit in the leg this morning, and he's out of the fight. Go up to the house and take over his equipment. We'll see to Scarlet.'

So back to the house went Simon, hotfoot, and mounted the steps of the terrace, where the winter jessamine sent a cascade of yellow stars over the low stone parapet, and Fairfax himself with a group of senior officers stood talking earnestly and watching the mustering troops in the deerpark below. A sentry passed him through, and told him where the wounded were bestowed; and a few minutes later he was out again, wearing Trooper Wagstaff's buff coat, luckily not much too big for him, and steel cap, and knotting a borrowed crimson sword-scarf about his middle as he went.

By the time he had rejoined his Troop, where Scarlet was now unsaddled and picketed, and enjoying his measure of corn with the rest, most of the troops had arrived, and were making an evening meal of the usual hard biscuit and strong yellow cheese which each man carried in his knapsack. Simon, investigating the wallet his mother had given him, found two large pasties in it; and he and Barnaby ate them, standing under a group of slender birch trees that were already flushed with the purple bloom of rising sap.

'What about Exeter?' Simon asked.

'Siege abandoned for the moment,' said Barnaby, with his mouth full, 'except for a few regiments left to watch like a terrier at a rabbit-hole.' He took another large bite of pasty. 'We marched from Chulmleigh at four o'clock s'morning, and there hasn't been much time for eating since.'

Simon had laid down his pasty and was fastening into his steel cap the sprig of furze which one of his troopers had given him.

'Why furze?' he demanded. 'A kerchief round one arm shows up better and doesn't—make one's fingers bleed,' for one of the sharp prickles had stuck into him.

'Question not the wisdom of your superiors,' Barnaby told him. 'We might have had to go into action with our shirts hanging out behind. I did that once. The idea was that if you turned round, your white scut didn't show any more, and your own men shot you in mistake for one of the enemy. Ingenious, that.'

They finished their meal in leisurely fashion talking over the prospects for tomorrow's engagement. They were sure that it *would* be tomorrow's, for at four o'clock on a winter's afternoon, with an Army tired after a full day's march, it did not seem likely that the General could have planned anything more than an advance skirmish for that night. The whole Army was mustered by now, and all across the deerpark the regiments were bivouacking, drawn up in battle order; and as the light thickened and faded, and the cold increased, many watch-fires began to glow, sending up great plumes of smoke into the sky, that was now clear and colourless as crystal above the bare trees. Here and there a man laughed or called to a comrade, or a horse whinnied. The rooks were flying home, cawing as they flapped overhead on lazy wings.

It was a peaceful scene, and nobody, looking out over it as Simon and Barnaby were doing, could have guessed that within a few hours one of the last battles of the Civil War would be raging round the barricades of Torrington.

In the first stage of the fighting, when it came, the General's Horse had no part. About five o'clock some scouts—a Forlorn of Foot—was sent out towards the town to reconnoitre and were met half-way by Royalist Foot. There was a sharp skirmish across the fields in the deepening twilight, and Lord Hopton, finding he could not hold the outposts, ordered his men closer in to the town defences.

Fairfax, judging that nothing more was needful for that night but to strengthen the positions gained, moved his men down into the townward end of the deer park, and stationed them in readiness for a general assault at dawn. Quietness settled down over the park and fields, save for the regular coming and going of the sentries between the watch-fires, and the low exchange of the watchword, 'Emanuel, God with us,' when patrols met.

But an hour later, through the frosty quiet, came the distant sound of a tattoo beating in the town. Attack, or retreat, which did it mean? Fairfax ordered a company of dragoons forward to the barricades to find out. The dragoons advanced down the road to the first barriers, and were met by a sharp volley from the Royalist musketeers lying in wait for them. Two more dragoon companies galloped down to their support, and the reserves of Foot, without waiting for orders, charged cheering after them. It was a valiant charge, but quite hopeless; and if more help did not quickly reach the troops at the barricades, they were going to be cut to pieces.

All this Simon heard afterwards, but at the time he knew only that something unexpected was happening; that dark regiments had gone past him at the double heading for the town, and that now the whole Army had been stood to arms. The quietness over the deerpark had frozen into a tense waiting silence, broken from time to time by the faint rattle of musketry from the town defences. And Simon, standing beside Scarlet in the midst of his Troop while the slow minutes crawled by, heard his own heart drubbing slowly, and the silken whisper of the Standard above his head as the light wind stirred it. It was very cold, with a bitter smell of frost in the air; overhead the sky had changed from crystal to a wonderful clear green, splintered with stars, and in the east the pearly glimmer of moonrise was spreading behind the black shapes of the trees.

'Parish Lantern's getting up. We'll have plenty of light presently,' Barnaby muttered over his shoulder.

'Yes,' Simon murmured back. 'Hullo! what's that?'

'Only an owl. Call yourself a countryman and don't know an owl when you hear one!'

'No, not that—it's a horse—someone in a hurry. Listen!'

They listened, and a few moments later they could all hear it: the sound of a horse being ridden at a furious gallop. They heard the hoof-beats ringing nearer and nearer up the frost-hardened bridle-way, until the wild rider swept past them on towards the house. Silence followed, a tingling silence that ended in another burst of hoof-beats, this time from the direction of the house, and a knot of horsemen loomed up through the darkness. One of the riders gave an order; and at the sound of his voice, the General's Own knew that Fiery Tom himself was at their head. Next instant the trumpets sounded *monte cavalo*!

Moving as one man, the troopers swung into the saddle. Simon felt the familiar balance of the Standard in his hand, and settled his feet into the stirrups, conscious of Scarlet's excitement thrilling through them both, as the troopers of his Standard Escort closed up on either side of him. Then the trumpets sang again, and five troops of Horse, with Fairfax at their head, were sweeping down at a purposeful trot towards the town, while three regiments of Foot, their drums rolling, swung forward to join them.

The park palings had been levelled on either side of the town-ward gate, making a wide gap for the advance of troops, and in a few minutes the whole force was out into the road and the open fields on either side. The moon was clear of the trees now, and sailing up into the glimmering sky, and hedge and tree sparkled with thickening hoar-frost, and the shadow of every man's head was blotted darkly on the moon-silvered shoulders of the man before him. A clear white night, and a moon that seemed disdainfully remote from the battle which was now raging all along the town defences, where King's man and Parliament's man struggled for every fortified hedge.

And into the conflict plunged the three regiments, with Fairfax at their head, the Cavalry wings spreading out on either side. Simon, in the main Cavalry wing, swung north to engage Lord Wentworth's Horse, which had swept round the town from the Commons; and for a while he knew nothing but a wild wheeling and flurry of Horse across the moon-drenched field, and the shock of charge and counter-charge, and had no idea how the main battle was going.

But after a time it seemed to him that the whole fight was drawing inward; and he realized that the Royalists were being driven back. Slowly, from hedge to hedge, from barrier to barrier, fighting for every yard of ground, they were falling in on their last lines of defence. The final barricades were reached at last, and without any clear idea how he got there, Simon found himself and most of his troop caught up in a fierce struggle for the barrier of piled tree-trunks across the mouth of Calf Street. The moonlight here was quenched, and the sky above the roof-tops darkened by contrast with the leaping light of flames, for somebody had fired the barricade, and the faces of defenders and attackers alike were lit by a fiendish red glare. The fighting was too close and quick for shooting now, and the men surging to and fro fought with their musket-butts, which rose and fell club-wise among the thrusting pikes.

Simon saw a surging mass of distorted faces, and in his ears was the roar of the password ' Emanuel, God with us ! ' answered and flung back by the defenders beyond the barricades. Then a fiercer yell went up, as the piled tree-trunks collapsed. For a moment the flames shot up in a wavering sheet, and a shower of sparks burst skyward, drifting away on the light cold wind; then the flames sank and were beaten out by a rush of feet, as the Parliament Foot surged forward, cheering. Simon saw a drummer leap upon the glowing remains, and then plunge down among the defenders, shouting to his comrades to follow the drum. Then above the uproar rose the brazen yelping of trumpets sounding the Charge, and the Horse were plunging forward into the mêlée through the gap that the Foot had made for them, scattering red embers from their horses' hooves.

With one roar of ' Emanuel, God with us ! ' the advance troops of the New Model poured into Calf Street, sweeping the enemy before them.

' Emanuel, God with us ! ' Simon's voice cracked at the full pitch of his lungs, and he stuck his heel into Scarlet's flank, and followed the Standard of the General's Troop to meet the desperate counter-charge which, led by Lord Hopton, came sweeping down upon them at that moment. The two squadrons came together with a crash and shock, in the narrow street, where scared faces peered from upper windows. For a while the struggle hung in the balance, and then Simon realized, with helpless fury, that Fairfax's squadron was being pushed back ! They steadied, and pressed forward again, following the General's Standard;

then, as another Royalist charge crashed into them, they gave ground once more, and could not check, until the still-smouldering barricades were reached. But there the Foot were closing in again with pikes levelled; and by their aid the Horse steadied once more, closing their thinned ranks.

It was a case of hanging on now, for once driven back into open country, it would be all to do again. Both Horse and Foot had lost heavily in storming the barricades, and to retake it was beyond those that were left. They must hang on, somehow, until reserves reached them or the attackers at some other point broke through and could take the enemy in the rear. The light was reddening again, for the sparks had caught the thatched roof of an outhouse; and full in the glare, Colonel Hammond, his sprig of furze burnt to a crisp, with his eyebrows singed off and his teeth grinning white in a blackened face, was encouraging his men at the top of his voice; while Fairfax's Cavalry strained heart and soul to fling back the Royalist Horse, who were making valiant efforts to break through into the open.

Minute by minute they held them, but only just. There were not enough men for the task. Simon, his Standard held high in the mingled light of fire and moon, snatched one glance behind him up the Stevenstone road, when the shifting *mêlée* opened for an instant, but saw it white and empty in the moonlight until it ran into the shadow of the trees. He had no leisure to look behind him again.

Would those reserves never come?

Then suddenly there was the thunder of a squadron's hooves behind him, and a sense of strength and increase that ran like heath blaze through the hard-pressed companies. 'Noll's here! Noll! Old Noll!' The reserves had arrived.

Simon heard the strident challenge of the trumpets, and with a roar like a bursting dam, the charge went home. Once again he was sweeping down the street, this time in the wake of Cromwell's leading troop. The Royalists broke back, Lord Hopton's Blue Coats, caught up in the retreat, were swept away like flotsam on a dark flood. Simon saw their Standard waver and go down. He saw Lord Hopton standing in his stirrups as he strove to rally his men, his face white in the moonlight and puddled with blood where a pike had torn his cheek open. Then the *mêlée* closed between them and he did not see Lord Hopton again.

How long the battle raged through Torrington, as one by one the defences went, Simon never had the least idea. He only knew that the moon was still high in the glimmering sky when the last desperate resistance of the main Royalist Horse swung into South Street, with Cromwell pressing after. Behind them the Square was in Fairfax's hands, and the Foot were coming up, and already the roar of battle was sinking. The trumpets were yelping like hunting-horns at the kill, and Cromwell charged again. The Royalist's defence had had the stubborn desperate courage of an animal when it turns at bay; but now, quite suddenly, it broke, and became a running fight that streamed away down the narrow street, past the old house that had been a second home to Simon when he and Amias were small.

All night long Simon had been looking for Amias, with a queer certainty that after their two encounters would come a third. He was still certain; but it was no use looking any more. Only backs to look at now, anyway. He settled down grimly in the saddle.

The pursuit down Mill Street was a nightmare, for in the light of the moon the cobbled street seemed to drop like a silver plummet to the dark valley below; and down it swept hunters and hunted, streaming out raggedly in dark skeins of horsemen, with the silver road between. Down and down, hooves slipping on the steep cobbles, and now and then the crash and flame-spit of a pistol as a hard-pressed Royalist turned in the saddle to fire his last shot, or a Parliament trooper fired into the flying shapes ahead. Simon was holding Scarlet well together, as they hurtled forward and down; once the horse slipped sickeningly, but he contrived somehow to steady him from a headlong fall. Other riders were less fortunate: a trooper just ahead of him came down with a slithering crash, the man was flung clear, and the mount lay kicking in the roadway. There could be no waiting to see what became of them: that must be left for others coming after. Simon plunged on. The dark woods of the valley seemed rushing up to meet him, and the moon was glinting on the swift water of the Torridge, flowing between the huddled cottages of Taddiport.

Horsemen were streaming away across the bridge and into the woods beyond ; on either side the quick-silver water was churned and darkened as the desperate riders for whom there was no room on the bridge, set their mounts to swim the river.

Barnaby's voice rose above the tumult, shouting to his troopers. ' Follow me, lads—the bridge is no use to us.' And he wheeled aside from the main pursuit, down the sloping river bank.

' Fifty yards farther down !' Simon yelled, ' A stickle. No need to swim for it !'

' Right ! Here goes !'

Other troops, glimpsing the broken brightness of the shallows, were following, as Simon, holding the Standard high in one hand, steadied Scarlet down to the water. ' Easy does it—steady, boy— now !' A smother of spray, a flash of sheeted silver boiling all around, full of the thrust and plunge of other horses, the icy water flung up in drenching showers; and then with a wild slipping and scrambling of hooves and a shout of ' Up, boy ! Up !' they had gained the farther bank.

As they did so, above the shouting and plunging there burst an appalling roar that seemed to leap down upon them from the town, a crash that flung backward and forth between the hills, making the solid ground tremble. Simon wrenched round as he rode, to stare behind him, and saw a livid glare spreading above Torrington, and the roofs of the houses along Castle Hill etched black against it. Other men were pointing and shouting, horses flinging this way and that in a shuddering panic.

' In Heaven's name, what was that ?' Simon shouted, with an instant's jagged vision in his mind of a moorland bridge exploding into red ruin, and men and horses flung from it, to lie broken and huddled in the water.

And out of the crowding shadows ahead, Barnaby's voice answered him. ' Powder store gone up, by the sound of it !'

Ahead of them, Cromwell's trumpets were calling up his scattered squadrons. They rounded the last cottages of Taddiport, and the muddy lane was beneath their hooves once more. The reddening glare in the sky above Torrington was left behind, and hunters and hunted swept on westward.

# XVII

## *The Man on Castle Hill*

IN the grey dawn, a dozen or more miles from Torrington, Cromwell called off the pursuit, and ordered his squadrons back on their tracks. And a few hours later the weary troops were bivouacking in the river-meadows below the old inn at Woodford, where the Holsworthy road crossed the upper reaches of the Torridge. The green valley-floor between hanging oak woods had become as busy as a market-place, with tired horses being rubbed down and made comfortable, camp-fires sending up jay's feathers of smoke into the wintry sky, and all the ordered coming and going of a bivouack. The frost of last night had gone, and there was a smell of coming rain in the air; and so presently, when a meal had been eaten and stray wounds bound up, there would be the business of finding quarters for close on four hundred men among the house and outbuildings of the inn and the few farms and cottages nearby; for Cromwell, in mercy on his weary squadrons, had decided against returning to Torrington that day.

Now, with several officers behind him, he was making the rounds of the temporary horse-lines; speaking a brusque but kindly word to a trooper here and there, inquiring into a wound, bending to examine the hock of a horse that had gone lame, all with the personal interest in horse and man that he had had when he was the leader of a troop and had not lost now that he was second in command of an army.

Simon, watering Scarlet at the stream, and talking to him softly the while, looked up to see Cromwell standing beside him. He drew himself to attention, trying at the same time to keep one eye on the horse, lest he drank more than was good for him, and found the square man regarding him with interest. He had never spoken to the Lieutenant-General before, nor, so far as he knew, had he been noticed by him; so he was surprised when Cromwell said, ' Back to the Colours again, I see.'

' Yes, sir.'

' Not going to miss the fun, eh? '

' No, sir.'

' But you have reopened that wound a bit.'

Simon had certainly had a bang on the head during the fighting for the barricades, but he had thought no more of it, and now, putting up his hand, he was surprised to feel the crumbly dryness of caked blood on his temple.

' Not good,' said Cromwell. ' And you scarce returned from —sick leave.' There was the least possible pause before the last two words, and Simon saw that the Lieutenant-General's bright hazel eyes were dancing like a boy's in his blunt ruddy face.

They grinned at each other like a pair of cheerful conspirators, and Simon felt, as people generally did when they were with Old Noll, his tremendous power of drawing men into fellowship with him.

' I forget your name,' Cromwell said.

' Carey, sir.'

' You're a local man, aren't you? What a fool question! Of course you are.'

' I come from four or five miles beyond Torrington, sir.'

General Cromwell nodded. ' But no doubt you are reasonably familiar with the roads this side of the town.'

' Yes, sir.'

' Good. Get a meal and give your horse an hour's rest; then report to me at the inn yonder. My Galloper is wounded, and I shall have dispatches for carrying back to the Lord-General.' And he tramped off to poke his blunt nose into the food being prepared for his men at the upper end of the meadow.

' I seem fated to bear-lead this disgusting troop by myself while you go gadding! ' Lieutenant Colebourne said resignedly, a few minutes later, when Simon reported to him what had happened. ' Why couldn't you have told him you hailed from Coventry or Clerkenwell, and then maybe he'd have picked on someone else.'

An hour later, as near as he could judge, Simon made his way

197

up to the inn. The Troop Standards had been formally housed in the room over the thatched porch, and were slanting out through the open window; and glancing up at them after he had looped Scarlet's reins over the hitching-post, Simon thought what a brave show they made in the faint sunshine, crimson and emerald and deepest blue, stirring a little as the breeze caught them. Then he turned his attention to the trooper on duty before the door, and explained that he had orders to wait on General Cromwell.

The man passed him on to another, and after tramping down a few worn steps and a sloping and uneven passage beyond, Simon found himself in the taproom of the inn. A low-ceiled room, with deep-set windows, and walls lined with the usual casks and demijohns and rows of many coloured bottles reflecting back in jewelled sparks the light of a fire that blazed on the open hearth. There was a strong smell of cider, and the air was blue with wreathing tobacco smoke through which Simon saw the figures of several dusty and weary officers. The Lieutenant-General was seated sideways on a settle by the fire, with a table before him. He was writing fast, with an inn pen which squeaked abominably, while with his free hand he supported the bowl of a long clay pipe, at which he puffed steadily.

Reaching the end of the page, he signed it and drew a final slashing line which spluttered ink all across the signature, sanded and folded the sheet, and held it out to Simon who was standing in readiness before him. 'I want this in Sir Thomas Fairfax's hands as soon as may be.'

'Sir,' said Simon, stowing the dispatch in the breast of his buff coat.

'But don't kill your horse for the sake of getting it there ten minutes earlier.' And he lounged up from the settle to kick the blazing logs together with a booted foot, as Simon saluted and turned to the door.

Outside once more, he unhitched Scarlet and, mounting, set out for Torrington, six or seven miles distant. Scarlet was very tired, despite his short rest, but he rallied valiantly to Simon's voice and hand, and changed his pace to an easy canter as they left the inn with its bivouacked troops behind them.

The first thing Simon noticed when he reached the near end

198

of South Street was a litter of broken glass crunching under-foot. He was leading Scarlet by that time; he never rode up Mill Street even with a fresh horse, and looking round, he saw that scarcely a pane of glass or horn was left clinging to a window-pane in all the length of the street, while the frames themselves were driven askew, and slates, chimney-pots and great lumps of thatch littered the cobbles. Suddenly he remembered the roar and the livid glare in the sky, which Barnaby had said was a powder store going up; and something seemed to turn over inside him. The powder store. Zeal and Podbury! Were they safely out of it, or had they gone heavenward with that rending glare? There was no time to find out now.

Simon called to one of the many passing soldiers. 'Where shall I find Sir Thomas Fairfax?'

'At the Black Horse, sir. Turn to the left at the Market.'

'Thanks. I know the place.' Simon walked on, turning up into the square. Here was a chaos of blown-out windows and stripped roofs, even worse than in South Street. Here also was a great coming and going of troops, wagons rolling in and horses being urged through the crowd. But scarcely any of the towns-people were to be seen, for though the good folk of Torrington had always been for Parliament, they had seen enough of armies in the past four years to distrust all of them, and they were keeping within doors.

Simon delivered up his dispatch to Fairfax in an upper room of the inn which he had taken over for his headquarters, and was ordered to join himself for the present to the General's Troop, which was quartered with the Third in some farm buildings on the north of the town. His nearest way lay through the churchyard, which had always been a thoroughfare from one part of the town to the other, and when he reached the head of the Square, and turned in between two old shops that seemed oddly crumbled and askew, he felt for an instant as though he had walked into some hideous dream. His eyes had been ready for the quiet of leaning headstones, ancient lime trees among whose bare topmost branches the rooks would be at their building, the grey well-remembered church with its friendly little leaded spire . . . But the rooks had flown from trees that were no more than blasted stumps stretching here and there a broken limb to the clouding sky, or lying uprooted across the hummocked turf. The old houses that had ringed the place were broken back, empty-windowed, roofless, with here and there a great breach in a tottering wall. And the church? The church was a fire-blackened and desolate shell, piled with rubble, among which soldiers were searching, under the orders of a sergeant.

Simon had brought Scarlet to a standstill, without knowing that he did so, and stood staring at the scene of desolation with a dull sense of shock lying cold and heavy in his stomach. Why the church? Why, in heaven's name, the church? His head was a trifle woolly from the bang he had received on it, and it was a few moments before he realized that he had never known where Zeal's powder store was. It must have been here, here in the church.

Leading Scarlet behind him, he made his way up what had once been a path, stepping over the fallen rubble to the place where the sergeant stood. 'What has happened here?' he asked, feeling as he did so how foolish the question sounded.

The sergeant turned on him a harassed face, and said wearily, 'Can't you see, sir?'

'I can see there's been an explosion; but what caused it?'

'Couldn't say, sir. Somebody or something must have touched off the powder.'

'Oh yes, the powder,' Simon said dully. 'It was stored here?'

'Aye, in the base of the bell-tower; but we didn't know that when we put the prisoners there.'

'Prisoners?'

'Close on two hundred.' The sergeant's voice was grim. 'And a dozen or more of Fortescue's Regiment on guard. Didn't you know, sir?'

'No, I didn't. Were many of them killed?'

'We've dug out a few wounded,' the Sergeant said, meaningly.

There was a long silence. Simon was staring down at a fragment of stone beside his foot. There were feathers chiselled on it, as though it came from a carved angel's wing, or a bird's.

'Oh,' he said at last, and turned away. He walked on, with his arm through Scarlet's bridle, and the weary horse clip-clopping after him, into Calf Street, and down one of the narrow ways leading to the Commons.

Captain-Lieutenant Meredith was down at the horse-lines when Simon found and reported to him; and presently, after Scarlet had been handed over to the care of a trooper, the two made their way back together to the big farm kitchen where several of the Regimental officers were gathered. They were standing round the fire, warming chilled hands in a few off-duty minutes; and they made room for the newcomer to get near the warmth.

'Carey! Where have you sprung from?' Cornet Fletcher greeted him.

Simon turned a shoulder and edged in to the blaze, carefully ignoring Denzil Wainwright, who was lounging in the chimney corner and just as carefully ignoring him. 'Woodford,' he said, 'if that conveys anything to you. Old Noll sent me back with dispatches for the Lord-General—his Galloper being out of action.'

Several voices demanded news of the chase; and he told them that Cromwell had called it off before Holsworthy, and that to the best of his knowledge the Royalist Horse were heading back over the border into Cornwall.

'I wonder how many of them will manage it,' said Meredith. 'Not that it makes much odds. The King's Army in the West is done.'

Simon took off his steel cap, which was chafing the place where the old scar had reopened, and reaching up, put it on the broad mantel. 'What happened after we left?'

Several people told him: while Fairfax's troops were gaining the Square, Lord Hopton had brought up his reserves of Horse for one last charge against the attackers on the north, but by that time his Foot had been in full retreat, and without their support the charge had failed. Defeat had become a rout, and despite all his efforts to rally them, the whole Royalist Army had gone streaming away over the Commons and down Castle Hill, so that while Cromwell was driving the Horse down through Taddiport, the Foot had been already running like red-shanks. By dawn it had all been over.

'What happened to Lord Hopton?' asked Simon.

'Got away with the rearguard of Horse,' Meredith told him. 'We had a bit of a brush with them at the lower bridge; that was when Major Disbrow got shot.'

'Killed?' Simon asked quickly.

'No, only flesh wound. Mostyn's gone, though, and Bennet's pretty bad.'

No one spoke for a little while, and then a cornet with a bloody rag twisted round one wrist asked abruptly, 'Did you hear the church blow up?'

'Yes, just as we were crossing the river. And I saw the wreckage on my way here, just now. The sergeant in charge didn't seem to have any idea what caused it.'

'There's a good many would like to know that,' said Meredith, 'and the whole place is buzzing with rumours. I've heard the Royalists did it themselves, to prevent their powder falling into our hands. Chaplain Sprigg is the leader of that school of thought; but with two hundred of their own men prisoned inside, it don't make sense.'

'I met the worthy vicar standing guard over the ruins this morning,' put in Cornet Fletcher, 'and he had the effrontery to tell me that *we* did it, to get rid of the inconvenience of two hundred prisoners.'

'Well, in that case, why haven't we blown up the other four hundred that we've got spread around the town?' It was he of the bandaged wrist who spoke. ''Sides, it was nearly the end of Fiery Tom. That bit of guttering only missed him by inches.'

'That last argument leaks like a sieve,' pointed out a new voice behind them. 'We couldn't have known that the General was going to be riding about South Street at that moment, or that a lump of lead was going to drop just where it did.'

They turned, as a muddy figure came in, shaking itself like a dog, for the day was turning wet.

'Oh, it's you, Anderson.' Lieutenant Meredith made room for him beside the fire. 'How did the search go?'

The other made a wry face, and sank wearily on to a bench. 'Every ditch in three parishes is choked with wounded. We've brought in a good many—Royalist for the most part, but a few of our men too. Major James is getting together another search-party now, but after a few hours of this rain there'll not be much point in bringing in any that are still out in it.'

Another silence fell on the company, which was broken by Fletcher, saying in a quiet hard voice, very unlike his usual one, ' When my brother was wounded and taken prisoner in Cornwall last year, they hanged him.'

' Rather a habit of Sir Richard Grenville's,' said Lieutenant Meredith.

The latest comer looked up. ' Talking of this magazine going sky high,' he said, ' one of my troopers swears he saw the man who did it.'

' *What?* ' shouted the company.

' Gammon! ' said Cornet Fletcher.

' All right; have it your own way.'

' No, but gammon apart, is it true, Anderson? '

' How should I know? He told me a long rigmarole about it, just now, when I handed my horse over to him. Wait a moment . . .' He got up, and crossing to the doorway, stuck his head out and shouted, ' Trooper Pennithorn!—Oh, Hughes, tell Pennithorn I want him.' He returned to the fire, and in a few minutes a lanky trooper appeared in the doorway, straightening his coat as he came.

' Sir? '

' Pennithorn, repeat the story you were telling me just now,' his officer commanded.

' You mean, about yon cove——'

' Yes, that's the one.'

Trooper Pennithorn drew a long breath, and began, speaking very fast, and staring straight before him with steady, rather stupid grey eyes. Evidently he had told the story a great many times. ' Well, sir, 'twas like this; I was making my way round below that ol' ruined castle, looking for any of the Men of Blood as might be in hiding. There was a good many of us beating the furze for 'em. Not long after midnight it 'ud be, and the moon was still high, and that was how I came to see a cove a-scrambling down one of them little sheep paths. A red-headed cove, with

203

a beak of a nose, and so bold as brass, and never a start when I challenged. " Emanuel, God with us," he says. " Good evening, Trooper, or should I say good morning? A fine night for catching mice ! " he says. I says, " Where might you be going to, sir ? " for I took him for one of our officers—him with a sprig of furze in his cap, and knowing the password and all. He says, " Out on the General's business." And he laughs a queer choking sort of laugh. *Then* he says, " Fine explosion up yonder. Fiery Tom won't be getting *this* lot o' the King's powder, as sure as unicorns ! " An' off he goes.'

Simon caught his breath, as though he had been plunged into icy water, and yet in some odd way he had known from the first mention of him who the red-haired man among the furze must be. It was so exactly like Amias to walk out like that, exchanging pleasantries with the enemy on the way.

The monotonous voice was going on :

' Sort of staggering a bit, if ye sees what I mean, like as if maybe he was wounded somewhere, but I didn't take much notice, not until I remembered something as I hadn't hardly been aweer on, at the time.' A dramatic pause. ' He smelled strong of singeing ! Burned powder and singeing ! Well, I thought 'twas queer, and 'tis my belief as he *was* wounded, and 'tis my belief as he got that way when he blew up the church. " Fiery Tom won't get *this* lot o' the King's powder," he says. And 'tis my belief——'

Simon realized that the dark eyes of Denzil Wainwright were fixed on him, rather curiously, and he pulled himself together with a jerk, just as the trumpets sounded in the distance for watch-setting. The group before the fire broke up instantly. Trooper Pennithorn was gone; and Simon heard his own voice, sounding surprisingly normal, asking Lieutenant Anderson, ' Did you say Major James was forming a relief party to carry on the search for wounded, sir ? '

' I did.'

He turned to Lieutenant Meredith, who had paused in the doorway to speak to a passing trooper. ' May I report to Major James ? I know every inch of this country. I might be of some use.'

' Yes, of course.   He'll probably be glad of you,' the Lieutenant told him, and went out, hitching at his sword-belt.

Simon went out, behind the rest of them, into the icy mizzle that was driving across the Commons before a rising wind.

## XVIII

## Loyalties

WITHIN half an hour, having yet again collected Scarlet,
Simon had reported to Major James and was once more
across Taddiport Bridge, and taking to the woods.
The searchers were splitting up, men and horses moving off to
quarter the rough country; and Simon found it quite easy, knowing every inch of the land as he did, to lose his comrades and get
away by himself on his own secret search.

Now, for the first time, as he wove Scarlet farther and farther
into the wet moaning woods, he had a chance to think. What
possible good could he do by joining this search? He didn't
know. He only knew that he had had to join it, because it was
his one chance of helping Amias: a desperately slim chance, he
knew, but the only one there was. Had Amias blown up the

church, blindly obeying orders left by Lord Hopton, or acting on some wild idea of his own? Simon remembered the fascination that mining and explosives had always had for the other boy. But whether or not Amias had engineered this explosion was beside the point; all that mattered was that if he was taken, there would be a black case against him, thanks to Trooper Penni-thorn.

By this time, what with the bang on the old wound and his utter weariness, Simon was not thinking very clearly; but he remembered very clearly indeed the stark shapes against the sunrise, of three men hanged by the Lord-General's orders, for looting, on the road to Taunton; two more gibbeted outside Oxford for burning down the cottage of a wise woman they believed to have overlooked them. Fairfax was completely merciless upon such crimes as damage to property and the wanton taking of life; and would he have more mercy on one of the enemy than on his own men? Also there was the likelihood that Amias was wounded. If that was the case, he might have been brought in already, and if he had been, then he was beyond Simon's help. But he might not have been brought in. He might be hiding up somewhere— if he was wounded, he was not likely to have got far—and it was the thought of Amias, wounded and hunted, crouching in some ditch, that kept Simon searching through the woods and coppices, in the haunts and hiding-places they had known when they were boys, in the desperate hope of finding him before anyone else did.

Presently the rain stopped, but above the tree-tops the sky was a cold lemon colour, against which clouds like grey snags of sheep's wool drove before the westerly wind. It was going to be a wild night. And still Simon kept up his search. It was already dusk among the trees, when, leading Scarlet behind him, he forced his way through a tangle of hazel and dogwood into a little clearing, and found himself looking down at a slight figure, lying spreadeagled face downward under the steep lift of a fox-holed bank, where two small boys had often dug for pig-nuts.

With a sickening dread, he dropped on one knee beside the still figure, and turned it over, very gently. The red of Amias's hair was darkened almost to black by the rain that had soaked into it, and his face was curd-white in the gathering shadows. In frantic haste Simon pushed back the sodden scarlet cloth of a pikeman's coat, and set his hand over the other's heart, giving a gasp of relief as he felt it beating faintly under his fingers. But Amias's doublet was sodden with something worse than rain, and when Simon withdrew his hand, it was sticky with blood. He opened the doublet, noticing now the spreading stain on it; noticing also, with a dull sinking of the heart, that it was torn and blackened, as by fire. He pulled it back, and the stained shirt with it, and laid bare an ugly wound in the other's shoulder. One glance told him that it had been made by flying fragments of some sort—shards that might very well have been set flying by an explosion—and they were still there. But getting them out must wait for the moment, and he set steadily to work with the green scarf from the other's waist, to plug the wound and staunch the blood that still drained sluggishly from the jagged hole.

Meanwhile Scarlet, who had remained close beside him, alternately slobbered at his shoulder and stretched down to nuzzle with soft lips and a kind of troubled bewilderment at Amias's red hair and white upturned face. Simon, straining the make-shift bandages tight, was talking to him, hurriedly and half under his breath, without knowing that he did so. 'Yes, it's Amias. You remember Amias, don't you? We've got to get him away from here—got to get him into shelter, where they won't find him.' He knotted off the bandages and drew the pikeman's coat back over the wound; then set about the next stage of his task. Amias was taller than he, but more slightly built, and Simon had all the strength of the small stocky countryman. Slowly, carefully, so as not to jar the wound, he raised the other across his knee, and then got up, rather unsteadily, braced under his weight. 'Steady, boy, steady now.' Scarlet stood like a trained pack-horse to receive his burden, and Simon contrived to get Amias across the saddle-bow; then he mounted himself, and gathering the limp body into the curve of his arm, set out for Solitude as fast as the tired horse could carry them. ("If Sir Walter Raleigh had hidden here, King James would never have found him to cut his head off!")

It was not much more than a mile to the hidden fastness that had been the Golden City of Manoa in the old days; but at least until they gained the farther woods, every moment might bring them face to face with some of the search-party; and always there was the possibility that even if they reached their goal, Pentecost might not be there. Simon prayed during that mile ride as he had never prayed before in all his life, that Pentecost might not have been driven away by the fighting; that he might be there to take Amias in and hide him.

Pentecost was there. He was lounging in the doorway of his hovel, when Simon came up through the wild-fruit trees, bending low in the saddle to shield his own face and Amias's from the wet whipping twigs.

' It's only me,' Simon gasped, as the Fiddler pushed off from the doorpost and came loping to meet him. ' I've got Amias here—wounded. Will you take him? '

A white owl swooped past them in the dusk, making Scarlet snort and side-step; but Pentecost had already put up his ragged arms and taken Amias from him, as matter-of-fact as though they had been two small boys again; and this their usual way of coming to call on him.

' It's his right shoulder,' Simon said, as he dropped from the saddle.

' I'll mind it,' said Pentecost. ' Hitch the horse to thicky bird-cherry branch yonder.' And not another word did he speak until they had carried Amias indoors and laid him on the piled bracken of the bed-place. Then, kindling the rushlight on its pricket, he asked, ' What be you up to, my dear? You bain't meddling with something ye'd better have left alone, be you? '

The little crocus flame of the rushlight sprang up, and steadied; and Simon, kneeling beside the still figure on the bed-place, began to undo the bandages, hurriedly explaining the state of affairs as he did so. ' He mustn't fall into the hands of our men,' he finished, ' not until we have found out the truth, anyhow. You see that, don't you, Pentecost? You must see that.'

' Aye, he'm better hid for the present, seemingly.' Pentecost was holding the rushlight close, to examine the wound. ' You've not tried to get out the shard? '

'No, I simply plugged the hole, and left the rest until I got him here.'

Pentecost Fiddler produced a knife from somewhere inside his ragged clothes. 'Us had better have a look,' he said.

But after a few minutes, Simon sat back on his heels. 'It's too deep bedded; we can't take the risk, Pentecost.'

'You'm right, I reckon. 'Tis too near the vitals for the likes of us to go a-digging and a-delving after it,' nodded the Fiddler.

'I'm going for Dr Hannaford,' Simon said, and got up.

'Ye'd best let me go, I'm thinking.'

'No, with things as they are I'm more likely to be able to find him. He'll be with the wounded, most like.' Simon stooped and felt for Amias's heart again; it was beating more strongly now, and he gave a quick sigh of relief. 'He's going to be all right.'

'Aye, he'll do well enough—but there's others,' said Pentecost, meaningly.

'If he's found here, you mean? You won't get into any trouble, my friend.' There was a flicker of scorn in Simon's voice. 'And as for Dr Hannaford, every surgeon is free to tend the wounded of both armies.'

'And that only leaves yourself,' said Pentecost, with the faint mockery that was so much a part of him; and Simon knew that he had done the fiddler an injustice. It was not his own skin he was bothering about.

'I'll be all right,' he said. 'I'll be back with the Doctor in a couple of hours, with luck.' He turned in the doorway, and looked back to where the fiddler was already spreading an old blanket over his charge. 'I'm leaving Scarlet here—less likely to be spotted without him. Keep an eye on him, will you, Pentecost?' Then he went out into the windy dusk and the first chill drift of the rain which was coming on again.

Being one of the search-party, he had no need to avoid the pickets on Rotherne Bridge, but walked boldly past them with a cheerful Good night and took to the Commons beyond.

It was almost dark when he crossed Mill Street and came up through the furze of Castle Hill, his head bent against the mizzle rain which drove into his face. The hill seemed higher than it had ever done before, and the steep sheep-tracks were slippery underfoot, but he reached the top at last. Far below him the rushlights blinked in the clustered windows of Taddiport, and he saw them for an instant through the rain-swathes, as he halted, feeling for the snib of a familiar gate. It opened under his hand, and he passed through into the swaying dripping tangle of guelder rose and gooseberry bushes at the foot of Dr Odysseus Hannaford's garden.

The faint apricot flicker of a firelit window showed ahead of him, and he made his way towards it, up the well-remembered path, and reaching the kitchen door, knocked softly. A sudden scuffle sounded inside, and then all was silent once more, save for the wind and the rain. Simon knocked again; and almost at once came sounds of bolts and bars being drawn. The door opened a little way, and in the gap appeared Tomasine Blackmore, a most valiant figure with a candle in one hand and a poker in the other. Seeing a buff-clad figure on the threshold, she made as though to close the door again, saying in accents of disgust, 'Roundheads! We've had enough of your kind hereabouts.'

The Roundhead propped himself wearily against the doorpost, with a squelching boot well inside. 'Tomasine,' he said, 'it's I, Simon Carey. Where's the Doctor?'

Tomasine let out a small screech and dropped the poker. Then she flung the door wide and hooked Simon over the threshold, shutting it again behind him, and turned with a hand spread-fingered on her large chest. 'Oh, my days! 'Tis Maister Simon, sure 'nough!' she wheezed. 'What be after, my dear?'

'I want the Doctor,' Simon said again.

'He'm out. Been out most of the day, a' has, helping tend the wounded.'

Simon had expected that, but the house had seemed the best place to start the search for him. 'Where?'

Tomasine jerked her head. 'Up along in the Square, I reckon.'

'Thanks. I'll ask again when I get there.' Simon turned to the inner door, but Tomasine laid a large imploring hand on his arm, holding him back.

'I—Maister Simon, my dear, is it Maister Amias?'

Simon nodded, then, seeing her face, added quickly, ' No, he's going to be all right, only I've got to find the Doctor. And, Tomasine, don't tell anyone you've seen me.'

' I won't, my dear. Not a soul!' she said fervently. She pushed by him in the dark passage, and drew the bolts and bars of the front door, as she had done of the back. ' There, quickly now.'

' Right. Leave the door on the latch,' Simon said, and went out into the street.

South Street seemed quite deserted, for most of the troops would be in quarters by now, and it was not a night when anyone would be abroad needlessly. But the Square, when he turned to it, was still full of comings and goings; and the lanterns which must be hung before the principal houses from Hallowtide to Candlemas flung their uncertain wind-swayed light on to wet cobbles and the hurrying figures of soldiers, and made a kind of golden smoke of the rain as it slanted by. Before the door of the Black Horse a sentry was pacing up and down, and two doors farther on some of the search-party were gathered, and something long and muffled in a cloak was being carried indoors. Evidently the wounded were still being brought in. Simon stood aside until they had gone; then turned quickly to the door, meaning to ask if Dr Hannaford was within, and if not, in which of the other houses he might be found. But in the doorway he met the Doctor himself, coming out, and accosted him breathlessly, ' Dr Hannaford——'

Dr Odysseus Hannaford swung round on him. ' Yes, what— *Simon !* ' His shaggy brows twitched together and his beak of a nose was disdainful. ' I have nothing that I wish to say to rebels,' he said, and made to turn away.

' Never mind that now,' Simon muttered. ' I *must* speak to you, sir, but not here. Go home and wait for me, and I'll join you in a few minutes.'

His face was clear in the light of the lantern over the doorway, and Dr Hannaford seemed to read the desperate urgency in it, for his manner changed, and he murmured back, his lips barely moving, ' Is it Amias?'

' Yes. For the Lord's sake go home, sir.'

'Very well.' The Doctor turned, wrapping his cloak about him, and set off in the direction of South Street.

Almost sick with relief, Simon moved into the shadows between two swinging lanterns, pretending, for the benefit of any passers-by who might notice him, to be making some adjustment to his sword-belt, for it seemed to him that, in the circumstances, it might be as well if he were not seen walking with Dr Hannaford. So far, so good. But he did not realize how noticeable he had been, bare-headed (his helmet was back at Solitude) and with the dark stain of blood on his temple, as he stood full in the lantern light with the Doctor, and he had not seen Denzil Wainwright check in passing, to watch him from the shadows, at first with malicious curiosity, and then with sudden hopeful suspicion narrowing his eyes.

A few minutes later, Tomasine, who had been on watch, opened the Doctor's door to him, and he slipped inside. As it closed behind him, he turned to the open door of the study through which taper-light shone out into the dark passage. Inside, the heavy curtains had been drawn across the window to cheat any prying eyes in the garden, and Dr Hannaford stood before the hearth, with his head bent and his back to the door. He turned round as his visitor hesitated on the threshold, and Simon saw that he looked suddenly an old man. But his rumbling voice sounded much as usual when he spoke. 'What about Amias? Is he killed?'

Simon shook his head, and closing the door, leaned heavily against it. 'No. He's at Solitude, in Pentecost Fiddler's care, and with some splinters of metal in his shoulder. Will you come and cut them out?'

Before the words were out of his mouth, Dr Hannaford had turned to his instrument cases. 'Why this so-extraordinary secrecy, may I ask?' he said, picking out a long bright probe. 'The houses round the Square are full of Royalist wounded. If your General's reputation be true, there'll be no harm come to them.'

Once again Simon explained the situation, and the Doctor's face grew more deeply lined as he listened, while all the time he was opening and shutting drawers and cases, and stowing the things he needed in his pockets. 'I have heard much of that story,' he said; 'but I did not connect it with Amias.'

Simon was looking at the Doctor's boots, noticing with satisfaction that they were long loose-fitting riding-boots like his own. 'We shall have to ford the river,' he said. 'There are pickets on both bridges. Luckily it's not coming down in spate any longer.'

'It won't be the first time I've crossed by the stickles, though I've not done it for thirty years.' The Doctor picked up his cloak and swung it round his shoulders. 'But there need be no " we " about it. There is no call for you to venture yourself farther in the matter. Go back to your fellows.'

'Do you know the way?' Simon demanded. But he knew that few people save himself and Amias and the Fiddler knew the exact position of Solitude, and those who did would be afraid to act as the Doctor's guide, especially at night.

'I can find it.'

'I doubt it, in this rain and darkness,' Simon said flatly. 'It's no good, sir; I'm coming with you.'

'So be it, then.' The Doctor's voice was tired and heavy, but his face had grown kinder as he looked at Simon. 'You know what you are doing, don't you?' he said, almost gently. 'You, a soldier—befriending one of the enemy.'

There was a long silence, while the Doctor clasped his cloak, and Simon stared at the candles. Somehow, until this moment the only thought in his tired mind had been to save Amias at all costs, and he had not had to choose between two loyalties. But now, Dr Hannaford had forced the choice on him. Two loyalties; and to keep faith with one meant breaking it with the other, and who should say which was the blacker treachery? 'Yes, I know what I'm doing,' he said at last; and his mouth felt dry. 'It's Amias, you see,' and he opened the door and stood aside for the other to pass.

'I see,' said Dr Hannaford. 'Yes, I see,' and he put a hand on Simon's shoulder for an instant, as they went out to the darkened kitchen, where Tomasine waited to open the back door for them.

Upwards of an hour later, soaked to the thigh from fording the stickle, and almost as soaked about the shoulders from the

rain, they emerged from the storm-lashed woods, on the edge of
Solitude, and saw a faint crack of light shining out through the
dripping branches of the wild-fruit trees.

'Here we are,' said Simon.

Scarlet stood dejectedly with hanging head where Simon had
left him under the bird-cherry; he raised his head with a faint
nicker at the sound of his master's voice, but Simon had no time
to do more than pat his neck in passing, and an instant later the
crack of light widened as the ramshackle door was opened to
let them in.

# XIX

## 'No Man shall Harbour the Enemy'

THERE was a certain rough comfort in the rush-lit cabin, where a red fire burnt on the hearth, and the lovely little *Destiny* on the mantel caught the light on the winged curve of her sails. Amias's sodden clothes had been spread before the fire, over which a crock was boiling; and Amias himself, quite conscious now, lay under the old blanket on the bracken-piled bed-place. He had raised himself on his sound arm at their approach, and lay staring at the door with strained eyes; then relaxed with a sigh as they came into the light and Pentecost shut the creaking door behind them.

'Oh,' he said, 'it's only you. I thought for a moment it was the Roundheads. Hullo, Father.'

'Telled 'ee Simon had gone for your father, didn't I?' said Pentecost soothingly, as one might speak to a small sick child. Then to the Doctor, 'There's water boiling for 'ee, Doctor, if 'ee should want; and a good red fire to heat the knife.'

Dr Hannaford slipped off his sodden cloak. 'Aye, thank 'ee,' he said, and knelt down by his son's bed, to loosen the stained bandages. 'Now let's take a look at this shoulder.'

Simon had brought the rushlight, and stood holding it while the Doctor uncovered and examined the wound, and Amias looked up at him across his father's shoulder and said, simply, as though there had been no four years' rift between them, 'Simon, your head's bleeding.'

'Not now,' Simon said. 'I got banged on it last night.'

Dr Hannaford seemed to pay no heed to this, but a few minutes later, getting up, he looked closely at Simon's head, apparently noticing the blood on his temple for the first time. 'You did not get that scar last night. No.'

'No, that was way back before Christmas. We took a

216

house that we needed for the siege of Exeter, and in the scrimmage somebody hit me on the head with a musket stock,' and as Dr Hannaford nodded and turned to the fire, the eyes of Simon and Amias met, and suddenly and most wonderfully, the memory of that wild night at Okeham Paine was become a bond between them.

The Doctor was setting out his instruments, intent on various preparations, with the help of Pentecost Fiddler; and the other two were left to themselves. Simon had not known that he was going to speak, until he heard the words, and they did not seem to have come from himself at all. 'Amias, did you blow up the church?'

Amias looked at him with blank astonishment. 'Blow up the church? No, of course I didn't. What on earth put that idea into your addled pate?'

Relief flooded over Simon, and with relief, he grew exasperated. 'It's in more pates than mine,' he said. 'What possessed you to talk all that moonshine about a fine night for catching mice, and Fiery Tom not getting the King's powder, to the corporal you met on Castle Hill? Of course he tumbled to it that you'd touched off the magazine, and he's spread the story through the whole Army, and what is more, he'll be able to swear to you again. The moon was full.'

'I suppose it does look a bit black against me,' Amias said blankly. 'That was why you came looking for me, and dumped me here on Pentecost?'

'Yes. Keep that shoulder still.'

'I—didn't do it, you know.'

'I know that now, but we couldn't prove it,' Simon said.

Dr Hannaford had turned back to them, and once more knelt down beside the bed-place. 'I am, I confess, relieved to hear that you have not the death of a couple of hundred men on your hands,' he remarked conversationally, producing the horn-rimmed spectacles out of habit, and then absent-mindedly putting them away again.

Amias looked at him with startled over-bright eyes. 'A couple of hundred—what do you mean, sir?'

'There were two hundred Royalist prisoners in the church,' Simon said. 'You didn't know that?'

Amias began to laugh, breathlessly. He looked at the palm of the one hand he could lift. 'It's quite clean, sir,' he said, 'quite clean; look——'

'Aye, quite clean,' said his father. 'Let's get this scrap-iron out now. Pentecost, here, and hold the arm steady for me.'

But Amias, who had command of himself once more, shook his head. 'If anybody's going to hold my arm steady, I want Simon.'

So Simon gave the rushlight to Pentecost, and knelt down beside his friend. Dr Hannaford showed him how to hold Amias's arm, twisted outward so as to keep the wound in his shoulder open. Then he gave Amias a soft leaden bullet to bite on, and taking up the first of his battery of probes and lancets, set to work.

The wind and the rain sounded very loud in the time that followed, as the wild wings of the rising storm beat against the thatch; but they seemed a long, long way off, and the only sound in the quiet cabin that had any meaning was Amias's quick, agonized breathing that filled it from wall to wall. Simon knelt rigid, holding his friend's eyes with his own, giving him the wrist of his right hand to grip, because to let Amias bruise his wrist was all he could do for him, just now. . . .

Time dragged so slowly that it seemed as if it was not moving at all and the beastliness would never be over. But at last Dr Hannaford straightened from his task with a sigh. 'Four,' he said, 'and that's the last of them.' And he held up a jagged splinter of metal.

After that everything was quick and easy and light of heart. The wound was bathed and dressed and presently, having been dosed with the Doctor's favourite evil-smelling cordial, Amias was grinning at them again, with a little colour beginning to creep back into his face, propping himself on his sound elbow to gulp down oatmeal gruel that had been warming for him. 'I shall turn into a calf,' he said, grimacing. 'That's the second lot of gruel Pentecost has poured down me tonight. Anybody'd think I was a puling brat.'

' 'Twill put new strength into 'ee,' Pentecost told him. ' And you'm like to need it.'

Amias's eyes grew sombre on the instant, and he said quickly, ' Yes, I'm like to need it. I must be away from here by morning.'

' You'll lie up for several days, with that shoulder,' said his father, busily cleaning stained instruments before the fire.

' Don't you believe it, sir. I'll be away into Cornwall after the others, and get the Colours back to Lord Hopton.'

' The Colours?' said Simon, who was squatting at his side. ' There were no Colours with you when I found you.'

' Down a foxhole,' Amias told him briefly.

Simon looked at him, and saw that he was like an over-stretched wire that might snap at any moment. With an instinct that it might do him good to talk he said, ' See here, suppose you tell us what really happened.'

' Not much to tell. We made a last stand on the Castle Green; us and the Prince's Guard and the ravellings of a couple more companies. We were just about done by the time the powder went up, and soon afterwards somebody's musket blew up too, and I got the bits in my shoulder and was knocked out for a while; and when I came to, the fighting was pretty well over, and there I was, with the Company Colours crumpled under me. I lay perdue for a bit, and when the coast was clear I managed to get the Colours off their pike and bind them round me. Then I took the coat and steel cap from one of your men who wouldn't be needing them any more, and got away down Castle Hill; that was when I ran into your nosy friend. I hoped to join up with the rest, but I couldn't stop my shoulder bleeding, and in the end I only just managed to stuff the Colours down a foxhole before I crumpled up completely—and the next thing I knew I was lying here, and Pentecost was pouring gruel down my throat, and telling me 'twas you who'd brought me in.' He shifted a little to ease the pain of his shoulder, and added, almost humbly, ' I say, Simon, haven't you ever got tired of digging me out of scrapes?'

It was not like Amias to be humble, and it bothered Simon, but before he could reply, the shrill whinnying of Scarlet brought them all to their feet, facing the door, while Amias sat up with a stifled gasp.

' Douse the lights,' said Dr Hannaford.

' Douse it is, Captain.' Pentecost reached out a long arm to the rushlight, and instantly the cabin was plunged in darkness, save for the red glow of the sinking fire.

' What startled him? ' whispered Amias.

' Maybe nothing more than a fox. Quiet, now,' answered his father.

The slow minutes crawled by, while the four within the hovel listened, breath in check, for any sound through the moaning wind and the swish and spatter of rain against the walls. Simon had drawn Balan, and stood with the long blade ready in his hand; but it had been only long habit that made him draw, and he did not know that he had done so. Minute followed minute, tense, twanging with expectancy, and then, as nothing happened, slowly the tension relaxed, and breath began to come more easily.

' Must have been a fox,' murmured Amias.

But it was not a fox. Even as he spoke, Scarlet whinnied again. There came a sound of movement from outside, a voice snapped an order; then the door was kicked open, and the golden radiance of a lantern flooded into the cabin. By its light they saw Parliament troopers, and the gleaming barrels of a pair of levelled horse pistols.

' Don't move,' said a voice. ' We have you all covered.'

Simon was the first to speak, slamming his sword home into its sheath as he did so. ' Denzil Wainwright,' he said.

Denzil entered the cabin, followed by two troopers, one with levelled pistols, the other carrying the lantern, by the light of which they could see more troopers outside. ' The virtuous Hodge,' said Denzil coldly. ' Busily engaged in helping the enemy. I guessed that was it. We've had rather a job tracking you down, Hodge, though the ground holds a track like butter along the stream-side after this rain. I don't think we'd have found you at all if that red brute of yours hadn't so obligingly given us your whereabouts by whinnying.'

The place was now flooded with a yellow radiance, and as it fell full on Amias's beaked nose and flaming hair, the trooper holding the lantern gave a yelp. ' Beg pardon, sir, but that's the man as blowed up the powder store; I'd know him anywhere! '

And Simon saw with a sinking heart that it was Trooper Pennithorn.

' *Is* it,' said Cornet Wainwright, obviously enjoying himself. ' General Fairfax will be interested to know that.' Then his voice changed and sharpened. ' Get up and dress, you.'

Dr Hannaford said, ' I am a surgeon; I have just removed several metal fragments from this lad's shoulder, and I assure you that he is in no fit state to move.'

' I am sorry, sir,' Denzil told him, courteously enough. ' I am not particularly interested in the welfare of Royalists and I must do my duty.'

' A fine thing is duty, when it don't look uncommon like spite,' said Pentecost, backed into the corner beside the little *Destiny*, and looking on with a shade more mockery than usual in his strange face. But no one paid any heed to him.

' Simon '—Amias's nose was in the air, and his voice at its most drawling—' give me a hand with my clothes,' and he began painfully to slip his arm out of the sling. Suddenly he gave a little broken laugh. ' Some vixen will have a fine nest-lining for her cubs, in the spring! I daresay she'll not mind a few stains on it.'

Dr Hannaford had stepped forward as though to help him, and then drawn back and left it to Simon. In grim silence, under the levelled pistols of the trooper, Simon helped his friend to drag on his still wet clothes. No one spoke again, until he picked up the stained and tattered doublet, and as he did so, something fell out of the inner pocket. He stooped for it, but one of the troopers was before him, and catching it up, gave it to Cornet Wainwright, with a meaning look.

It was a kinked and tangled length of oiled bed-cord; the usual makeshift for slow-match or fuse when the real thing was not to be had.

Every eye in the cabin was fixed on the deadly piece of evidence, as Denzil took and examined it, with raised brows. ' This also will interest the General,' he said softly, and slipped it into the breast of his buff coat.

' Then be sure to give it him,' drawled Amias. ' Hand over my doublet, Simon.'

Simon helped him settle his arm back in its sling, and pull the wreck of his doublet over it. But when he reached for the dead pikeman's coat, Amias shook his head. 'Nothing doing. I'm through with borrowed plumage,' he said, and then, with a very set mouth, 'Help me up.' When Simon had done so, he staggered clear of his supporting arm, and took up Balin, which was propped in the corner.

Cornet Wainwright moved forward to take it, but Amias rounded on him with blazing eyes and his most insulting sniff. 'I may be your prisoner,' he said, 'but I'll be hanged before I give up my sword to anyone save your commander. Belt it on for me, Simon.'

Denzil shrugged. 'As you will. It makes no difference.'

So Simon belted the old sword on for him, while he stood glaring at his captor, with his sound hand against the wall to steady himself.

'It seems that we are ready,' Amias said, when the buckle was secure. He looked at Simon, with a small crooked smile. 'This is once too often you've tried to pull me out of a scrape, old lad.'

'Snuff!' said Simon, and put a steadying arm round him as he lurched towards the door. 'Put your good arm round my neck. That's better.'

'I am allowed to go with you?' demanded Dr Hannaford.

'As you please, sir,' Wainwright told him formally. 'As a surgeon you have, of course, the usual immunity. I have no orders concerning you.'

'Thank you.' The Doctor picked up his cloak and swung it round his shoulders.

Simon looked round at his brother officer, addressing him directly for the first time. 'No, nor have you any orders concerning *me*, my dear Denzil; you merely thought how pleasant it would be to see me disgraced.'

'My dear Hodge, how intelligent you have grown in these last few weeks,' said Denzil Wainwright. 'I said I'd square the account with you, for that night in Mess, didn't I?' And he drew back from the door to let them through.

So the grim little company passed out into the wild February

223

night, leaving Pentecost Fiddler still standing against the wall of his deserted hovel. A few minutes later they set out for Torrington, Amias drooping on Scarlet's back, and Simon following with his hands bound behind him.

'I can't bear the thought that I might lose you in the dark,' Denzil had said, when his bonds were being tied, and Simon had choked on his furious retort. One of the troopers walked beside Amias to steady him in the saddle, and Dr Hannaford, who had been refused leave to walk with the prisoners, tramped grimly in the rear.

And as they went, there rose suddenly behind them the wailing notes of a fiddle, playing, not a tune, but simply an accompaniment to the wind in the trees.

To Simon, stumbling down, pinioned, through the storm-lashed woods, that march was a nightmare. The lantern jigging ahead like some hateful will-o'-the-wisp, the troopers all around him—several of them men of his own Regiment—Amias slumped on the back of a weary horse, and at the end of the march? But it did not do to look so far ahead.

They passed the picket on Rotherne Bridge, and straggled up the hill to the town. The Square was emptier now, but still the lanterns shone on wet cobbles and gilded the mizzle as it drove by them; and still the sentry marched up and down before the door of the Black Horse. He called over his shoulder to a comrade, as they halted. Amias half slid, half tumbled from the saddle into the arms of the nearest trooper, who steadied him with rough kindness, saying, 'Hold up, lad; thee's as groggy as an hour-old calf.'

Simon was already being urged into the taproom, but he contrived to call back to the troopers remaining outside, 'Will one of you see to my horse? He's not had his evening feed yet, and he's just about foundered.'

The huge begrimed face of Mother Trimble appeared round the door of an inner room as they entered, and crumpled into relief at sight of Dr Hannaford. 'Oh, Doctor, thanks be you've come! Surgeon Morrison do be away somewheres, and there's a poor lamb just brought in as is beyond my skill!'

For an instant, the Doctor did not answer; and his eyes were on

Amias. Then he said, 'I'll come at once,' and disappeared after her, without a backward glance.

Simon and Amias were hustled into the far end of the taproom, where they were kept under guard of Trooper Pennithorn and an orderly, while Cornet Wainwright spoke aside with one of the General's staff. After a few moments he returned to them, and perched himself sideways on a barrel, swinging one foot and examining his nails, while the Galloper went tramping upstairs. Simon had been unbound by now, and stood rubbing the crimson weals on his wrists, where the bonds had cut into the flesh, and feeling rather sick. He watched Denzil; watched his guards; watched Amias standing propped against the panelling, and noticed anxiously a small bright stain that was beginning to spread through the shoulder of his sling. Behind the door through which Dr Hannaford had disappeared, a man cried out suddenly and sharply, in pain.

After what seemed a very long time, a door opened somewhere above stairs; voices sounded, and several officers came down, still talking together.

'You can go up now,' said the Galloper, who had followed them, and Simon found himself stumbling upstairs with Amias behind him. Another sentry stood aside from an open door, and the two of them were thrust into the upper room where Simon had handed over his dispatch only that morning, into the presence of the very weary man who stood with his arm along the mantel; staring down into the sea-coal fire.

'Cornet Wainwright, sir,' said the Galloper.

Fairfax turned slowly. 'Thank you, Peter,' he said. 'Is John Rushworth on hand?'

'Below stairs, sir. You wish him here?'

'No. Tell him, my compliments to Colonel Walley, and will he favour me as soon as may be with the list of casualties in his Regiment? If I need you again tonight, I'll send for you.'

'Sir,' said Peter, and departed.

'Yes, Cornet Wainwright?'

Cornet Wainwright drew himself up, doffing his steel cap in salute. 'I would not have troubled you but that Major

Disbrow is wounded. Sir, I have to report the capture of a Royalist officer, suspected of being responsible for the explosion in the church; also of Cornet Carey, taken in the act of harbouring the same.'

Fairfax seated himself without a word at the paper-scattered table, and looked long and searchingly at the three before him. There was a suggestion of triumph in Denzil Wainwright's bearing that did not seem altogether to please him, and he turned his attention to the prisoners. They were a disreputable pair, haggard with exhaustion, both wet through and mired to the eyebrows, their clothes torn and stained; one with his arm in a sling and the sleeve of his doublet hanging empty, the other with dried blood clotted on his temple. But they stood before him with their heads up, and met his gaze eye to eye, as though they felt no need to be ashamed of themselves. The General was a good judge of men.

Then Amias, who had been fiddling with his sword-belt while they waited below stairs, slipped the buckle free. 'I regret that owing to my right arm being out of action, I am unable to proffer you my sword in the correct manner,' he said, and bowing with a gesture as proud as that with which his old hero, Sir Walter Raleigh, might have yielded up his sword to a captor, laid Balin on the table before General Fairfax.

The General put out a hand and touched the hilt in token of acceptance. There was an instant of silence, while still he scanned the faces of the three before him. Then, with a quiet courtesy and not at all as though he were speaking to a prisoner, he asked of Amias his name, rank and regiment.

'Amias Hannaford, Ensign of Major General Molesworth's Regiment of Foot.'

'Thank you, Ensign Hannaford. Are you responsible for setting off the powder stored in the church yonder?'

'No, sir.'

Fairfax turned to Denzil Wainwright. 'What grounds are there for making this charge against the prisoner?'

A great weariness was growing on Simon. As in a dream, he saw Denzil produce Trooper Pennithorn like a fairground conjuror producing a rabbit out of a hat. As in a dream, he

heard the trooper's story again. 'Smelled sort of singed, he did; of burned powder like, and I thought 'twas a bit queer.'

The General glanced an instant at Amias, at the rent and blackened cloth of his doublet, on the side on which the sleeve hung empty. 'If you thought it was so queer, why did you let him go?'

'He had the watchword, sir.'

'Seeing it had been used for a battle-cry, probably half the Royalist Army had it by that time,' said the General drily. 'Very good, you may go now,' and as the crestfallen trooper drew back, he turned again to Denzil. 'Have you anything to add to that?'

Denzil produced from the breast of his buff coat the length of oiled bed-cord, and laid it before the General. 'This, sir. It was in the inner pocket of the prisoner's doublet when I found him. It could be fuse, sir.'

' It could scarcely be the fuse that blew up the church.'

' No, sir, but it could have been the piece from which the fuse was cut, if you see what I mean, sir.'

' I see what you mean. Personally I would rather use a powder trail than anything as slow as this would be.' Fairfax laid down the cord, and addressed himself to Amias. ' I do not need to ask you what you were doing when you encountered Trooper Pennithorn.'

' No, sir. Getting away.'

' What did you mean by your very peculiar remarks to him? '

' I did not mean anything in particular. I'd heard the explosion, and guessed it was our magazine going up. I didn't know about our men being prisoned there—and I was glad that at least there was something of our war supplies that wouldn't fall into the hands of the King's enemies.'

' Good,' nodded Fairfax. ' How did you come to have these obvious marks of an explosion on you? '

' Somebody's musket blew up,' Amias said, and his voice was bitter. ' It must have been a very old musket, ill-cared for, I suppose. The King's Army, you doubtless know, has been running very short of such things for a long while past.'

General Fairfax leaned forward to touch the length of cord, his bright dark eyes fixed on the other's face. ' This is bed-cord, oiled to serve as emergency slow-match. But you are not a musketeer, and so you had no need of slow-match. How did you come to have this in your pocket? '

A small twisted smile curved Amias's mouth. ' I used it to mend the cords of my Company's Colours. They were shot through during the assault. That cord was the first thing that came to hand to mend them, when there was a lull. Later on, when I cut the Colours from their pike for—bringing away, I suppose I stuffed the cord into my pocket without thinking.'

' You had the Colours with you, then, when you encountered the trooper yonder? '

' Naturally, sir. I should scarcely be leaving without them.'

' No,' said Fairfax, consideringly. ' No, I imagine not. What did you do with them afterwards? '

'I hid them.'

'Where?'

'I regret, sir, I have forgotten.'

Fairfax nodded. 'You realize that you have given me no proof of all this? If you could remember where you had hidden the Colours, and they proved to have the cords shot through, it would at least bear out part of your story.'

'I regret, sir, I think it—most unlikely that I shall remember.'

'So do I,' agreed General Fairfax. Then he raised his voice quickly. 'Orderly, a chair for the prisoner.'

For Amias had suddenly begun to sway on his feet, and his eyes looked blind in the candlelight. A chair was brought, and he crumpled slowly into it, and sat there with drooping head. 'I beg your—excuse, sir—a little weak,' he mumbled.

The General left him to recover himself, and turned his attention to Simon's share in the business. 'Cornet Wainwright, I should like now to hear your grounds for the charge you have made against Cornet Carey, and also, as a matter of general interest, how you came to hunt him down.'

Still in his dreamy state, Simon heard Denzil's voice, a little flurried now. 'Well, sir, when we first heard Trooper Pennithorn's story, Carey looked—odd—as though he guessed who the man was. Then at about seven o'clock this evening, as I was passing through the Square, I saw him clearly in the light of a lantern, talking very urgently to the local doctor, who has been helping tend the wounded.'

Simon heard the story in snatches, with foggy blanks between. 'Thought he looked as if he was up to something, so I followed him . . . doubled back while he was in the Doctor's house, and got a few men together . . . We picked up his trail when he left the garden with the Doctor . . . lost him twice in the woods, but . . .'

Presently he found that the recital was over, and Fairfax had turned on him a very bleak face. 'Cornet Carey, there is no point in my asking you whether or not you are guilty of the charge, since you have been taken in the act.'

Simon struggled desperately to clear his foggy wits. 'No, sir.'

'You know the Articles of War.'

229

' " No man shall harbour the enemy, under penalty of death ",'
said Simon, steadily.

' Have you anything to say to me in your own defence?'

' No, sir,' said Simon again.

Amias suddenly raised his head. 'He always got me out of
scrapes in the old days, and it became a habit.'

' A dangerous habit, seemingly,' said Fairfax; but all at once
there was the hint of a smile in his eyes. 'I take it that you two
are friends of long standing?'

' Yes, sir,' said both together.

General Fairfax made an abrupt movement in his chair, and
reached for the embroidered bell-pull beside the hearth. ' This
matter of the magazine will of course have to be gone into in the
normal way. Personally, Ensign Hannaford, I am inclined to
accept your story; but it is for the Court of Inquiry to decide,
and in the meantime you will understand that I must give orders
for your close confinement. As for you, Cornet Carey——'

But the sentence was never finished, for at that moment the
door opened to let in an orderly sergeant with an urgent message.

' Beg your pardon, sir,' said the orderly sergeant, saluting.

' Yes, Sergeant?'

' One of the wounded as was dug out of the church last night
has come to hisself, sir. Says he knows how it come to be
blowed up, sir.'

' *Does* he?' said General Fairfax. 'Very good, Sergeant; I'll
be along shortly.'

' Beg pardon, sir, the Doctor says he can't last many minutes.'

# XX

## *The Call Home Comes for Ishmael*

FAIRFAX got up, reaching for his sword, which hung from the chair back. ' It seems that this may alter the complexion of certain matters we have been discussing,' he said, as he belted it on. ' Cornet Carey, you had better come with me, since your friend, whom it chiefly concerns, is in no state to do so,' and he turned to the door, asking of the sergeant as he passed out to the stairhead, ' Where is the man? '

' Only in the long parlour, below stairs, sir.'

Close behind the General, and with the strange dreaminess coming between him and his own feet, so that he had to walk carefully, Simon went downstairs and turned into the long inner room, where the furniture had been pushed aside, and wounded men were bedded down in duffle blankets all over the sanded floor. A horn lantern hung from the rafters and under it, his Bible held so that the light fell on the pages, stood Chaplain Joshua Sprigg, his black gown and Geneva bands sadly rumpled, for he had been working among the wounded since the previous night. He was reading aloud as they entered, his voice filling the crowded room.

' " I have smitten you with blasting and mildew. I have sent among you the pestilence after the manner of Egypt. Your young men have I slain with the sword, and have taken away your horses, and I have made the stink of your camp to come up unto your nostrils. Yet have ye not returned unto me, saith the Lord." '

Not a yard off, quite undisturbed by his thunderings, Mother Trimble sat on her immense haunches, tenderly spooning broth into a wounded Royalist. Friend or foe meant little to Mother Trimble, if he were but hurt or sick.

At the far end of the room, Dr Hannaford was bending over one of the blanket-muffled figures, which lay very still.

Behind Fairfax Simon made his way towards him, and found himself looking down at Zeal-for-the-Lord. Zeal-for-the-Lord, not much marked by the explosion, but most cruelly changed by the months before it that had turned his hair from black to white. Meeting him only in the dark, for the light of the shielded lantern had never reached his face, Simon had not realized the change in him, and it was a few moments before he knew him. Then the dreaminess that had seemed to clog his brain burst like a pricked bubble, and everything became very real again, with clear hard edges. He saw that General Fairfax had not recognized the man at all; there was no particular reason why he should. In the same instant he saw the appeal—no, it was a command—in the eyes of his old Corporal, fixed on his, and he did not betray him.

'You're almost too late,' the Doctor muttered.

Fairfax bent over the still figure, saying quietly, 'You know what caused the explosion in the powder magazine?'

Zeal did not answer at once. It seemed as though his clear command to Simon had taken all the life that was left in him. 'We made a clatter getting down from—the bell-tower. The Guard—came in on us,' he said at last, in a harsh whisper, so faint that it was hard to catch his words. 'Slow-matches alight, and there—must have been—loose powder.'

The dry whisper trailed into silence; and for a few moments Sir Thomas Fairfax stood looking down at the dying man, with the look of someone trying to lay hold of a half memory. 'What is your name?' he asked.

A shadowy smile fluttered for an instant on the other's cracked mouth. 'Ishmael Watts.'

'Watts,' said the chaplain, who had closed his Bible and joined the group. 'And a desperate villain, sir, by the look of things.'

'We do not know that,' said Fairfax. Then, very slowly and clearly, 'What were you doing, above the magazine?'

No answer.

Joshua Sprigg, convinced that he had to deal with a villain, and bent on bringing him to repentance, far more than on finding out the cause of the explosion, had dropped on his knees beside him. 'Sinner!' he thundered. 'Through you, two hundred souls have gone untimely to their Maker!'

'A heavy harvest from—a small sowing.'

'Sowing? What sowing do you speak of?'

Zeal's lips were scarcely moving. 'Thirty pounds, all in silver,' he said. 'And a white—just thirty pounds.'

'O vile and wretched man——' began Joshua Sprigg.

Dr Hannaford looked round with the beginning of an angry protest; but Zeal-for-the-Lord was beyond any reviling now. He turned his face to Simon's, and it was peaceful as the boy had seen it only once before, on that spring day beside the river, when he had talked of his little holding and the breeding of flamed and feathered tulips. He stretched himself out with a long quiet sigh, as though he were very weary. And Simon knew that, in this world, it was all over for his old Corporal.

'Poor devil,' said Dr Hannaford; and got up, dusting the sand from his knees.

'A most hideous mishap,' said Fairfax.

The chaplain turned to him in surprise. 'You believe that cock-and-bull story, Sir Thomas?'

'I don't know,' said the General. 'I don't know.'

'You'll notice he refused to say what he was doing in the magazine, at all?'

'In the bell-tower above it, rather. He may have been hiding for some cause. Does it matter, now?'

'Would any sane man hide over a powder-store? For my part, I believe him to have been some rogue left behind by the Man of Wrath, Hopton, to destroy the magazine. The thirty pounds were obviously his fee for doing it.'

'Joshua, Joshua, men risk their lives for many things, but would you or I, or any sane man face almost certain death for a fee that we should not have the spending of? There is some mystery about all this, that we shall not find the answer to.'

Simon said nothing. That was the one last thing he could do for Zeal, to obey him, and say nothing. The old Ironside had paid his debt, and the fact that it had all been in vain could not alter that. He had made peace with his own hard unbending conscience in his own way, and it was not for Simon to meddle.

Fairfax had turned to leave the room, and Simon, once more following him, missed the anxious question in Dr Hannaford's eyes, and blundered against the doorpost as he passed, because he was not seeing very clearly. For the first time since he was nine, years old, when his dog died, he was crying; crying for an unknown man called Ishmael Watts, who had once been Corporal Zeal-for-the-Lord Relf, of the General's Horse, and erstwhile of Cromwell's 'Lovely Company'.

He shook his head angrily to clear his sight as they remounted the stairs and turned once again into the panelled parlour. Cornet Wainwright, who had been leaning against the table, straightened hurriedly as the General entered; while at the same moment Amias got unsteadily to his feet.

General Fairfax crossed to the hearth and stood looking down into the flames, frowning a little; then he seemed to make up his mind and turned to face the three pairs of eyes fixed on him. 'Ensign Hannaford,' he said, 'it seems that the matter of the magazine explosion is closed. You are no longer under suspicion.'

'I'm—relieved to hear it, sir.'

'Tomorrow I shall offer to take into the New Model Army any of the Royalist prisoners who care to change their allegiance. Quite a large number will probably accept.'

'Those who do will do no credit to their new Colours,' said Amias.

'Privately, I am inclined to agree with you; but like the Centurion, "I also am a man under authority". I am not going to make the offer to you, because I think you would refuse it.'

'I should.'

'Instead, I am going to release you on parole into your father's care. I take it that Dr Hannaford now tending the wounded below stairs *is* your father?'

'Yes.'

'Very well. Then I suggest you join him. He will be anxious about you.'

Amias stared at him for an instant, then drew himself up. 'Sir,' he said, as though to his own Commander, and turned to the door.

Fairfax halted him. 'You are forgetting your sword.'

Amias looked from the dark scarred face of the Parliament

General to the long rapier on the table, and back again. ' You're —you're going to let me have it back?' he stuttered, quite forgetting his formal manner.

' I do not release a man on parole and keep his sword.'

' I——' began Amias, and broke off. He picked up Balin, and made for the door once more. The orderly who had been half his guard opened it for him. But on the threshold, Fairfax halted him again.

' Oh, and Ensign Hannaford, touching the matter of your Company Colours.'

' Yes, sir.'

' It is of course your duty to keep them out of enemy hands; and while I naturally regret that you have so completely forgotten where you hid them, I don't quarrel with any man for carrying out his duty.'

Amias grinned from ear to ear, and suddenly his eyes were dancing in his grey face. ' Thank you, sir,' he said, and disappeared unsteadily into the passage.

When the door had closed behind Amias and the orderly, Fairfax turned to the two who remained. ' Cornet Wainwright, your conduct in this affair has been most praiseworthy, if perhaps —somewhat over-zealous.'

Denzil flushed crimson. ' Sir?' he said.

And Simon noticed that the General's eyes were uncomfortably deep-seeing.

' A few weeks ago,' said Fairfax, ' there was, I believe—I ask no questions—a trifle of unpleasantness in Mess one night.'

' That wasn't my doing, sir,' said Denzil deliberately.

A shadow of distaste crossed Fairfax's face, and he was silent a moment, as though waiting for Simon to speak; but Simon said nothing, and he went on: ' I do not ask whose doing it was. I merely say, there was a trifle of unpleasantness—and now this. Gentlemen, we are at war, and it is no time for schoolboy games of tit-for-tat. I say this to both of you: *I will not have feuds among my officers.*'

' No, sir,' said Denzil.

' No, sir,' said Simon.

' Very well. Good night, Wainwright.'

The crimson flush had drained away from Denzil's face, and he was almost as white as Simon had been on the night Fairfax had just spoken of. 'Good night, sir,' he said, and stalked from the room.

The door closed again, and Simon was alone with his General. He had begun to hope a little, in the last few minutes, but as he met Fairfax's bright compelling gaze, he braced himself for what might still be coming. 'So, Carey, we now have only your part in all this to bring to a satisfactory conclusion.'

'Yes, sir.' Simon met his gaze steadily, but his mouth felt dry.

'Do you remember the Covenant that you took when you became an officer of this Regiment?'

Simon said, 'I do, sir.'

'Yet you forgot it, today,' said Fairfax, in a quiet voice that fell like splintered ice into the silence. 'What am I to do with one of my officers who forgets his duty to the cause he serves, for the sake of a private friendship?'

Simon said nothing. There seemed nothing to say. The silence dragged on, while, facing the cold accusation in the General's eyes, he had time to think of all the things that Fairfax intended him to think of. Those moments were some of the worst that he had ever known.

Suddenly and most surprisingly, the General's dark harsh face lit into his rare smile. 'I shan't hang you, this time,' he said.

'No, sir,' said Simon, standing rigidly to attention.

The General made a small gesture of finish, with his open palms on the back of the chair. 'In fact, I suggest that we consider this matter closed. Go back to your quarters, get yourself a meal, and turn in. You must make your own peace with the Regiment.'

Simon drew a quick deep breath, dizzy with relief. 'I'm— I'm to return to the Regiment, sir? I mean—you're not going to——' His voice stumbled away into silence.

'Since we enlisted the South Devon levies we have scarcely enough officers to go round. We certainly cannot afford to hang or cashier any of them. Furthermore, though it is no shadow of an excuse, I do not suppose you are the first to act as you did today, since Jonathan stole out the of King's Camp to

236

comfort David in the wilderness of Ziph.' Fairfax was gazing down into the red heart of the fire, as he spoke. After a moment he added, ' If the fortunes of war had gone otherwise, I might have sorely needed a friend to forget his duty for me. Pray God I should have found such a one.'

There was a little silence, and then he turned back to his chair beside the littered table. ' Good night, Carey.'

' Good night, sir,' Simon said fervently. ' And thank you, sir.'

And somehow he got himself out on to the stairhead.

The fog inside his head was gathering thick and fast again, as he stumbled downstairs into the taproom on his way to the street door; and it was a few moments before he realized that the voice shouting after him ' Simon ! *Simon* !' meant himself, and that it was Amias's voice. Then the fog cleared a little, and looking round, he saw Amias wrapped in a blanket lying on the deep settle beside the fire; Amias straining up on one elbow to look after him with very anxious eyes.

' Amias !' he exclaimed, and was across the room to his side on the instant, heedless of the soldiers who glanced at him curiously as he passed. ' I thought you'd have gone home by now.'

' I'm to stay here for the night. Father and a long-legged Scotsman who came in just now have decided it between them. But anyway, I couldn't have gone home till I knew how things went with you.'

' My orders are to go back to my quarters, get a meal and turn in,' Simon told him.

' Not a stain on your good Roundhead character? '

Simon considered. ' I don't think so. No, not a stain,' he said.

' A great man, your General.'

' Yes,' said Simon.

Amias dropped flat on his back, and thrust his free hand out from the blanket. ' Oh, curse you, Simon, you're the best friend a graceless numskull like me ever had,' he said ruefully.

Simon shook the hand warmly. ' You'll not be feeling so humble when your shoulder stops hurting.'

'Of course not,' Amias grinned. 'Who did blow up the church?'

'Oh, it was an accident—a stupid accident. Your father knows the story. Look, old lad, I've got to be marching. See you again when——' He broke off. He had almost said, ' when the war is over ', but that was not a thing you could say to a friend on the losing side.

A sudden gust of wind, higher than any that had gone before, dashed the rain against the broken shutters and swooped rumbling down the chimney, driving a stinging cloud of smoke into the room. When it cleared, the two were still looking at each other, with no trace of laughter left between them.

'When the war is over; that's what you were going to say, isn't it?' Amias said. 'That won't be long now. The King's cause is finished; the Army is a rabble.' Suddenly his voice cracked a little. 'We had such high hopes.'

There did not seem to be anything that Simon could say. He touched Amias's sound shoulder for an instant, a poor sort of comfort, but it was the best he could do and Amias would understand. Then he turned away. Old Davey Morrison was at work in the next room, and softly whistling his one tune as he cleaned instruments. Passing the open door, Simon caught the slow-falling melody; and it seemed to him that the ' Flowers of the Forest ' was a lament, not for Flodden alone, but for all lost causes since the world began; for all lost causes, and for all broken men, even for Zeal-for-the-Lord.

Then he went out past the sentries into the wild February night, hunching his shoulders against the driving rain, with only one thought left in him, that soon he would be able to lie down and sleep.

Next day Cromwell returned with his squadrons from Wood-ford, and that afternoon, it being Sunday, Pastor Hugh Peters preached a thanksgiving sermon to the assembled Army from a balcony in the Square. And Simon, still rather gummy-eyed and unsteady on his feet, was back with his Troop, carrying the gay silken Standard that stirred like a great flower-petal in the light February wind.

That day almost half of the Royalist prisoners accepted Fairfax's offer, and enlisted in the New Model Army; and the remainder he discharged, each man with two shillings to get him to his own home.

Eight Colours and Standards had been taken, among them Lord Hopton's own, with its scroll bearing the words, ' I will strive to save my Sovereign King ', and several bare pikes, broken across, from which the Colours had been stripped by the men who carried them back into Cornwall to the last rally of a lost cause. But the stained and shot-torn Colours of Amias's Company remained undisturbed in their foxhole, which chanced to be a deserted one; and the spring rains washed it into the ground, and next autumn a squirrel made a store in the folds, and then, after the way of squirrels, forgot the place. One of the nuts sprouted and took root, and presently there was a fine hazel sapling growing through the old Royalist Colours.

During the five days that the Army remained in Torrington, Simon worried ceaselessly about his report to Major Watson. He would have to tell the truth, and he would have at the same time to keep faith with his old Corporal, and he did not quite see how he was going to do both. But he was never called on to make that report at all. Major Watson's methods were rough and ready : if the job was done, he seldom asked for details afterwards. He did make a few inquiries about his missing scout, and pieced together the facts that he had been taken as a spy, and had escaped; and when the man did not return to duty, he simply assumed that he had got tired of the service—not at all an unusual thing to happen among the scouts.

During that time, also, Simon had to make his peace with the Regiment, as Fairfax had said; for the whole story was public property within a few hours. But he did not have very much difficulty. Denzil, on the other hand, had rather a lot. The General's Own felt a good deal more sympathy with a man who had risked everything to stand by a friend in the wrong camp, than they did with one who, out of malice, had seized quite so zealously on the chance to break a brother-in-arms. Denzil, who had spent so much time and care in trying to make life unpleasant for Simon, now found himself cold-shouldered, and, worse still, slightly ridiculous.   Within a few weeks he obtained a transfer to another regiment; and the General's Own did not grieve to see him go.

But that was still in the future when Fairfax marched his troops west once more, in drenching rain that had turned the deep lanes to running torrents.

At Stratton, Lord Hopton had been rejoined by the shreds of his Army, but judging it useless to try to hold a place so near the Devon border, he retreated to Truro.   There, he would have made a last stand, but his ragged troops were beyond any more fighting, and at Truro, on a gleamy March day, he laid down his arms.   The Prince of Wales had already fled to the Scillies on his way to France, and Lord Hopton, refusing the offer of a Command in the Parliamentary Army which was accepted by many of his officers, followed him overseas, a very faithful servant.   Simon watched him board the ship which was to take him into exile, and wondered whether Prince Charles, who seemed by all accounts to be a wild and rather unpleasant youth, deserved the loyalty of such a man.

Exeter fell, and then Newark.   By early May nothing was left to the King but Oxford, and he, vainly trusting in the Scots as his last hope, had already slipped out of the city, and was heading northward in disguise, with his little beard shaved off.

For six weeks the New Model sat down before Oxford, and then it too was forced to yield.   On Midsummer's day, with the trees in young leaf against a milky sky, Simon watched the Garrison march out with full honours of war: drums beating, colours flying, slow-matches lit.   Last of all, Prince Rupert and his companions rode out over Magdalen Bridge, with the sun bright on their cuirasses; fluttering cloaks, fine laces, and tossing feathers that had mostly seen better days, still brilliant against the tender green of the trees; and the fretted grace of Magdalen Tower rising over all.   A scene as richly beautiful as a page from some old missal, limned in gold and lapiz-lazuli to the Glory of God.   And underneath, the bitterness of defeat.

The Civil War was over.

## XXI

## *After Many Days*

O N an April evening, Simon and Amias came up through
the lower spinney. They had been busy most of the day
dyking up the bank of the Jewel Water where the spring
rains had torn it away, and they were tired and contented.
Joram, Jillot's last-born, trotted at Simon's heels, dripping wet and
also contented, for Joram loved water, and he loved Simon, and
all day long he had had both of them.

It was more than a year since the bitter January morning when
the King had stepped out from the window of his banqueting
hall on to the waiting scaffold; more than four since the battle of
Torrington; but the two friends had seen very little of each other
in all that time.

Simon had remained with his Regiment after the fall of Oxford, and when the King from his "honourable confinement" had contrived to stir up the war again, he was at the storming of Maidstone, and was promoted Lieutenant; but he held his new rank only a few months.   Then Parliament had decided that it was hopeless to treat with Charles any longer, since he obviously did not understand treaties, and would go on making trouble as long as he lived.   For the welfare of England, the King must die. Cromwell and most of the Army leaders were of the same mind, but not Sir Thomas Fairfax.   Simon's General had gone to war because he loved justice and freedom, and felt it to be his duty. But the execution of the King, he said, was not his duty; it was not justice but only expediency, and he would have nothing to do with it.   He refused to sign Charles's death-warrant, knowing that the refusal would cost him his Army Command; and when he gave up his commission, many of his officers did the same, amongst them, Simon.

So Simon had returned to take over the Mastery of Lovacott, for that was what it amounted to.   His father had finally returned home late in the summer that ended the war, and with old Diggory to help him, had contrived to keep the farm and the Manor going, without quite enough men or quite enough money, as so many farmers and landowners were doing in the lean years after the war.   But it had been gruelling work for a rather sick man lacking a leg; and when Simon came home, he had thankfully given the reins of government into the young man's hands.   They were still "the Maister" and "the Young Maister"; John Carey was there for Simon to turn to for advice, for counsel, out of his experience of land and men and cattle that Simon had not yet had time to gain; but none the less, it was Simon now to whom the farmhands came for orders, and who decided what crop should be sown in Sanctuary, whether a villager's pigsty really needed rebuilding, and when a new team of plough oxen should be bought.

For Amias, the story had been quieter.   He had been unpleasantly ill after the battle of Torrington, and by the time his wound was healed and he was fit for service again, the war was over.   So he had become apprenticed to his father, as both of them had always intended.   When the King's Standards were raised once more, he had answered the call, but the rebellion had flickered out almost before it touched the West Country, and Amias had gone back to his father's surgery. By the time Simon had returned to Lovacott, Amias was away in London, taking instruction at St Bartholomew's Hospital; and only a few days since, he had come home to finish his apprenticeship and settle down, as he said, into a staid and respectable country surgeon. Not that he showed the least signs of becoming either staid or respectable at the moment, mooning contentedly through the hazel-scrub, with his red hair wildly on end and his ancient green doublet split at one shoulder from a misadventure with a sharp alder root.

The lower spinney was hazed with green, and full of the wing-flitter of nesting birds; primroses and wind-flowers held up small clean faces among the fern and brambles, and away over open country the curlews were crying. Amias sniffed the springtime smell of wet moss and green things growing, flinging up his head like a colt into the light west wind. ' Listen to the curlews! I've not heard a curlew calling for a whole year; and, by heaven, I have been hungry for that bubbly call of theirs! '

They had come out from the woodshore, as he spoke, on to the steep grass verge of the lane, and suddenly he checked. 'Hullo, who have we here?' For a solitary wayfarer had appeared at that moment, loping along from the direction of the village. He wore loose-fitting faded clothes with a smack of the sea about them, and on his head a red seaman's bonnet. Simon did not know any seamen, yet there was something familiar about this one.

' What on earth is a sailor doing, so far from the beaten track? ' Amias said.

But Simon was not listening. ' Good Lord! It's Podbury! ' he exclaimed, and dropped into the lane, calling, ' Podbury! Hi! '

' Long-lost relation? ' inquired Amias, following; but got no answer.

The seaman quickened his pace at sight of Simon, and came up with a broad smile splitting his rogue's countenance in two. 'Why, if 'tisn't Cornet Carey! I been asking for you in the village. 'Tisn't so easy to find your place from this side.'

Simon said in bewilderment, 'I thought you were killed when the powder store went up, four years back.'

'Not me, sir; just come from Bideford, I have, and afore that from Jamestown in the New World. I'm a honest seaman now, ye sees.'

'Yes, I can see that. What happened in the church? What really set off the powder? How did you escape?'

'Nay now, sir, 'tis all ancient history by this time.'

'Maybe,' said Simon. 'But the man who was with you in hiding was a friend of mine. He died of his wounds, without being able to tell us much, and I want to know that ancient history.'

'You'll be meaning Ishmael Watts?' inquired Podbury.

'Yes.'

'Now I'll tell you what, sir'—in the tone of one trying to oblige a friend—' I'll tell you all I knows, honest and above board; but I didn't come here for that. I comes here because I says to meself, "Benjamin Podbury, here you are, just landed on your native soil, and here's Cornet Carey as would be pained to think as you'd gone your way, with no soles to your shoes, so to speak, and never come a-nigh him for to allow him to assist you. And 'oo are you to pain Cornet Carey, as is a old comrade of yours?" So here I am, and——'

'Is it work you want?' Simon interrupted.

'Work? Lor' no, sir. I did think to turn thimble-rigger again, but fairs and suchlike is out of favour now, it seems, and consequently don't pay like they used; so I'm on my way to Plymouth to pick up another ship; but I thinks to meself that for the sake of days gone by, and comrades in arms, and so on, you might feel disposed to help a deserving object on me way.'

'I'll give you what I can. In these days we none of us have much to spare.'

'Bless you, sir, I know that. I'm a reasonable man, and not one to hold it agin a comrade that his pockets ain't so well lined as I could wish,' Podbury assured him kindly. 'You throw a square meal in with it, and there'll be no ill-feeling, I do assure you. And speaking of square meals, s'pose we goes and gets this one now, and I'll tell you what you wants to know as we goes along.'

Simon realized that they had been standing stock-still in the middle of the lane all this time, while Amias and Joram looked on, and a little red heifer, with her head thrust through the hedge, peered down at them with soft long-lashed eyes.

' Come on,' he said. ' Down the wagon-lane yonder.'

' Well, now,' said Podbury, as, with Amias strolling a few paces behind, they turned into the narrow track. ' Ask away, sir. '

' I want to know what happened from the time Watts hid you above the powder store.'

' Well now, for a while nothing happened, and precious cold quarters 'twas up there too, and me bruised and basted all over and scarce able to move, and never daring to groan or sneeze for fear of being overheard, and the hard-tack going green and not too much of it. (Not as I means to complain, mind you, sir; real grateful I was to that cove, even if he did look a sight too like the prophet Isaiah for my taste.) Then things must o' got too hot for him, and he nips in past the guard in a snow-flurry one night with a sack of biscuit and " Benjamin ", says he, " don't neither of us stir out of this place again till you're fit to run the gauntlet or the New Model arrives ", he says. And there we was.'

' What then ? ' demanded Simon.

' I'm a-telling you, ain't I? There we was, three days, maybe, till we decided to make a dash for it after the next nightfall. I was pretty well mended by that time, as right as a cove could be in such a doghole, on mouldy biscuit. But about dusk we hears a great to-do in the town, drums beating to action quarters and such like; then a lot of coves comes into the foot of the tower and starts taking out some of the powder, and presently we hears the rattle of musketry. " 'Tis Fairfax at the gates," says Watts. " Now let us forth and smite the Amalekites," says he, and then we finds as some fool has took away the ladder ! We couldn't pull it up after us, ye sees, 'cos that would have been sure to make some suspicious-minded cove get ideas in his head. Well, 'twas a long drop from the ringing-chamber, and no knowing how we might land in the dark, and I were still a bit weakly; so we decided to wait a bit, afore risking a pair of broken necks, hoping as the church'd fall into the hands of our own men, by and by. The fighting comes nearer, and presently 'tis all around us, and then it seems to pass on a bit, and we hears a mortal lot of men being herded into the church like as they might be prisoners; but with only a li'l slit window to squint through, and the thick walls and all, we can't make out no details, nor whose hands the church is in, nor nothing, which aren't a comfortable thing, seeing as how we're sitting on dunno how many kegs of gunpowder like a hen on addled eggs.

' " I'm getting out o' this," I says. " I'd sooner break me neck than be blowed to flinders." Watts says to me not to be a fool, and makes a grab at me in the dark, but I leaves me coat in his hands and drops down through the hole where the ladder should 'a been, like a pea into a thimble. As ill luck will have it, I lands all a-sprawl, with enough noise to rouse old Davy Jones hisself; and next instant the li'l door in the churchyard flies open, and a whole lot of nosy rogues comes busting in, *with* their slow-matches well alight too, and then Ishmael Watts lands on top of me, hollering, " Get out, you fools! 'ware powder! " But whether they never takes it in, or what . . . Howsomever, I wriggles clear and finds meself near the door, so I ducks under a cove's arm, and runs for it; (wonderful how easy a cove forgets his bruises in a emergency!). And afore I'd run twenty yards the whole place goes up behind me like a catherine wheel. I comes to, after a bit, and I'd had a fair sickener of this spying lay, and I says to meself, " Benjamin Podbury, with your record, you ain't going to be none too popular with those in authority, and the sooner you slings your hook out of here the better ", so I slings it.'

They had almost reached the house by now, and Podbury looked about him with an approving eye. ' 'Tis a'most enough to make a cove turn respectable,' he said. ' You said Ishmael Watts was killed? I allus thought he must have been. Well, he were a gloomy sort; didn't seem to get much pleasure out o' life.'

Simon, who had listened in silence to this recital, felt a hot rush of anger. ' At least he saved yours, and lost his own thereby,' he said furiously, as they turned in through the farm buildings.

246

'Ah, so he did,' agreed Podbury. 'I'd have been hanged, but for Ishmael, and *I* gets a deal of pleasure out o' life.' And he sniffed loudly at the savoury smell that was floating out from the kitchen.

Simon handed him over to Phoebe and left him deep in mutton pasty, with Amias a-sprawl in the deep window-seat looking on with a kind of distasteful interest; while he went upstairs and got out the money with which he had meant to buy a new saddle. He knew quite well that Podbury was not a deserving object, but it was not for Podbury's sake that he would do without the saddle: it was for Zeal's. It was a kind of thank-offering, because he knew now for a certainty that although the whole black business had indeed sprung from that long-ago betrayal and Zeal's wild questing after revenge, yet it was Podbury's blunder and not any fault of Zeal's that had brought the last hideous tragedy on the church and its prisoners. Zeal-for-the-Lord had kept the Faith in his own way, and Simon tipped the jingling coins into the palm of his hand.

He did not go downstairs again at once, but strolled in to see his father, who was having a bad day. In four years, Simon's father had learned to do without his left leg quite well. On good days he hobbled about the farmstead and demesne, generally with Jillot, who was growing old, at his heel; the same rather stern, quiet figure that he had always been, quite unchanged save for his long crutch and for certain lines about his mouth that had not been there when he rode out to join the forces of Parliament. He would never ride again, but he took an expert's interest in Simon's horses, and would spend hours leaning on a gate to watch Simon and Tom breaking a colt, with cold light grey eyes that took in every point and detail, every least success or failure, and sometimes made Tom feel that his fingers were all thumbs, though they never seemed to worry Simon. But the four-years-past explosion had played havoc with the nerves and muscles of his maimed side, and from time to time there would be a bad day, or several, when the old wounds throbbed almost unbearably and every movement twinged to the quick, and there was nothing for John Carey to do but lie still and wait until the pain died down again. He was doing that now, lying very long and flat under

247

the tumbled blankets and staring out of the window to the blue beyond; but he turned his head when Simon came in. 'Ah, Simon, how is the Jewel Water?'

'We'll have to plant willows down there in the autumn to bind up the bank,' Simon told him. 'But it's all right for the present; *and* so it should be: Amias and I have been working on it the whole day, and Joram of course. Joram is convinced he's a water spaniel.' He sat down carefully on the edge of the bed. If one sat down carefully, it was all right, but if one sat down with a jolt, it hurt. His father had never said so, but Simon knew. He knew rather a lot about his father by that time. 'How is it? Any easier?'

'Unpleasant, but less unpleasant than an hour or two ago. I'll be a sound man again in the morning. In fact, I'd make a push for it and come down to supper, but that it would worry your mother.'

They smiled at each other in perfect understanding. Simon's mother might remain unruffled when a rick caught fire or Civil War broke out, but where Simon's father was concerned she was a hen with one chicken. She took the greatest care not to let him know it, but there was one infallible sign which always told her family when she was anxious.

'Nice Nourishing Broth,' said Simon softly.

The smile deepened in his father's eyes. 'Exactly. If your mother's Nice Nourishing Broth could grow me a new leg, I should be a centipede by now.'

He shifted a little, searching for an easier position, and Simon leaned forward to slip a hand under his braced shoulder and help him. 'Speaking from a purely selfish point of view, I should intensely dislike to have a centipede for a father,' he remarked. Then, as the other relaxed and lay still again, 'We've got company downstairs. An old comrade of mine, just landed at Bideford and come up " to allow me for to assist him ". They're feeding him in the kitchen now.'

Mr Carey showed no surprise. Derelict soldiers were everywhere, left behind by the war like driftwood when the tide goes out. He asked, 'One of your troopers? What are you going to do about him?'

'*Not* one of my troopers,' Simon said emphatically. 'And I'm going to give him some money—more than I can afford—and bid him a very good day.'

His father's brows lifted for a moment in cool inquiry, and Simon shook his head quickly. 'No, he doesn't want work. Steady employment and Benjamin Podbury don't mix very well. He's been a lawyer's clerk, and a fairground thimble-rigger; he was one of our scouts when I ran up against him, and the only evening I ever passed in his company, he spent in cheating a trooper of Grenville's out of one and ninepence with loaded dice. He tells me he is now an honest seaman, so I should think that if he hasn't yet turned pirate he'll do it on his next voyage.'

'What remarkably odd company you seem to have kept in your soldiering days,' said Mr Carey with amusement. 'If this specimen is as plausible as your account of him would suggest, it appears to me that you had best pay him off before your mother finds him and gives him everything we possess.'

Simon got up, grinning. 'Maybe you're right.' He half turned to the door, then back again. 'Job Passmore's coming up tomorrow to start re-thatching the cow byres. Look, sir, when you're feeling up to it, will you come and inspect the linhay? Diggory says it ought to be re-thatched too, and he can't abear to have the place looking such a proper mucksey-pie; but the thatch seems to me sound enough to last another year—and anyhow we honestly can't afford to have it done now, so soon after the new plough oxen.'

'You told him that?'

'Ye—es, but he only muttered darkly.'

'Diggory, alas! still lives in the spacious days before the war,' said his father. 'It's hard for old men and old dogs to alter their ideas.'

'That's why I think he'd take it better from you, than from me—if you agree with me about the thatch, when you've had a look at it that is.'

'More than likely. And I have not the slightest doubt that I shall agree with you about the thatch ... So be it then; I'll come and act as reinforcement for the routing of Diggory in the morning, but you will probably have to give me an arm.'

'Thank you, sir. That is good of you.' Simon hesitated, looking down at him. 'It's really better?'

'It is,' said John Carey. 'Go and look to your disreputable friend.'

Simon was satisfied. He was the one person in the world whom his father honoured with the absolute truth on such occasions, and he knew it.

Podbury had begun on his third pasty and was deep in a great leather-jack of cider. Joram was sitting bolt upright in a corner, with his back turned on the interloper and disapproval in every line of him from his feathery topknot to the last long hair at the end of his tail; but Jillot, a shameless beggar, sat at Podbury's feet, quivering nose upraised and mournful eyes fixed on what remained of the pasty.

'That,' drawled Amias from the window seat, 'makes two of them. Different methods, but——' He broke off to watch a piece of pasty disappear down Jillot's throat, '' 'zackly the same result.'

'Nay, now, young sir, you'd not grudge a trifle to a man as has fought for his country?' said Podbury, pained, but with his mouth full.

Amias's only reply was a sniff.

'Here you are,' said Simon, giving the money into the ready hand which came out for it. 'It's maybe less than you hoped for, but 'tis all I've got.'

Podbury examined the coins, nodded, spat regretfully and put them in his pouch. 'Ah well, it might be worse. No need to fret yourself about it.'

'I wasn't,' said Simon, with the ghost of a grin.

Amias lounged up from the seat, stretching. 'It's too fine an evening to waste indoors. Come on, Simon, let's go and be lazy in the high orchard until supper-time.'

'Just coming.' Simon turned back for an instant to the old scout. 'Good luck and fair winds, Podbury. I hope you'll never be hanged.'

'Thank 'ee, sir; much obleeged, I'm sure!' said Podbury, beaming.

They left him still eating, with Jillot cuddled on his feet, the

250

centre of a half-admiring, half-disapproving group made up of Phoebe and the maids. Joram came with them. A few minutes later, with the dog between them, they were sprawling at their ease in the high orchard, where the new young cider trees, planted to replace those cut down by Grenville's troopers, were putting out the first hesitant blossom of their lives.

'I do not,' said Amias, peering down between the young trees at the quiet huddle of house and outbuildings below, 'no, I do *not* find myself drawn to your old comrade.'

Simon grunted, his nose in the long cool orchard grass. 'Anyhow, he told me what I've wanted to know for four years.'

'About the magazine going up, you mean, and that fellow Watts?'

'M'm.'

Amias screwed round. 'Why were you so interested in him— the other man? Who was he?'

'My old Corporal,' Simon said.

'Your—but what on earth was he doing there? What was Podbury doing there, for that matter? Look here, what *is* all this about?'

Simon did not answer at once, then, very quietly, his eyes on the shadow of a blossoming apple spray among the grass, he told Amias the whole story. It was not breaking faith with Zeal to tell Amias, as it would have been to send in that report to the Army authorities. He was very sure of that.

'Poor devil,' said Amias softly, when the story was done. 'Poor crazy valiant devil.'

'He was the best Corporal a man ever had,' Simon said.

Neither of them spoke again until, a little later, they caught the glint of a red seaman's bonnet jigging down the wagon-way.

'There goes friend Podbury,' Amias said. 'Odd, to think he was the spy we ransacked Lovacott for, and you working with him all the while. I'm glad I didn't know that—about you, I mean—at the time.' He turned on his elbow to look at Simon as the full truth dawned on him. 'If I had known, I should have had to take you. You'd probably have been hanged,' he said deliberately, and then he asked, 'Simon, if it had been like that, would you have hated me?'

251

'No,' said Simon. 'It would have been just the fortune of war. I should have known that it was the only thing you could do.'

The sudden tenseness went out of Amias. 'Anyhow, I didn't know; and I hope Podbury gets a ship to suit him—no work and lots of loot.' They watched the speck of scarlet out of sight, before he spoke again; 'By the way, I fell in with Pentecost Fiddler yesterday. *He* was talking about going back to sea.'

'Pentecost going back to sea—after all these years? He can't have meant it.'

'He did, though. He said that now dancing is counted sinful, there's no place for a fiddler ashore, but he reckoned no Parliament could stop sailormen needing a fiddler aboard ship, so he was off where he was wanted, and I don't blame him. England's a dreary place, under the Commonwealth.'

'Yes, but look here,' Simon began, and broke off to get his argument straight in his own mind. 'You're a surgeon, least-wise you will be soon. You know how you deal with a man who's sick; you knock off all the things he likes doing, and make him eat plain food, and bleed him and give him black draughts; and maybe he doesn't like you while the treatment lasts. But he's all the better for it afterwards.'

'Aye, but is there going to be an "afterwards"?' Amias countered.

'Surely. This isn't—natural, somehow, not for England. One day we shall have a King again.'

'So even you admit that the Commonwealth isn't all honey?'

'Maybe,' Simon said. 'There are a lot of good things about it, though. More justice, for one thing, than ever there was under King Charles, and we're getting back our old place among the nations, the place that men like Sir Walter Raleigh won for us, and our last two Kings threw away.' It was odd, he thought suddenly, when they were boys, and the trouble between King and Parliament yet a-brewing, they had not been able to talk about it to each other; the subject had been like a sore place that is better not poked at. But now they no longer had to avoid it, they could argue and disagree if they wanted to, and it did not matter.

'Well, I still don't think much of your brave new England

without a King,' Amias was saying. 'even if we do have another King, one day. What about the old one?'

'It wasn't meant to be like that,' Simon said quickly. 'We went to war to make the King see reason, to make him understand that ordinary folk must be free to worship in their own way, and —and things like that; never to get rid of him. Something went wrong at the end.'

'Something went wrong, sure enough, and the King died for it.' Amias was plucking up grass stems with a sharp snapping sound. 'You know, I'm glad your General Fairfax stood out against the rest, and wouldn't sign the King's death-warrant.'

'He's the sort of man who'd go to the stake for what he thought was right.'

'And so he's sitting in his native Yorkshire mud, I suppose, ruling a few cottages, and a trout stream while the men who signed rule England.'

Simon laughed. 'You sound as indignant as though he had been your commander, not mine.'

'I liked your General Fairfax,' Amias said thoughtfully. 'That night when you and I were brought up before him . . . I'd sooner serve under him than any man I've ever come across—except Lord Hopton.' Abruptly, he flopped flat on his stomach, pillowing his head comfortably on his arms, and no more was heard for a while.

Joram's soft ears pricked, and he opened one eye as two girls came out through the garden close into the near corner of the paddock, where the old mare Rizpah was grazing with a foal beside her. Amias raised his head to watch them coaxing the little bright-eyed, feather-tailed creature, while its mother looked anxiously on. 'I'll wager that's the last of the long-biding apples,' he said.

'Candy sugar,' Simon said, with the glimmer of a smile. 'They keep the long-biders for Scarlet.'

Amias was watching the smaller of the two, who had turned, the foal's muzzle in the hollow of her hand, to look up at the other with an air of rather shy triumph. 'You know, I'd never have believed that whey-faced little oddity I used to catch sight of at Okeham Paine could have grown into such a happy maid.'

'Mistress Killigrew doesn't approve of happiness, so she never had much chance until she came to us,' Simon said.

'How did you win her mother over into letting her come visiting up here?'

'Oh, I don't know. Mother and Mistress Killigrew had been writing to each other for years about still-room management, and Mouse made a splendid impression when she visited them last year. Mouse can always be relied on to rise to an occasion; but you know that. And then Father and I both having fought for Parliament was a help, of course; and I think she felt that Father having lost a leg in the Cause somehow vouched for the principles of the family as a whole, though I can't myself quite follow that line of reasoning.'

'You aren't Mistress Killigrew,' said Amias. 'How was he getting on when you went upstairs just now?'

'Father? On the mend again. He says he'll be all right by the morning, and he always seems to know.'

Amias nodded. 'You'll be able to enlist his aid in this desperate business of the linhay roof, then.'

'I've already enlisted it. I have his solemn promise to come and help me rout Diggory in the morning,' said Simon, his fingers very gentle in the soft hollows behind Joram's fluttering ecstatic ears. 'Game as a pebble, the Old Man,' he added, in a tone of proud and affectionate disrespect.

The two girls had gone in again; the light was fading, and away over the western hills the sky was flushing pink behind quiet cloud-bars that were as faintly coloured as a dove's breast.

'Going to be another fine day tomorrow for the thatchers,' Simon said contentedly, after a long pause.

'I hate to dash your hopes, but it's going to rain.'

'You're mazed! Look at that pink sky!'

'I am looking. I don't care if it's scarlet with green spots; my shoulder aches, and that means a change of weather, as sure as unicorns.'

'I can't compete. My head doesn't act as a weather-vane,' Simon said, and laughed. 'What a walking hospital we are! By the way, how *is* the shoulder?'

'Pretty good, on the whole. I've had to learn to use a sword left-handed; but what's the odds? They do say a left-handed swordsman is the most deadly, anyway.' Abruptly he turned on Simon with one of his sudden bursts of enthusiasm. ' I've brought a new rapier back with me from London; no, of course I couldn't afford it, I sold most of my clothes; but wait till you *see* it! A French blade, the very latest thing; triangular, you see, supple as a withy wand and deadly as an asp. You fight with the point only. Oh, but I'll show you when we get a chance.'

' And what do you suppose a respectable country leach wants with a blade like that? ' Simon demanded lazily.

' Even a country leach might run into adventure.' Amias's eyes had begun to dance. ' My dear Simon, don't be so lacking in ideas. " Amias Hannaford, the Duelling Doctor." You take exception to the cock of a man's eyebrow, or the way he ties his collar-strings, call him out, drill him through the brisket, and then plug the hole. It might be very good for trade.'

' Zany! ' said Simon, and waited for more.

But instead they heard Mouse calling from the wicket gate. ' Simon! Amias! where are you? It's almost supper time.'

Amias cupped his hands and called back, ' Up here in the cider orchard,' and an instant later, as the two girls came out through the gate, rose to his feet and went strolling down to meet them. Simon hung back a few minutes, for the pleasure of seeing them coming up between the blossoming fruit trees; Mouse with her dark skirts caught up to show the gay murrey-striped petticoat beneath, Susanna with a knot of periwinkle tucked into the wide square collar of her grey puritan gown. Then he strode down after Amias, and the four of them came together just where the young apple trees of the high orchard met the ancient leaning ones of the lower slopes.

Susanna went at once to Simon, and Mouse to Amias, for that had become the established order. But Mouse's first words were for her brother, and they were hotly indignant. ' Simon, I don't think it was at all nice of you to tell that poor old soldier that you couldn't afford to give him anything but a mutton pasty, especially when he was an old comrade of yours! We shouldn't have known anything about it, Susanna and I, if we hadn't chanced to come out from the still-room just as he was leaving.'

'And he told you I wouldn't give him anything but a mutton pasty?'

'Oh, he wasn't complaining, you know, but I think he was a little hurt. Susanna and I gave him sixpence each, which was all we had, and he was *touchingly* grateful!'

'I'm sure he was,' said Simon.

But Amias subsided into the low branches of a quince tree, with a crow of laughter.

Mouse turned on him with raised brows. 'It appears that we amuse you,' she said.

'No, oh no.' Amias hiccoughed. 'Only—I gave him a crown, and Simon bestowed his life's savings on him. A deserving object. Oh, bless my soul.'

'Well!' began Mouse indignantly; and then she too dissolved into laughter, and Simon joined in, until, catching sight of Susanna's pointed face, grave and puzzled and a little shocked, he managed to stop himself.

'I'm sorry about your sixpence, Susanna,' he said.

'Oh, I don't mind about the sixpence,' Susanna told him. 'But—but would you say we had been encouraging that man in the Path of Wickedness?'

'Bless you, Podbury don't need no encouraging,' Amias cut in, wiping the back of his hand across his eyes, as he disentangled himself from the quince tree.

'I wouldn't say any such thing,' Simon said. 'And I'm sure he'll find your sixpence very useful.' He felt the corners of his mouth twitching, and tried desperately to straighten them, lest he should hurt Susanna's feelings.

She looked at him gravely. 'I don't always quite understand about things being funny,' she said, rather wistfully. 'I hope you don't mind. I am trying to learn.'

Simon reached out and touched her hand. 'Sukey, I'm rather a dull sort of fellow. I like you as you are,' he said, and then felt that he had not chosen his words very well.

But Susanna found nothing amiss. She did not speak. She simply went on looking at Simon.

There was some magic about the lower orchard that evening, that seemed to hold them there, though it was really time to go in to supper. Dusk was creeping through the long grass, but it had not yet risen high enough to dim the delicate radiance of the blossom starring the old knotted branches of pear and apple, quince and damson and cherry trees, and the faint cool fragrance of the apple bloom was all about them, seeming to float on the quiet twilight air. Then a little wind came soughing up the valley, bringing the scent of rabbits to flutter Joram's nose, and scattering a flurry of petals like an elfin snow-storm on to the grass.

'Supper,' said Mouse sensibly, and held out a hand to Susanna, as they turned back towards the wicket gate, with Joram dodging about in front of them. Simon and Amias dropped behind, each with a hand on the other's shoulder, as they strolled through into the garden close.

It was almost a year since Simon had returned from his soldiering, but this evening, as he entered his mother's garden, he had all at once a vivid sense of homecoming. He remembered how, in those weeks before the battle of Torrington, he had felt that he did not belong here, but was only a passage-hawk and had not yet earned his right to come home. Now, quite suddenly, it was as though Lovacott had opened its innermost door to him; the door of some secret sanctuary that he had not known existed before, swept and garnished, with a fire burning in the hearth, to welcome him home.

'Look,' Mouse called back over her shoulder, 'the jonquils mother got from Spalding are flowering beautifully this spring!'

The jonquils grew close under the parlour window, and inside the candles had been lit already, and the room was as golden as the jonquil petals. Glancing in, as they passed, Simon saw Balan hanging in its familiar place above the mantel; but now, the single blade, in its worn sheath that had been made for two, did not look lonely, any more.

'I think,' Amias was saying, beside him, 'that next time I come, I shall bring Balin back. I shan't be using it again; it's too long and heavy for the new style of sword-play, and it seems a shame to break up a case of rapiers. It will still be mine, of course, but we'll house it in its old place, along with your Balan; they belong together, after all.'